Mind and Brain

Mind and Brain
The Many-Faceted Problems

Edited by Sir John Eccles

An ICUS Book

PARAGON HOUSE PUBLISHERS
New York

Published in the United States by
Paragon House Publishers
2 Hammarskjold Plaza
New York, NY 10017

Second printing, 1987.

An International Conference on the Unity of
the Sciences Book

"Adaptability of the Nervous System and Its Relation to
Chance, Purposiveness and Causality" © 1974, Ragnar A. Granit

"The Scientist at His Last Quarter of an Hour" © 1974,
L.V.P.R. de Broglie

"Some Thoughts on the Matter of the Mind-Body Problem"
© 1977, Daniel M. Robinson

"Bridging Science and Values: A Unifying View of Mind and
Brain" © 1975, Roger Sperry

ISBN: 0-89226-016-5 (hardbound)
       0-89226-032-7 (softbound)

Library of Congress Catalogue Card Number: 82-083242

Contents

Preface

The annual International Conferences on the Unity of the Sciences (ICUS) have been the occasion for the exploration of a wide range of topics covering a large part of human culture—from the natural sciences to the social sciences and to the humanities as exemplified in art, philosophy and religion. The proceedings of seven of these conferences (1972 to 1978) have been published, and it is from these published records that I have compiled this book, selecting those contributions that could be considered as relating to a theme of discourse and argument that rightly has now become a topic of great interest, namely the body-mind or mind-brain problem.

I have chosen to interpret this theme very broadly on the grounds that this problem has a quite unique relationship to the human quest for a meaning and value for life. In fact the question is that of ultimate concern especially when this mysteriously wonderful conscious life is viewed as ending in death. There is a termination of our consciously experiencing selves and our memories with the death of the brain.

The topics assembled in this book extend in a spectrum from evolutionary biology through to the philosophy of life and death. I have organized them into four main sections: I) Philosophical contributions to the mind-brain problem; II) Cerebral correlates of consciousness; III) The biology of consciousness; and IV) Meaning of life and death in the context of the mind-brain problem. In these sections there are contributions from some of the foremost thinkers of the world, who do in fact present widely different beliefs. Thus it is hoped that this book provides an excellent educational opportunity for the reader to view a wide variety of beliefs. Since the papers necessarily are limited to a brief text for presentation in 30 minutes or less, references to more extensive works by the authors are appended to each paper. Unfortunately there has been no recording of many of the interesting discussions aroused by the presented papers and the associated commentaries.

Sir John Eccles
Locarno, Switzerland

Introduction

Sir John Eccles

I. Philosophical Contributions to the Mind-Brain Problem

The contributions in this section, present a wide range of speculative thought by scientists who have pondered deeply on a great variety of problems oriented around the mind-brain problem.

In his philosophical essay *Gunther S. Stent* views the failure of positivism in relation to its successors, particularly structuralism. He attempts to relate the structure and functioning of the neural machinery of the brain to the subconscious and the conscious, as exhibited particularly in language in Chomsky's structuralist linguistic theory. *Marius Jeuken* follows with penetrating comments and criticisms.

Daniel N. Robinson presents an historical and critical appraisal of the mind-body problem. Robinson's perspective is that this is a bona fide issue for science and central to the attempt to understand homo cogitans. No solution is offered, but the way to a solution is indicated.

By a masterly logical analysis *J.W.N. Watkins* develops a seemingly insuperable objection to the Identity-hypothesis, particularly as defined by Moritz Schlick. He concludes that: "if . . . physiology were ever to show that the above-mentioned properties of consciousness are *also* properties of the brain, then the brain would be utterly different from the brain as described by contemporary physiology and, indeed, from *any* physical system so far known to us."

On the same theme *Grover Maxwell* contemplates the possibility that the neural machinery of the brain may have completely different properties from anything yet discovered, having mental attributes *per se*; hence there could be a strict identity of mind and brain.

Sir John Eccles critically evaluates all materialist theories of the brain-mind problem and discounts the suggestion that the neurosciences will eventually provide a complete explanation of all mental phenomena, which is labelled as promissory materialism. The alternative hypothesis of a strong dualist-interactionism is outlined. Further consideration of this hypothesis is provided in Chapter 7.

Karl H. Pribram gives a general and critical survey of the mind-brain problem in which he favors a structuralist basis for a solution (cf. Chapter 1).

H.D. Lewis gives a very well argued account of the philosophical concept of persons. An historical account of the idealism-materialism controversies leads him to develop his own critical attack on materialism. He then presents his philosophy of dualism and the human person (for a similar account see Chapters 7 and 18). He insists on the "notion of the distinct and ultimate identity of persons," which he suggests continues after death. *Mary Carman Rose* comments in a well reasoned, wise and deeply thoughtful paper on the philosophy of the human person as conceived in the great religions. *Bradley T. Scheer* also comments on the Lewis paper. He develops a good synthesis of biology and personhood, stressing in particular that the person represents a history of expression, reception, creation and transmission of information. Finally he considers the person as having "the property of eternity" in conformance with the "Will of the Creator."

II. Cerebral Correlates of Consciousness

This section embraces papers that are concerned in one way or another with the responses of the brain and their relationships or conscious experiences.

The first paper of this section, by *Sir John Eccles*, embraces the theme of intimate association of the human person with its brain and follows on thematically from the last paper of the preceding section (Chapter 6). In particular there is an account of the modular structure and operation of the neocortex with conjectures about the way in which mind can relate to the enormous complexity of the spatio–temporal modular patterns, so giving the unity of conscious experience.

Empirical evidence on the mind-brain interaction is presented by *Benjamin Libet*. The temporal discrepancy between brain events and the related conscious experiences provides a difficulty for any variety of identity theory (cf. Chapters 16, 17 and 18).

Robert J. White describes remarkable surgical interventions on primates whereby brains or heads (cephalons) are transplanted and remain viable, as shown by electroencephalograms and reactions. The vexed question of human head transplants arises as a menacing spectre.

W. Horsley Gantt's contribution is of particular interest for its rich historical material. He is one of Pavlov's most famous pupils, but developed scientifically and philosophically away from Pavlov. It is remarkable for its wisdom and deep insight into the mind-brain problem.

Holger Hyden presents the outcome of many years of neuro-chemical investigations on the brain, particularly in respect to learning. He has always stressed the important role of messenger ribonucleic acid and the subsequent protein synthesis. As the discussant *Robert J. White* indicates, it is important to synthe-size these concepts with the neurophysiological mechanisms of the brain—with synaptic actions, impulse discharges, modular patterns, etc.

Sir John Eccles discusses the philosophical problem of the freedom of the will in the light of the hypothesis of dualist-interactionism (cf. Chapter 7). Suggestions are given as to how the mind influences could provide information modifying the spatio-temporal modular patterns of the neocortex.

Ragnar A. Granit approaches evolutionary theory from the standpoint of a neurophysiologist, and stresses the importance of concepts of purposiveness and adaptability, even speaking of immanent teleology with which I approve.

III. The Biology of Consciousness

The papers of this section of the mind-brain problem are grouped around biological ideas, particularly evolution and purposive-ness. The chairman's introduction by *Karl H. Pribram* helps to orientate our thinking to evolution and to consciousness in its many states.

Henry J. Jerison gives an excellent account of the factors probably concerned in that most wonderful of all evolutionary achievements, the creation of Homo Sapiens. Necessarily atten-tion is concentrated on brain performance with the superposition of consciousness and language.

Diane McGuinness develops the provocative idea that the role of females in the evolution of Homo Sapiens has been overlooked because of the preoccupation of evolutionists, particularly Darwin, with natural selection by prowess in hunting and warfare. She makes a most convincing case for the dominant female influence in important aspects of human evolution, such as food-gathering, food-sharing and language. In his discussion paper *Roger W. Wescott* in part agrees, but outlines a balanced position.

J.W.S. Pringle presents a rich field of speculative thought. He regards the human brain as being central to *all* problems. There is an initial section on temporal patterns of oscillators, which are presented as a possible model of brain action, in contrast to the customary spatial relations. The treatment becomes more general with valuable sections on the evolution of consciousness and the emotions. In his commentary *Brian D. Josephson* raises important points with respect to the blocks produced by the conditioning of scientists to consider only material happenings. He offers as examples the understanding of such phenomena as ESP and even of the possible intervention of God in the natural world.

Sir John Eccles uses the three-world philosophy of Popper to illuminate the process of cultural evolution, which is exclusively human. Homo Sapiens has created culture, and each human being (Nature) has to be created as a person by the culture he is immersed in (Nurture).

IV. Meaning of Life and Death in the Context of the Mind-Brain Problem

There can be no doubt but that the mind-brain problem must be of paramount concern because of the key position it necessarily occupies in the human quest for meaning, not only of life, but also of death. Given the complex nature of this topic, it is appropriate that this series of papers offer widely differing and even antagonistic viewpoints.

In his plenary [ICUS] lecture *W.H. Thorpe* concentrates on the human search for meaning that has been threatened by "the monistic views of so many scientists and humans of the present day." He counteracts these threats first by reference to the recent revolution that suggests a deep relationship between ourselves and the whole cosmological story from the Big Bang onwards. Second, he postulates a real disposition of the world for the evolution of mental awareness. He concludes that "the human mind and soul which operates in liaison with it has latent possibilities and capacities for further emergence and transcendence—capacities to which we can set no limit."

The late *Duc de Broglie* presents the quest for meaning, as it appears to a great physicist immersed in the materialist philosophy of science, though spiritual overtones are lightly sketched in.

Philosophical implications of the brain-mind problem are discussed at length by *Roger Sperry*. He states that his aim is to show that the traditional separation of science and values and the related limitations it has implied for science as a discipline are no longer valid in the context of the current mind-brain theory. He develops a wholistic concept of the mind-brain relationship that is opposed to reductionism and materialism on the one hand and to dualism on the other. This closely reasoned paper deserves critical attention. He concludes that "Science deals with values as well as with facts."

Kai Nielsen develops a philosophical position diametrically opposed to that of Lewis and his commentators. He presents a clever atheistic argument which essentially mirrors that of the majority of scientists and humanists of this day. He attempts to show that for an atheist life can have meaning and moral commitment, and even hope.

W. Norris Clarke's paper is in great contrast to Nielsen's. He presents a very clear and authoritative account of the traditional Christian position on death and the meaning of life. With the coming of the Christian message death "becomes no longer the ultimate darkness, the end without issue, but rather the gateway to a new and indestructible fullness of life." He finishes with reference to "the mystery of the total meaning of human life, as seen in the partly revealing, partly concealing light of death."

Ravi Ravindra presents the Hindu response to death and the meaning of life, which is in great contrast to the views expressed in Chapters 26 and 27. There is a relativity of life and death, of death and rebirth. The meaning of life consists in the opportunity it affords for liberation from this endless repetition of life and death and rebirth.

Sir John Eccles attempts to bring to a conclusion this extraordinary variety of contributions. He outlines a position that can be developed from the principles of Natural Theology, but which is not in conflict with the Christian tradition.

Part I

Philosophical Contributions to the Mind-Brain Problem

1.
Structuralism and Biology

Gunther S. Stent

For the past two centuries, scientists, particularly in English-speaking countries, have generally viewed their attempts to understand nature from the epistemological vantage of positivism. All the while, positivism had been under attack from philosophers, but it is only since the 1950's that its powerful hold on the students of nature finally seems to be on the wane. There is as yet no generally accepted designation for the philosophical alternatives that are presently replacing positivism, but the view of man known as "structuralism," which has informed certain schools of psychologists and social scientists, appears to be central to the latter-day epistemological scene. As I shall try to show here, in addition to the philosophical and psychological arguments that have been advanced in its behalf, structuralism can draw support also from biological insights into the evolutionary origins and manner of function of the brain. The principal tenet of positivism, as formulated in the 18th century mainly by David Hume and the French Encyclopaedists, is that sensory experience is the source of true knowledge about the world. According to this view the mind at birth is a clean slate on which there is gradually sketched a representation of reality built on cumulative experience. This representation is orderly, or structured, because, thanks to the principle of inductive reasoning, we can recognize regular features of our experience and infer casual connections between events that habitually occur together. The possibility of innate, or *a priori*, true knowledge of the world is rejected as a logical absurdity.

It is unlikely that the widespread acceptance of a positivism had a significant effect on the development of the physical sciences, since physicists have little need to look to philosophers for justification of their research objectives or working methods. Moreover, once a physicist *has* managed to find an explanation for some phenomenon, he can be reasonably confident of the empirical test of its verity. Thus, the positivist rejection of the atomic theory in the late 19th century, on the grounds that no one had ever "seen" an atom, did not stop chemists and physicists from then laying the groundwork for our present understanding of microscopic matter. However, in the human sciences, particularly in psychology and sociology, the situation was quite different. Here positivism was to have a most profound effect. One reason for this is that practitioners of the human sciences are much more dependent on philosophical support of their work than are physical scientists. For in contrast to the clearly definable research aims of physical science, it is often impossible to state explicitly just what it really *is* about human behavior that one wants to explain. This in turn makes it quite difficult to set forth clearly the conditions under which any postulated causal nexus linking the observed facts could be verified. On the one hand, positivism helped to bring the human sciences into being in the first place, by insisting that any eventual understanding of man must be based on the observation of facts, rather than on armchair speculations. On the other hand, by limiting inquiry to such factual observations and allowing only propositions that are based on direct inductive inferences from the raw sensory data, positivism constrained the human sciences to remain taxonomic disciplines whose content is largely descriptive with little genuine explanatory power. Positivism clearly informed the 19th century founders of psychology, ethnology, and linguistics. Though we are indebted to these founders for the first corpus of reliable data concerning human behavior, their refusal to consider these data in terms of any propositions not derived inductively from direct observation prevented them from erecting a theoretical framework for understanding man.

Structuralism transcends the limitation on the methodology, indeed on the agenda of permissible inquiry, of the human sciences imposed by positivism. Structuralism admits, as positivism does not, the possibility of innate knowledge not derived from sensory experience. Furthermore, structuralism not only permits propositions about behavior that are not directly inducible from observed data but it even maintains that the relations between observed data, or *surface structures*, are not by themselves explainable. According to this view the casual connections which determine behavior do not relate to surface structures at all. Instead, the overt behavioral phenomena are generated by covert *deep structures*, inaccessible to direct observation. Hence any theoretical framework for understanding man must be based on the deep structures, whose discovery ought to be the real goal of the human sciences.

Probably the best known pioneer of structuralism is Sigmund Freud, to whom we owe the fundamental insight that human behavior is governed not so much by the events of which we are consciously aware in our own minds or which we can observe in the behavior of others, but rather by the deep structures of the subconscious which are generally hidden from both subjective and objective view. The nature of these covert deep structures can only be inferred indirectly by analysis of the overt surface structures. This analysis has to proceed according to an elaborate scheme of psychodynamic concepts that purports to have fathomed the rules which govern the reciprocal transformations of surface into deep and of deep into surface structures. The great strength of Freudian analytical psychology is that it does offer a theoretical approach to understanding human behavior. Its great weakness, however, is that it is not possible to verify its propositions. And this can be said also of most other structuralist schools active in the human sciences. They do try to explain human behavior within a general theoretical framework, in contrast to their positivist counterparts that cannot, or rather refuse to try to do so. But there is no way of verifying the structuralist theories in the manner in which the theories of physics can be verified through critical experiments or observations. The structuralist theories are, and may forever remain, merely plausible, being, perhaps, the best we can do to account for the complex phenomenon of man.

For instance, positivist ethnology, as conceived by one of its founders, Franz Boas, sought to establish as objectively and as free from cultural bias as possible the facts of personal behavior and social relations to be found in diverse ethnic groups. Insofar as any explanations are advanced at all to account for these observations, they are formulated in *functionalist* terms. That is to say, every overt feature of behavior or social relation is thought to serve some useful function in the society in which it is found. The explanatory work of the ethnologist would be done once he had identified that function and verified its involvement by means of additional observations. Accordingly, the general aim of this approach to ethnology is to show how manifold and diverse the ways are in which man has adapted his behavior and social existence to the range of conditions which he encountered in settling the Earth. By contrast, structuralist ethnology, according to one of its main exponents Claude Levi-Strauss, views the concept of functionality as a tautology, devoid of any real explanatory power for human behavior. All extant behavior is obviously "functional" since all "dysfunctional" behavior would lead to the extinction of the ethnic group which exhibits it. Instead of functionality, so Levi-Strauss holds, only universal and permanent deep structural aspects of the mind can provide any genuine understanding of social relations. The actual circumstances in which different peoples find themselves no more than modulate the overt behavior to which the covert deep structures give rise. In other words, the point of departure of structuralist ethnology is the view that the apparent diversity of ethnic groups pertains only to the surface structures and that at their deep structural level all societies are very much alike. Hence, the general aim of that other ethnology is to discover those universal, deep mental structures which underlie all human customs and institutions.

Positivist linguistics, as conceived by its founders such as Ferdinand de Saussure and Leonard Bloomfield, addresses itself to the discovery of structural relations among the elements of spoken language. That is to say, the work of that school is concerned with the surface structures of linguistic performance, the patterns which can be observed as being in use by speakers of various languages. Since the patterns which such classificatory analysis reveals differ widely, it seemed reasonable to conclude that these patterns are arbitrary, or purely conventional, one linguistic group having chosen to adopt one, and another group having chosen to adopt another convention. There would be nothing that linguistics could be called on to explain, except for the taxonomic principles that account for the degree of historical relatedness of different peoples. And if the variety of basic patterns of various human languages is indeed the result of arbitrary conventions, study of extant linguistic patterns is not likely to provide any deep insights into any universal properties of the mind. By contrast, structuralist linguistics, according to one of its main proponents, Noam Chomsky, starts from the premise that linguistic patterns are *not* arbitrary. Instead, all men are believed to possess an innate, *a priori* knowledge of a *universal grammar*, and despite their superficial differences, all natural languages are based on that same grammar. According to that view, the overt surface structure of speech, or the organization of sentences, is generated by the speaker from a covert deep structure. In his speech act, the speaker is thought to generate first his proposition as an abstract deep structure which he transforms only secondarily according to a set of rules into the surface structure of his utterance. The listener in turn fathoms the meaning of the speech act by just the inverse transformation of surface to deep structure. Chomsky holds that the grammar of a language is a system of transformational rules that determines a certain pairing of sound and meaning. It consists of a *syntactic component, a semantic component* and a *phonological component*. The surface structure contains the information relevant to the phonological component, whereas the deep structure contains the information relevant to the semantic component, and the syntactic component pairs surface and deep structures. Hence, it is merely the phonological component of grammar that has become greatly differentiated during the course of human history, or at least since the construction of the Tower of Babel. The semantic component has remained invariant and is, therefore, the "universal" aspect of the universal grammar which all natural languages embody. And this presumed constancy through time of the universal grammar cannot be attributable to any cause other than an innate, hereditary aspect of the mind. Hence, the general aim of structuralist linguistics is to discover that universal grammar.

Now, in retrospect, at a time when positivism and its philosophic and scientific ramifications appear to be moribund, it seems surprising that these views ever did manage to gain such a hold over the human sciences. Hume, one of the founders of positivism, already saw that the positivist theory of knowledge has a near-fatal logical flaw. As he noted, the validity of inductive reasoning—which is, according to positivism the basis of our knowledge of the regularity of the world, and hence for our inference of causal connections between events—can neither be demonstrated logically nor can it be based on experience. Instead, inductive reasoning is evidently something that man brings to rather than derives from experience. Not long after Hume, Immanuel Kant showed that the positivist doctrine that sensory impressions are the sole source of human knowledge derives from an inadequate understanding of the working of the mind. Kant pointed out that sensory impressions become experience, i.e., gain meaning, only after they are interpreted in terms of a set of innate, or *a priori* concepts. Induction (or causality) is merely one of these concepts, time and space being others. But why was it that although Kant wielded an enormous influence among philosophers, his views had little currency among scientists? Why did the positivism of Hume, rather than the "critical idealism" of Kant, come to inform the explicit or implicit epistemological outlook of much of 19th and 20th century science? At least two reasons can be advanced for this historical fact. The first reason is simply that many positivist philosophers, especially Hume, were lucid and effective writers whose message could be readily grasped after a single reading of their works. The texts of Kant, and of his mainly Continental followers, are, by contrast, turgid and hard to understand.

The second reason for the long scientific neglect of Kant is more profound. After all, it does seem very strange that if, as Kant alleges, we bring such concepts as causality, time and space to experience *a priori*, these concepts happen to fit the world of our experience so well. Considering all the ill-conceived ideas one *might* have had about the world prior to experience, it seems nothing short of miraculous that our innate notions just happen to be those that fit the bill. Here the positivist view that all knowledge is derived from experience *a posteriori* seems much more reasonable. It turns out, however, that the way to resolve the dilemma posed by the Kantian *a priori* has been open since Darwin put forward the theory of natural selection in the mid-19th century. Nevertheless, few scientists seem to have noticed this until Konrad Lorenz drew attention to it thirty years ago. Lorenz pointed out that the positivist argument that knowledge about the world can enter our mind only through sensory experience is valid if we consider only the *ontogenetic* development of man, from fertilized egg to adult. But once we take into account also the *phylogenetic* development of the human brain through evolutionary history, it becomes clear that individuals can also know something of the world innately, prior to and indepen-dent of their own sensory experience. After all, there is no biological reason why such knowledge cannot be passed on from generation to generation via the ensemble of genes that deter-mines the structure and function of our nervous system. For that genetic ensemble came into being through the process of natural selection operating on our remote ancestors. According to Lorenz, "experience has as little to do with the matching of *a priori* ideas with reality as does the matching of the fin structure of a fish with the properties of water." In other words, the Kantian notion of *a priori* knowledge is not implausible at all, but fully consonant with present mainstream evolutionary thought. The *a priori* concepts of causality, time and space, happen to suit the world because the hereditary determinants of our highest mental func-tions were selected for their evolutionary fitness, just as were the genes that give rise to other innate behavioral acts, e.g., sucking the nipple of mother's breast, which require no learning by experience.

The importance of these Darwinian considerations transcends a mere biological underpinning of the Kantian epistemology. For the evolutionary origin of the brain explains not only why our innate concepts match the world but also why these concepts no longer work so well when we attempt to fathom the world in its deepest scientific aspects. This barrier to unlimited scientific progress posed by the *a priori* concepts which we necessarily bring to experience was a major philosophical concern of Niels Bohr. Bohr recognized the essentially semantic nature of science, pointing out "as the goal of science is to augment and order our experience, every analysis of the conditions of human knowledge must rest on considerations of the character and scope of our means of communication. Our basis [of communication] is, of course, the language developed for orientation in our surround-ings and for the organization of human communities. However, the increase of experience has repeatedly raised questions as to the sufficiency of concepts and ideas incorporated in daily lan-guage." The most basic of these concepts and ideas are precisely the Kantian *a priori* notions of causality, time and space. The meaning of these terms is intuitively obvious and grasped auto-matically by every child in the course of its normal intellectual development, without the need to attend physics classes. Accord-ingly, the models which modern science offers as explanations of reality are pictorial representations built of these intuitive concepts. This procedure was eminently satisfactory as long as explanations were sought for phenomena that are commensurate with the events that are the subject of our everyday experience (give or take a few orders of magnitude). For it was precisely for its fitness to deal with everyday experience that our brain was selected in the evolutionary sequence that culminated in the appearance of *homo sapiens*. But the situation began to change when, at the turn of this century, physics had progressed to a stage at which problems could be studied which involve either tiny subatomic or immense cosmic events on scales of time, space and mass billions of times smaller or larger than our direct experience. Now, according to Bohr, "there arose difficulties of orienting ourselves in a domain of experience far from that to the description of which our means of expression are adapted." For it turned out that the description of phenomena in this domain in ordinary, everyday language leads to contradictions or mutually incompatible pictures of reality. In order to resolve these contradictions, time and space had to be denatured into generalized concepts whose meaning no longer matched that provided by intuition. Eventually it appeared also that the intuitive notion of cause and effect is not a useful one for giving account of events at the atomic and subatomic level. All of these developments were the consequence of the discovery that the rational use of intuitive linguistic concepts to communicate experience actually embodies hitherto unnoticed presuppositions. And it is these presuppositions which lead to contradictions when the attempt is made to communicate events outside the experiential domain. Now, whereas the scope of science was enormously enlarged by recognizing the pitfalls of everyday language, this was achieved only at the price of denaturing the intuitive meaning of some of its basic concepts with which man starts out in his quest for understanding nature.

In addition to explaining in evolutionary terms how the human brain and its epiphenomenon, the mind, can gain possession of *a priori* concepts that match reality, modern biology has also shown that the brain does appear to operate according to principles which correspond to the tenets of structuralism. By this statement I do not mean that the neurological correlates of any of the structuralist theories, particularly not of Freud's subconscious, or of Levi-Strauss' ethnological universals, or of

Chomsky's universal grammar have actually been found. Such a claim would be nonsensical, inasmuch as it is not even known in which parts of the brain the corresponding processes occur. What I do mean, however, is that neurological studies have indicated that, in accord with the structuralist tenets, information about the world reaches the depths of the mind, not as raw data but as highly processed structures that are generated by a set of step-wise, preconscious informational transformations of the sensory input. These neurological transformations proceed according to a program that preexists in the brain. The neurological findings thus lend biological support to the structuralist dogma that explanations of behavior must be formulated in terms of such deep programs and reveal the wrong-headedness of the positivist approach which rejects the postulation of covert internal pro-grams as "mentalism."

One set of such neurological findings concerns the manner in which the nervous system of higher vertebrates, including man, converts the light rays entering the eyes into a visual percept. For the purpose of this discussion it is useful to recall that the nervous system is divisible into three parts: (1) an input or *sensory* part that informs the animal about its external and internal environment; (2) an output, or *effector*, part that pro-duces motion by commanding muscle contraction, and (3) an *internuncial* part that connects the sensory and effector parts. The most elaborate portion of the internuncial part is the brain. The brain does much more than merely connect sensory and effector parts, however: it processes information. This processing consists in the main in making an *abstraction* of the vast amount of data continuously gathered by the sensory part. In order to abstract, the brain destroys selectively portions of the input data and thus transforms these data into manageable categories, or *structures* that are meaningful to the animal. It is on the basis of the perceived meaning that the international part issues the relevant commands to the effector part which then result in an appropriate motor response.

For vision, the input part of the nervous system is located in the retina at the back of the eye. There a two-dimensional array of about a hundred million primary light receptor cells—the rods and the cones—converts the radiant energy of the image project-ed via the lens on the retina into a pattern of electrical signals, much as a television camera does. Since the electrical response of each light receptor cell depends on the intensity of light that happens to fall on it, the overall activity pattern of the light receptor cell array represents the light intensity existing at a hundred million different points in the visual space. The retina contains not only the input part of the visual system, however, but also the first stages of the internuncial part. These first internuncial stages include another two-dimensional array of nerve cells, namely the million or so *ganglion cells*. The ganglion cells receive the electrical signals generated by the hundred million light receptor cells and subject them to information processing. The result of this processing is that the activity pattern of the ganglion cells constitutes a more abstract representation of the visual space than the activity pattern of the light receptor cells. For instead of reporting the light intensity existing at a single point in the visual space, each ganglion cell signals the light-dark *contrast* which exists between the center and the edge of a circular *receptive field* in the visual space. Each receptive field consists of about a hundred contiguous points monitored by individual light receptor cells. The physiological mechanisms by means of which the input point-by-point light intensity information are more or less understood. They can be epitomized simply by stating that the light receptor cells reporting from points at the center or the edge of the receptive field make respectively excitatory or inhibitory connections with their correspondent-ganglion cell. Thus the ganglion cell is maximally excited if the field center receptors are struck by bright light while the field edge receptors are in the dark. In this way, the point-by-point fine-grained light intensity information is boiled down to a somewhat coarser field-by-field light contrast representation, thanks to an algebraic summation of the outputs of an interconnected ensemble of a hundred contiguous light receptor cells. As can be readily appreciated, such light contrast information is essential for the recognition of shapes and forms in space, which is what visual perception mainly amounts to.

For the next stage of processing the visual information leaves the retina via the nerve fibers of the ganglion cells. These fibers connect the eye with the brain, and after passing a way station in the midbrain the output signals of the ganglion cells reach the cerebral cortex at the lower back of the head. Here the signals converge on a set of cortical nerve cells. Study of the cortical nerve cells receiving partially abstracted visual input has shown that each of them responds only to light rays reaching the eye from a limited set of contiguous points in the visual space. But the structure of the receptive fields of these cortical nerve cells is more complicated and their size is larger than that of the receptive fields of the retinal ganglion cells. Instead of representing the light-dark contrast existing between the center and the edge of circular receptive fields, the cortical nerve cells signal the contrast which exists along straight line edges whose length amounts to many diameters of the circular ganglion cell receptive fields. A given cortical cell becomes active if a straight line edge of a particular orientation—horizontal, vertical or oblique—formed by the border of contiguous areas of high and low light intensity is present in its receptive field. For instance, a vertical bar of light on a dark background in some part of the visual field may produce a vigorous response in a particular cortical nerve cell, and that response will cease if the bar is tilted away from the vertical or moved outside the receptive field. Actually, there exist two different kinds of such nerve cells in the cerebral cortex: *simple* cells and *complex* cells. The response of simple cells demands that the straight edge stimulus must not only have a given orientation but also a precise position in the receptive field. The stimulus requirements of complex cells are less demanding, however, in that their response is sustained upon parallel displacements (but not upon tilts) of the straight edge stimuli within the receptive field. Thus the process of abstraction of the visual input begun in the retina is carried to higher levels in the cerebral cortex. The simple cells, which evidently correspond to the first cortical abstraction stage, transform the data supplied by the retinal ganglion cells concerning the light-dark contrast within small circular receptive fields into information concerning the contrast present along sets of circular fields arranged in straight lines. And the complex cells carry out the next cortical abstraction stage. They transform the contrast data concerning particular straight line sets of circular receptive fields into information concerning the contrast present at parallel sets of straight line sets of circular receptive fields.

It is not clear at present how far this process of cerebral abstraction by convergence of visual channels can be imagined to go. Nerve cells have already been found in the cerebral cortex which respond optimally to *straight-line ends* or *corners* in the receptive fields. Evidently, the output of these cells represents an even higher level of abstraction than the parallel straight lines of a given orientation to which the complex cells respond. But should one suppose that the cellular abstraction process goes so far that there exists for every meaningful structure of whose specific recognition an animal is capable (e.g., "my grandmother") at least one particular nerve cell in the cerebral cortex that responds if and only if the light and dark pattern from which that structure is abstracted appears in its visual space? This could very well be the case for lower vertebrates, with their limited behavioral repertoire. For instance, there is neurological evidence that the visual system of the frog abstracts its input data in such a way as to produce only two meaningful structures, "my prey" and "my predator," which, in turn, evoke either of two alternative motor outputs, attack or flight. But in the case of man, with his vast semantic capacities, this picture does not appear very plausible, despite the fact that the human brain has many more nerve cells than the frog's brain. Somehow, for man the notion of the single cerebral nerve cell as the ultimate element of meaning seems worse than a gross oversimplification; it seems qualitatively wrong. Yet, so far at least, it is the only neurologically coherent scheme that can be put forward.

Here we encounter what could turn out to be a barrier to the scientific effort to understand man. I think it is highly significant that in working out his structuralist linguistic theory, Chomsky has encountered the greatest difficulty with the semantic component. Thus far, he has been unable to spell out how that presumably universal component manages to extract meaning from the informational content of the deep structure. It is over just the problem of meaning that disputes have arisen between Chomsky and some of his students, and it does not seem that any solution is presently in sight. The obstacle in the way of giving a satisfactory account of the semantic component appears to reside in defining clearly the problem that is to be solved. That is to say, for man the concept of "meaning" can be fathomed only in relation to an even more elusive notion, namely that of the *self*, which is both ultimate source and ultimate destination of semantic signals. But the concept of the self, the cornerstone of Freud's analytical psychology, cannot be given an explicit definition. Instead, the meaning of "self," or of its old-time, pre-scientific equivalent "soul," is intuitively obvious. It is another Kantian *a priori* concept, one which we bring to man, just as we bring the concepts of space and time to nature. The concept of self can serve the student of man as long as he does not probe too deeply. However, when it comes to explaining the innermost workings of the mind—the deep structure of structuralism—then, just as microscopic physics or cosmology, this attempt to increase the range of understanding raises, in Bohr's terms, "questions as to the sufficiency of concepts and ideas incorporated in daily language." From this ultimate insufficiency of the everyday concepts which our brain obliges us to use for science it does not, of course, follow that further study of the mind should cease, no more than it follows from it that one should stop further study of microscopic physics. But I think that it is important to give due recognition to this fundamental epistemological limitation to the human sciences, if only as a safeguard against the psychological or sociological prescriptions put forward by people who allege that they have already managed to gain a scientifically validated understanding of man.

Commentary

Marius Jeuken

It was a pleasure for me to comment on Dr. Stent's paper, for in it I found some ideas which I myself had been thinking over in my reflections on the relation between philosophy and natural science, especially biology. My commentary is divided into three items, each of which is a praiseworthy element of Dr. Stent's paper.

These items are:

1. The decline of positivism

2. The emphasis on the so-called deep-structure

3. The reference to the problem of the mind-matter relation.

1. With regard to the decline of positivism (in its dual form: the positivism of Hume and the neo-positivism of Wiener Kreis), Stent sees structuralism as an answer to modern problems, and illustrates it, referring to the role of the subconscious (Freud), to ethnology (Levi-Strauss) and to linguistics (Chomsky). I would like to point out that structuralism is not the only answer to positivism. Stent too says that there are philosophical alternatives, and it is my opinion that they must not be underestimated.

That positivism was one-sided was already acknowledged in philosophies more or less in the positivist tradition, especially in so-called analytical philosophy. Some examples:

 a. *G. E. Moore* emphasized the common sense idea. Common sense is expressed in ordinary everyday language. In

17

his ethics, common sense and intuition are basic concepts. Some innateness must be assumed.

b. *Bertrand Russell* on the contrary had not much confidence in common sense, and ordinary language, but sought after an ideal logical language. Maybe there is some relationship with Chomsky's deep structure of language. The co-author of *Principia Mathematica*, Whitehead, became the great metaphysicist of Harvard University, and certainly cannot be called a positivist.

c. *Ludwig Wittgenstein* wrote his *Philosophical Investigations* during his Cambridge period (1953) in which he proposed his theory of language games. The statements which in the positivist's theory were senseless, such as statements on aesthetics and metaphysics, gained sense by means of the language games principle.

Other reactions on positivism are known as well, more from outside the positivist tradition:

a. Reactions of philosophers of dialectical materialism, as in Marcuse. His criticism of the one-dimensional man who in his alienation is incapable of realizing his real self-development, his responsibility and his freedom, is an indication that Marcuse cannot be called a positivist. He expects little or nothing from science, it is true. According to him science is too much tied to the study of existing reality, whereas the not-yet-existing must also be explored.

b. The position of the renewed Aristotelian philosophy is far removed from positivism.

c. The idea of structure is not a new one. In biology we have the holist theory, already brought forward by Smuts. Afterwards followed organicism, being Von Bertalanffy's solution for the mechanicism-vitalism controversy. "The whole is more than the sum of its parts." In cybernetics the functioning organized structure is the central idea. In psychology we have Kohler's Gestalt theory. We can say: what organicism is in biology, is structuralism in ethnology and linguistics.

However, I think that the main reason why Dr. Stent emphasizes structuralism is that in structuralism we find the idea of the so-called deep structure, innate in man, *a priori* given. And this brings me to the second item.

2. *The emphasis on the so-called deep structure.*

In biology the need for philosophical reflection and for a sound philosophical basis has always been felt. There is a famous saying: "When you scratch a biologist, you find a philosopher under the skin." Contrary to theoretical physics, theoretical biology was from the beginning philosophy of biology. Only later did biomathematics come into existence.

Likewise contrary to modern physics, where mathematical explanation is almost the only explanation admitted, we have in biology various kinds of explanation, such as causal explanation, teleological explanation, historical explanation, morphological explanation, etc. So in the study of animal and human behavior we know the idea of the innate, and it is precisely the innate where the deep structures lie. Innate can be explained as: "given with our being." Maybe this notion of the innate in biology has been transferred to other fields of thinking like ethnology and linguistics. One can call the innate also the *a priori*, but in my opinion it is not necessary to refer to Kant. Other modern philosophical systems know the contents of this notion too. In connection with this I would like to indicate some points in which I disagree with Stent—a disagreement however that may enliven the discussion.

- When Stent uses the term "verification" he seems only to have in mind the positivist's conception of verification. However, I think that nowadays the term verification tends to the generic meaning on "making true in general;" so that in the various fields of knowledge—biology, philosophy, theology—the concomitant specific kind of verification must be sought out.

- When Stent discusses Bohr's and Levi-Strauss' ideas on ethnology, he seems to agree that functionality has no explanatory power. This is not in accordance with data of modern biology. Here we acknowledge the value of functional or teleological explanation, not as a substitute for causal explanation, but as another way of seeing the phenomena. So functional explanation cannot be opposed to causal explanation; both explain the whole phenomenon in one of its aspects. The total explanation of the phenomenon is the result of all the aspects together: causal, teleological, mathematical, historical, morphological and maybe more still.

- The structure of our chromosomal pattern and the structure of cytoplasmic elements are the basis of our being Homo Sapiens. That natural selection is conditional for the coming into existence of this pattern, is a valid theory. However, the question is whether natural selection, if it is a necessary condition, is also a sufficient condition in evolutionary theory. Natural selection certainly leads us to a historical explanation, but I doubt whether it is also a causal explanation, I think, however, that evolutionary theory is not necessary to explain our *a priori* concepts.

- In his interesting description of the way our visual pattern works, Stent finally points out the structures in our brain cortex. He calls them "the depths of mind," but the question is whether this notion of the "deep" is the same as in "deep structures." And are these structures necessarily correlated with the deep structures of the mind? Of course in the unity of mind and matter, there must be a material correlate for our mental activities, but it seems premature to me to indicate already certain structures as the material basis for the mental deep structure. Moreover the term "structure" has a different meaning in the various language games of biology, ethnology and linguistics. And this leads me to the third item.

3. *The problem of the mind-matter relation.*

Stent indicates this problem at the end of his paper. The real problem for our knowledge is how concrete, individual representations and perceptions of the object in the brain cortex can yield abstract universal ideas in our mind. This is the problem of extracting general meaning from concrete information.

In my opinion Chomsky is on the wrong track in looking for an explanation in brain structures. Not only is the language of natural science insufficient, it is incapable. For an explanation we have to change over to another language game, the language of metaphysics. The concept of meaning belongs to the metaphysical language, whereas the description of brain structures is on the level of scientific language. Perhaps a renewed positive metaphysical understanding of matter may offer a clue for solution.

2.

Some Thoughts on the Matter Of the Mind/Body Problem

Daniel N. Robinson

In his oft-cited and regularly misunderstood *De Anima*, Aristotle sought to establish the boundary-conditions within which a purely naturalistic science might address itself to the facts of life. As every undergraduate learns, Aristotle found little difficulty in relating the nutritive, sensitive, reproductive, and locomotor functions of the soul to the physiological processes of the organism. However, on the question of *intellect*, he is found to be rather more diffident. It was Aristotle's thesis that there must be some common elements shared in any causal sequence. Or, as his Scholastic commentators put it, nothing can be the cause of anything unless the two events have a likeness. On this construction of causation, the empirical knowledge of man and brute pose no difficulty for the materialist. A knowledge of *things* can, somehow, be acquired by anything capable of being impressed or otherwise stimulated. But the rational knowledge of man—a knowledge which includes *universal* truths—cannot be imparted by things, or by particulars of any kind. Thus, such knowledge is not the gift of our sensitive faculty.

Aristotle's relaxation of this epistemological tension was to accord transcendental status to the rational faculty, and to render intellect "impassable." This summit of mental achievements was, on his account, attained only by human beings, and represented a condition of mind which was indestructible. After all, to be destroyed or to undergo degeneration, an entity must be material; to be material, it must be particular; but to be particular, it

23

cannot partake of the universal. Accordingly, and with the legislative authority of the syllogism, Aristotle was able to conclude that the feature of mind which communes with "universals" is, itself, eternal. Lest this analysis make a modern audience too hopeful, it is sadly necessary to note that the eternal life granted here is not a *personal* survival after the death of the body. Persons, after all, are *individuals!*

Even in this very sketchy summary of *De Anima*, we begin to see the scientific implications of the Mind/Body problem, and also the complexity of the web of suppositions surrounding the problem. It is clear, for example, that Aristotle was forced to his position on the "impassability" of reason by the prior position he had taken on the question of causation. As I shall discuss further on, there is still a close connection between the two issues in modern scholarship, although it is a different sort of connection from the one established by Aristotle. It should also be clear that at least since the Hellenistic period, philosophers have recognized that the peculiar properties of *mind* would constitute the acid-test of any naturalistic metaphysics.

Since Aristotle's day, countless figures in the history of ideas have faced the Mind/Body problem, and a fair share of them were persuaded that they solved it—once and for all! A review of their efforts is beyond the scope of this treatment. Instead, it will be sufficient to summarize the several categories into which all these attempts can be placed.

At the coarsest level of classification, the entire history of speculation can be reduced to the two headings, "Monism" and "Dualism." Monists and dualists, however, present themselves in a variety of forms. There are, for example, *mentalistic* monists such as George Berkeley, and *materialistic* monists such as La Mettrie. There is also the rarer species—the so-called "neutral monist"—who will not commit himself either to a universe that is exclusively spiritual or to one that is exclusively material, but who rejects duality. In his formative years, Bertrand Russell was pleased to espouse this position, but even his charisma could not attract many disciples to this position.

Perhaps the most popular form of monism is that which serves as the foundation of "double-aspect" theories. This is the monism of many of the great names in nineteenth century science: Thomas Huxley, C. Lloyd Morgan, Ernst Haeckel, Alexander Bain (on certain accounts). The "double-aspect" theorist has the laudable penchant for conciliation. He insists that the organism is unitary, but that it displays two aspects; a mental and a physical. Neither is completely reducible to the other; neither is more valid than the other. Indeed, there are not two *realities*, but two *aspects* of a single reality. Here, of course, we have a monism almost shamelessly courting dualism.

As for dualism, it, too has been served up in various fashions and has enjoyed the support of famous and accomplished figures in science and philosophy. The most common form of dualism, and the form which seems to dominate our contemporary metaphysics, labors under the title, "epiphenomenalism." Adherents of this thesis accept the validity of Mind, but insist that all mental events, states, and processes are uniquely caused by physical events, states, and processes. The physical work required by this thesis is generally regarded as taking place in the brain, or in the nervous system at large—thus, the Mind/Brain problem instead of the more ambiguous Mind/Body problem.

The two remaining major categories of dualism are "two-way interactionism" and "psychophysical parallelism." In polling my own students from time to time, I have ascertained that the former is most popular among upperclassmen majoring in psychology. The latter enjoys some support from our Theology majors. But the latter also was adopted by Leibniz and by Wilhelm Wundt and, opinion-polls aside, has something to recommend it.

Each of these traditional solutions to the Mind/Body problem has its own body of facts, convictions, and hunches to back it up. Berkeley's *Immaterialism*—as odd as it is irrefutable—begins with the indubitable claim that we can know only the contents of our own minds, and that these are *ideas*. Every knowledge-claim we make which contains non-ideational elements can only be an inference, and cannot be tested except ideationally. Accordingly, the knowable universe is furnished exclusively with ideas. (I put aside the more Delphic entity of "spirit" in the interest of brevity). A thoroughgoing refutation of Berkeley must begin, then, with a demonstration of material existence independently of any *idea* of the putative matter. This, of course, is impossible. The shortest refutation on record is that registered by the foot of Dr. Johnson. Perhaps in kicking the stone, this impatient genius of the *Enlightenment* acted for legions of practical men and women who would find it easier to ignore or ridicule Berkeley than to rebut him. We do, however, find echoes of Berkelean metaphysics in the *phenomenalism* of J.S. Mill, where matter is defined as the "permanent possibility of sensation."

Leaving Berkeley—for we must—we arrive at his polar –opposite, *materialistic* monism. In its modern dress, it is called the "Identity Thesis," and is closely associated with the works of J.J.C. Smart. If I were to permit myself a bold speculation, I would insist that the question of the "unity of sciences" will be settled completely by the fate of this thesis. If, as Professor Smart maintains, sensations are not caused by processes in the brain but are, in fact, these very processes, then there would seem to be no reason for psychology not to prepare itself for imminent absorption by physics. The dream of Epicurus will be a reality, and the song of Lucretius a veritable Book of Knowledge. But if, as I suspect, the thesis is either wrong or unintelligible, then the disunity of sciences is likely to be a very long season.

What can be said for the "Identity Thesis" and its older cousins is that they are parsimonious. The history of physics, from the seventeenth century until a few decades ago, lent credence to the antique belief that Nature is not profligate in her laws and operations. For many centuries, scientists have groomed their sensibilities with Ockham's razor and, for the past century, psychology has followed suit on the strength of Lloyd Morgan's famous *canon*. It is less clear, however, what else might be said in favor of *materialistic* monism. The facts of neurophysiology and clinical neurology—to the extent that they are relevant to the issue—will support *epiphenomenalism* and *two-way interactionism* as well as they are said to support the "Identity Thesis." And there are other facts which the "Identity Thesis" cannot confront without embarrassment. There is, for example, the uncontestable authority of percipients in the matter of their first-person reports of sensations. When Mr. Jones insists that he has a toothache, we discover that, in principle, there is nothing we can do to refute the claim. If we assume that Jones is not a liar, we accept without hesitation not only that, indeed, he has a toothache, but that his sensation will serve as our only means of ever developing impersonal methods of detecting such events. Thus, even if we choose to test Jones's credibility—for example, by recording the discharge-patterns from his dental nerves—we can only do so with instruments which have been "calibrated" against the claims of other Joneses.

This status which attaches to cooperative (i.e., non-deceptive) first-person reports of sensation is unique. There is no statement which Jones might make about nerves, brains, or glial cells which, in principle, cannot be proven to be wrong. But what Jones says about his aches, hopes, and passions is, in principle, irrefutable. The implication of this to the "Identity Thesis" should be obvious. If everything one might say about processes in the brain is, in principle, refutable, and if nothing said by Jones about his sensations is, in principle, refutable, then Jones's brain processes and sensations are not identical.

This is not the only problem which infects the "Identity Thesis." In an almost perverse way, the thesis pushes its adherent firmly in the direction of Berkeley's curious metaphysics. It converts all mental events to events in the brain, and all reports of mental events into reports of processes in the brain. It is not at all clear that an external world can survive this analysis. And, as in the case of Berkeley's argument, it revives the vexing problem of "other minds." It does this by converting the problem of "other minds" to that of "other brains," but it offers us no means by which our brains can be conversant with these other brains. Nor does it tell us how, given a nervous system which is probably never in the same state on any two successive occasions, there can be continuity of "self," or of "self-identity."

With respect to this latter problem the "Identity Thesis" is hardly alone in its awkwardness. All materialistic accounts of "self," when examined closely are found to be incredible. This is due principally to the historical tendency of materialistic metaphysics to ally itself with empiricistic epistemologies. The usual argumentative chain is as follows: (a) all we know is furnished exclusively by experience; (b) experiences are the consequence of sensory events which are impressed upon the nervous centers; (c) a history of experience is possible as a result of residual *traces* or chemical codes formed in these nervous centers pursuant to stimulation; (d) one's sense of "self"—as a continuing personal identity—is but these memories.

It was Descartes who introduced the fashion of doubting one's own existence, but it has had a longer life than most fashions in philosophy. Locke was the first of many to settle the issue by taking recourse to memories, but Thomas Reid's utter devastation of this theory has not prevented others from following in Locke's footsteps. Examining the proposition that "self" is identical to "memories," Reid offered this illustration:

1. There is a brave officer who remembers being the small boy punished years earlier for stealing from the orchard.

2. There is a decorated General who recalls being the brave officer, but who has no recollection of the small boy punished in the orchard.

On Locke's account, the small boy is identical to the brave officer; and the brave officer is identical to the decorated General; but the small boy and the decorated General are not identical. In other words, A ^{5} B and B ^{5} C, but A $^{5/}$ C. Thus, the thesis bears the double-burden of implausibility and self-contradiction. I might note that the modern Lockeans who would use the findings resulting from surgical separation of the hemispheric connections to challenge the concept of a "unified self" fall into the same trap. The patient never doubts his "personal identity," but does provide conflicting responses on tests of memory. For such facts to sustain the claim that multiple identities are involved, it would be necessary to reduce "self" to "memory"—and we see that this cannot be done with logical impunity.

Berkeley's *Immaterialism* is something we have agreed to praise and to bury, and the "Identity Thesis" is bloated with difficulties even when it is expressed coherently. Thus, among the *monisms*, we are left with the Double-Aspect theory. It promises to give us the same parsimoniousness and it also allows us to continue speaking intelligibly and scientifically about minds. Moreover, it seems to be at least metaphorically related to that lingering dualism in physics whose demon has been named the *wavicle*. But the metaphor cannot be said to be entirely apt. There are electromagnetic phenomena which are best explained in terms of quantum-effects; others in terms of wave-mechanical effects. But both classes of effects are amenable to identical procedures of quantification, and both classes fit into that matrix of explanatory devices known as the laws of radiation and matter. The *wavicle* in physics should, on the "double-aspect" account, have a corresponding entity—let us call it the *mentasome*—in the realm of Mind/Body. But the plain fact is that virtually *none* of the predicates ordinarily assigned to mental events can be plausibly assigned to somatic events. Merely on the face of it, there would seem to be no two entities drawn from the universe of realities which are less similar than the mental and the somatic.

All the events in one are explicable in the scientific language of *causation*, but most of the truly interesting events in the other seem not to be. This is not to say that the actions of psychological beings are inexplicable; only that the explanations are not of the scientific, causal sort.

What I mean by "truly interesting" are those events which, for want of a clearer term, might be called *historical*. These are the events which have significant effects on the personal or social history of a species—and here I am considering only our own species. When we attempt to provide an explanation for such events, we generally take recourse to the language of *reasons*, not the language of *causes*. This gets us back to the remarks I made regarding Aristotle, and the connection between the Mind/Body problem and theories of causation. If we ask, "Why did Pericles urge Athenians to destroy their possessions on the eve of battle with the Spartans?," we surely do not want to be told, "Because of neuromuscular discharges in his tongue and larynx." The question seeks to penetrate the *reasons* Pericles had for making such a speech, and not the physical causes by which speech of any kind is produced.

Here we have another difference between the *wavicle* in physics and the *mentasome* in psychology. Whether the physicist is concerned with waves or particles, the fundamental logic of explanation is the same. But those who would seek to understand why Pericles spoke as he did, or why Smith sold his properties in Wales, or why Jack chose the train over the airplane, will only be satisfied with a *rational* account of such actions. If treated to a *causal* account, they will assume their correspondent is being droll. It is like being told, when asking why so many men have died in war, that their blood pressure dropped.

This is not to say, however, that no form of Double-Aspect theory is likely to be satisfying. Over the past decade, Professor Pribram has attempted to develop a *holographic* theory of perception and memory; a theory which, like its *Gestalt* ancestors, proposes an isomorphic resemblance between the structure of psychological events and the structure of neural correlates. Professor Pribram is not to be faulted for the historic habit of modeling the human nervous system after the most current productions of technology. Descartes had his hydraulic pumps, J.S. Mill his "mental chemistry," Sherrington his cables, and Hebb his "assemblages." Why should we deny Dr. Pribram his holograms! But the point, of course, is not whether holograms are apt. The point is that a Double-Aspect theory which goes no further than the one bequeathed by the nineteenth century is little more than religious science. Pribram has set forth a *substantive* rather than a polemical theory and has, in my view, given Double-Aspect theories a new lease. More importantly, he is to my knowledge the only Double-Aspect theorist who has stated the case in a manner which, at least in principle, is amenable to experimental refutation. This will be no easy trick, but it is not arrantly impossible, whereas experimental refutation of the "Identity Thesis" is.

It is probably all too evident from what I have said that I judge the historic attempts to reduce Mind to Body as failures, and that—from my own reading of this literature—I do not see much by way of encouragement on the horizon. It is by no means clear, however, that even if my own estimations are correct, the "unity of sciences" is a casualty. Behaviorism and its twin —associationism—diverted the intellectual energies of psychology for far too many years. All sorts of facile and occasionally agile evasions were promoted by this perspective such that, even today, many otherwise serious scientists accept reductionism as the official method of the sciences. The leaders of the behavioristic schools—and these schools are ancient—have always tied their claims to the achievements in physics and biology; often corrupting the facts and theories established in these other disciplines. Ironically, behaviorism has always leaned on evolutionary biology for support. Yet, there is nothing in the theory of evolution which requires all species to develop the same adaptive mechanisms. Quite the contrary. Evolutionary biology leaves as much room for the appearance of *mind* in the natural world as it does for prehensile forelimbs or for feathers. Thus, psychology need not fear that, in accepting the *facts* of human mental life, it somehow is cutting itself loose from Darwin's science.

Associationism infected modern psychology with a quieter but equally lethal notion. It convinced a woeful number of psychologists that the final product of associative learning contained all the elements involved in all the stages leading to the final product. On the traditional associationistic account, then, we should expect the accomplished pianist to repeat all the errors made in the course of his training! This was the line of reasoning that led to the otherwise incredible notion that the richest expressions of human cognition were, in principle, reducible to elemental forms of associational learning. Let us agree that there are good and bad forms of reductionism, and that the bad form invariably asks us to eliminate facts for the sake of the theory.

I noted that a failure on the part of reductionism does not, *ipso facto* spell doom for the "unity of sciences." Doom can be averted by the expansion of the established sciences to embrace the logical and geometric coherence of *homo cogitans*. Physics, after all, can trace as many of its triumphs to an expansion of the conceptual bandwidth as to a narrowing. Not everything in physics must be *reduced* to principles of sub-atomic interactions. And if astrophysics can proclaim its scientific status even while ignoring xi-zeta particles, one would think that psychology can proceed scientifically even if it cannot cram a thought into a neuron. Moreover, we already have refined models of human cognition, although we have yet to come to think of them as models. Let me mention a few: Euclidean Geometry, Model logic, Constitutional Law, Algebra, Music. In reciting this short list I do not intend to display my "humanistic" credentials, nor am I offering a veiled defense of romanticism. In as hard-nosed a fashion as is possible, I am suggesting that these subjects and achievements are veritable working-diagrams of human mental organization. They are star-charts for astronomers of the mind and blueprints for architects of the mind. They tell us far more about the intrinsic "design" features of the human nervous system than can be gleaned in a millenium of bar-presses and key-pecks. Like the geological records which waited for a Darwin, these records of mental evolution are already there. It requires no experiment to unearth them, no technology to assess them. What is required is that nemesis of so-called "objective psychology," a *theory*. And, in light of the manner in which psychologists have approached this mission over the past fifty years, there would seem to be no reason for physicists to be sheepish.

3.

A Basic Difficulty in the Mind-Brain Identity-Hypothesis

J.W.N. Watkins

The hypothesis that every mind-event or process is, as a matter of fact, identical with some brain-event or process, is popular today. I think that one reason for its popularity is this. It is still widely held that dualist interactionism is quite implausible. Those who hold this can avoid the depressing doctrine of epiphenomenalism (roughly: mind-events are but the shadows or echoes of brain-processes) and retain their belief in "the casual efficacy of the mental," that is, the belief that what we think makes a difference to what we do, by adopting the Identity-hypothesis; for this allows one to hold that our bodily behavior is strongly influenced by our beliefs, values, and decisions just because these mental entities *are* at the same time casually efficacious brain-processes.[1]

For my part, I hold that there are no insuperable objections to dualist interactionism, but I will not argue for that here.[2] I shall argue only for the negative thesis that there is a seemingly insuperable objection to the Identity-hypothesis.

An early statement of that hypothesis was given by Moritz Schlick.[3] I am going to take this as my starting-point for several reasons. First, it remains to this day one of the clearest and boldest statements of the hypothesis. Second, it has been largely ignored in the rapidly expanding literature on mind-brain identity.[4] My third and main reason is this. Schlick treated *both* sides of the mind-brain divide with the utmost seriousness. Some contemporary identity-theorists are like Schlick in this respect. I am thinking especially of David Armstrong[5] and Grover Maxwell.[6] But others take the mind-side of the divide less seriously. It has been claimed that Ryle in *The Concept of Mind* succeeded in reducing nearly all allegedly private and ghostly inner happenings to publicly observable behavior, leaving only tickles and other "raw feels" to be mopped up. In earlier times there were identity-theorists who did not take matter altogether seriously, but only paid it a kind of lip-service. I am thinking of Russell's neutral monism and his idea that matter is a logical construction from sense-data, and of Mach's sensationalism and his idea that some configurations of sensations constitute minds while others constitute material objects.

By contrast, Schlick was both an unrepentant mentalist and an unrepentant physical realist (to begin with, at least; he reneged on his physical realism later). He held that the last thought of a dying man is something *real*, though private and without causal effects. He also held that, for instance, an unobservable physical atom is real (as real as a loaf of bread). Moreover he was an eager explorer of both sides of the divide. He came to philosophy from theoretical physics (he had studied under Max Planck and written a book on space and time in contemporary physics). At the same time he was fascinated by various features of human consciousness, especially the peculiar *unity* of consciousness. Although highly critical of many of Kant's ideas, Kant's doctrine of the "synthetic unity of apperception" was one which, considered as a psychological thesis, he wholeheartedly endorsed, reinforcing it with striking arguments of his own.

In short, my main reason for going back to Schlick is that, instead of softening up the problem for the Identity-hypothesis by first so redescribing one side of the mind-matter divide that it becomes not unlike the other, he hardened the problem by going out of his way to highlight features on one side which seem to have no analogue on the other. He presented a contrast between mind and brain which was strong and stark, and then boldly claimed that, notwithstanding this, each item on the mind-side is actually identical with some item on the brain-side. I shall argue that the peculiar features of consciousness which he rightly highlighted do in fact constitute a basic difficulty for the Identity-hypothesis.

One formulation he gave to that hypothesis was the following:

. . . in place of the dualistic assumption we introduce the much simpler hypothesis that the concepts of the natural sciences are suited for designating every reality including that which is immediately experienced. The resulting relation between immediately experienced reality and the physical brain processes is then no longer one of causal dependency but of simple *identity*.[7]

He also called his view "psychophysical parallelism," making it clear that the parallelism was only *linguistic*: there is the language of psychology and the language of physics and physiology (not necessarily as it is today but as it would be if these sciences were in a final form); and any mental event which can be designated by an expression in the former language can also be designated by an expression in the latter language; the two expressions designate the same thing:

. . . the expression "psychophysical parallelism" is entirely suitable for characterizing our view that one and the same reality—namely, that which is immediately experienced—can be designated both by psychological concepts and by physical ones.[8]

In this section I will try to arrive at a rather more precise formulation of the Identity-hypothesis as adumbrated by Schlick. I will begin by distinguishing three different types of non-analytic identity-statements, which I will call respectively: (i) singular; (ii) universal and one-one; (iii) universal and one-some. (i) A contingent singular identity-statement has the form 'a^5b', where 'a' and 'b' are both uniquely designating phrases, as in "The Morning Star is the Evening Star." An example of (ii) is: "Each President of the USA is the Commander-in-Chief of the US forces." Let 'P_1', 'P_2', 'P_3' . . . denote respectively the first, second, third . . . President of the USA, and 'C_1', 'C_2', 'C_3' . . . the first, second, third . . . C in C US forces; and let 'i' be a variable which ranges over the indices of 'P' and 'C'. Then this universal one-one identity-statement could be formulated thus:

$$'a = b', \quad (\forall i)\,(P_i = C_i) \quad \text{for } i = 1, 2, 3 \ldots$$

In words: the i-th US President is always the i-th US C in C. As an example of (iii) I take this feature of the British peerage: at any given time there is *one* Earl Marshal and *several* Dukes, and the

Earl Marshal is always one of the Dukes. Let 'M_1', 'M_2', 'M_3' . . . denote respectively the first, second, third . . . Earl Marshal; and assume that all past and present Dukes are numbered off (say, according to their date of accession) and denoted by 'D_1', 'D_2', 'D_3' . . . ; and let 'i' and 'j' be variables which range over the indices of, respectively, 'M' and 'D'. Then this universal one-some identity-statement could be formulated thus:

$$(\forall i)\ (\exists j)\quad (M_i = D_j) \text{ where } i = 1, 2, 3 \ldots \text{ and } j \geq i.$$

In words: each i-th Earl Marshal is always some j-th Duke.

I have dwelt on this last type because Schlick's version of the Identity-hypothesis concerns type (iii) rather than type (ii) or type (i) identity-statements. For him, as for other identity-theorists, a mental state is not identical with a total brain state: "Certainly the correlate is not the total brain process, but only *some part* of it" (my italics).[9]

To formulate Schlick's Identity-hypothesis I will invoke the idea of a psychological language M which is complete in the sense that, for any mental event or process, M can provide an expression which denotes it, and likewise a physiological language B which is complete in the sense that, for any brain event or process, B can provide an expression which denotes it. To make things more manageable I will relativise M and B to a particular person, who may as well be myself; and I will restrict the denoting expressions in M and B to those which actually succeed in denoting, respectively, a mental event or process in my consciousness, or a physical event or process in my brain.

However, the Identity-hypothesis cannot be formulated *within* M and B. To formulate it we need to postulate a metalanguage above M and B which is complete in the sense that it can provide a name for each denoting expression in M and in B. Assume that the names in the metalanguage for these denoting expressions in M and B are lexicographically ordered, and let them be 'm_1', 'm_2', 'm_3' . . . and 'b_1', 'b_2', 'b_3' . . . Let 'i' and 'j' be variables which range over the indices of, respectively, 'm' and 'b'. We can now formulate the Identity-hypothesis in this metalanguage as follows:

$$(\forall i)\ (\exists j)\ (m_i = b_j)$$

In words: for any mental event or process of mind depicted by a psychological expression m_i there is an event or process in my brain depicted by a physiological expression b_j such that what b_j denotes *is* what m_i denotes.

I now turn to two conditions which any contingent identity-statement must satisfy for it to be possible that the statement is true. I begin with type (i) statements.

For it to be possible that a singular statement of the form 'a^5b' is true, one condition is that 'a' and 'b' are both denoting phrases each of which, at least in principle, picks out or individuates one definite person, thing, object, event, process, etc. (I say "in principle" because we do not want to exclude phrases like "the tallest man in Tibet" which may fail in practice to pick out one definite individual.) A second condition comes into operation where 'a' and 'b' are neither of them purely denoting phrases but also have some descriptive content; or, to put it in Frege's terminology, where each of them has a sense as well as a reference. In that case it must be conceptually possible that the thing as (denoted and) partially characterised by 'a' is the thing as (denoted and) partially characterised by 'b'. Let us consider these two conditions in their application to the following putative identity-statements:

(1) Sir Isaac Newton is the author of *The Compleat Angler*;

(2) The Noble Savage is the author of *The Compleat Angler*;

(3) The mountain called Mount Everest is the tallest man in Tibet.

Sentence (1), though false, satisfies both conditions: "Sir Isaac Newton" picks out one person and so does "the author of *The Compleat Angler*," and it is not conceptually impossible that the former is the latter. Sentence (2) violates the first condition: "The Noble Savage" is not a genuine denoting phrase; it does not, even in principle, pick out one individual. Sentence (3) violates the second condition: it is conceptually impossible that a mountain is a man.

We can extend the above considerations to type (ii) statements, like our '$\forall i(P_i = C_i)$', by requiring them to be such that our two conditions are met by the singular statements which can be obtained from them by dropping the quantifier and putting a particular value on i; for instance, '$P_{10} = C_{10}$' must satisfy our two conditions. And we can likewise extend them to type (iii) statements, like our '$\forall i \exists j (M_i = D_j)$' by requiring these to be such that our two conditions are met by the singular statements which can be obtained from them by dropping the quantifiers and putting particular values on i and j; for instance, '$M_{10} = D_{100}$' must satisfy our two conditions.

I now turn to Schlick's striking ideas about human consciousness. One way to introduce them is by contrast with Hume's psychological atomism. As well as declaring that a self is "nothing but a bundle or collection of different perceptions" Hume declared that

> All perceptions are distinct. They are, therefore, distinguishable, and separable, and may be conceiv'd as separately existent, and may exist separately. [10]

On this view, a perception occurring in a bundle of perceptions is similar to an atom located in an aggregate of atoms in that it could exist separated from the others. (Notice that this psychological ontology promises well for the Identity-hypothesis: for the left-hand side of the equation it provides neat units waiting to be picked out by *m*-expressions, which would then await pairing with *b*-expressions.)

As Schlick pointed out, Hume's view implies that a sequence of such unit-like perceptions occurring in one individual could be conceived "as being distributed among different individuals." [11] So let us in imagination despatch the first perception in the sequence to one oyster, the second to another oyster, and so on; and let us suppose that each oyster has just this one momentary perception in its life. We could hardly say that the oysters attained *consciousness* in virtue of a momentary sensation (of light, sound, pain or whatever) which then vanished totally. Let us now, instead of despatching each perception to a different oyster, despatch them one at a time to the same oyster but with intervals of total blackout between each perceptual unit. Clearly, the oyster's condition would differ only numerically from its previous condition: if it did not attain conscousness from one momentary sensation with a blackout on either side of it, the oyster will not attain consciousness from a sequence of momentary sensations with a blackout on either side of each of them. Now let the blackout intervals become shorter and shorter. This again will not change the oyster's condition in any significant way, *even if the intervals become vanishingly short.* For the oyster will not be having a continuous flow of experience, but only a chopped up series of unit-sensations. (Schlick acknowledged that Wundt had already stated that momentary "consciousness" is not really consciousness.)

Schlick's view could be summed up thus: no *consciousness* without *unity* of consciousness. He wrote:

> And where there is unity of consciousness, the individual moments of consciousness then exist not for themselves but, as it were, for each other. That is, they cannot be considered independently of their neighbors. Torn from their interconnection with them, they would no longer be the same; the interconnection is of their *essence.*[12]

This "indescribable interconnection," as he at one point called it,[13] is both intersensual and temporal. Although he did not actually use the term "specious present" he endorsed the idea: we "experience temporally adjacent elements of consciousness not merely as succeeding one another but also as being simultaneous."[14] The conscious *present* always has "*some* duration."

Let us now consider the bearing of Schlick's unity of consciousness thesis on his Identity-hypothesis. It will help to have a simple example before us. Yesterday evening I was, let us suppose, at an official dinner. The port having been circulated the presiding officer rose, rapped on the table, raised his glass and said: "Ladies and gentlemen, let us drink a toast to Her Majesty the Queen." A tape-recording was made of this performance: it took ten seconds. What does the Identity-hypothesis say concerning what went on in my mind/brain during those ten seconds? Presumably something like this:—It would in principle be possible to give, in that ideally complete physiological language B, a full description of all the changes that took place in my brain during the first, second, third . . . tenth second. And in the psychological language M there are expressions to denote what I was experiencing during the first, second, third . . . tenth second. For convenience, suppose these expressions to be numbered m_1, m_2, m_3 . . . m_{10}. Then within the physiological description of my brain during the first second there will be something which denotes what m_1 denotes, and so on for each subsequent second. We could express this by:

$$(\forall i) \ (\exists j) \ (m_i = b_j) \text{ for } i = 1, 2, \ldots, 10$$

Let us now ask whether this putative one-some identity-statement meets the first of the two conditions presented in Part 3 above: if we form a singular identity-statement from it by dropping the quantifiers and putting a value between 1 and 10 inclusive on i and some value on j, will both the m-expression on the left and the b-expression on the right of the identity-sign be genuine denoting phrases?

So far as I know there is no reason why the b-expression should not be. Admittedly, it might need to be enormously long and complicated. According to Eccles, one fifth of a second of neuronal activity is already

> . . . very long indeed. The time for transmission from one nerve cell to another is no longer than 1/1000th of a second; hence there could be a serial relay of as many as 200 synaptic linkages between nerve cells before a conscious experience is aroused. Many thousands of nerve cells would be initially activated, and each nerve cell by synaptic relay would in turn activate many nerve cells. The immensity of this patterned spread throughout the neuronal pathways of the brain is beyond all imagining.[15]

But length and complexity do not debar an expression from being a denoting phrase. Imagine a faithful stone-by-stone description of Westminster Abbey, prefaced by "The building which satisfies the following description:" that would constitute a genuine denoting phrase, even if it ran to millions of words.

But what about the left-hand side? Let us consider my experience in the light of Schlick's unity of consciousness thesis. This suggests that it would be most misleading to say that I had a sequence of visual perceptions (of a man rising, raising his arm and moving his lips) running alongside a sequence of aural perceptions (of a rap on the table followed by vocal sounds). I perceived someone proposing a toast. And it would be quite wrong to say that I heard "Ladies and" during one second, then stopped hearing that and heard "gentlemen" during the next second, and so on. What I first heard lingered on and merged into what came after. I was still in a way "hearing" "Ladies and gentlemen" when he got to "the Queen:" I did not have to *recall* how his sentence began.

To make things definite let us select m_9, which is supposed to denote what I experienced during the ninth second. Erasing the first eight seconds and the tenth from tape we find that the ninth consists of ". . . to her Maj . . . " Schlick's unity of consciousness thesis clearly implies that my flow of experience did not provide any distinguishable unit for m_9 denote some (no doubt very complicated) process which went on in my brain during that ninth second.

Then

$$m_9 = b_{90}$$

is a putative identity-statement; but I say that it does not meet our first condition: the left-hand term is not a genuine denoting phrase.

I do not say that there are no denotable and, as it were, unitary items in human experience. There surely are: hearing a click, a stab of toothache, feeling a pinprick, the first taste of an iced drink, and so on. Rather surprisingly, Schlick seems to have regarded such essentially *simple* experiences as the main threat to his Identity-hypothesis. Suppose that a sleeper is half-awakened by, say, a steady drone which he drowsily hears for a while and then sinks back into sleep. Then he briefly has an essentially simple experience. But its physiological correlate

> . . . is apparently extremely complex. The physical processes . . . are enormously complicated. From among the innumerable cells of which the brain is composed, a goodly number go into action when a sensation takes place . . . And now the concept of a brain process . . . is supposed to designate a single quality, namely, this simple sound! Is this not a truly unsolvable contradiction? This objection is so basic that there seems to be no escape from it.[16]

Actually, there is a fairly easy escape from this objection, and Schlick had no difficulty in finding it. Given an m-expression which, as in this case, succeeds in picking out a definite item ("this simple sound"), the Identity-hypothesis makes the merely existential claim that there exists a b-expression which denotes what the m-expression denotes. This claim is irrefutable, a fact of which Schlick took advantage in answering his own objection:

> But we do not know *which* [brain] process is to be associated with a simple sensation as its physical correlate . . . Thus it may be a very small partial process, one that is extremely simple.[17]

But Schlick would have been the first to agree that simple sensations, raw feels, episodic perceptions of bangs, flashes, and the like do not constitute a major part of ordinary experience. If I look back over my experience during the last hour to find how many isolable, denotable episodes it contained, how many instantiations it provided for the 'm_i' in $(\forall i)\,(\exists j)\,(m_i = b_j)$, I find hardly any: the telephone rang and I heard the front-door open and shut; otherwise there was practically nothing of that kind.

In order to secure something definite for his m-expressions to denote, the identity-theorist might take as his unit a person's entire experience from each first awakening until he next falls into unconsciousness. (This would exclude dreams, but let us ignore that complication here.) Let us allow that m-expressions thus conceived constitute genuine denoting phrases. And let us take m_n to denote all that I experienced yesterday between 0715 and 2340. Applied to this particular chunk of experience the Identity-hypothesis will now say

$$\exists j\,(m_n = b_j)$$

This is not itself an identity-statement. It is analogous to '$Ex\,(x^5$ of *The Compleat Angler*)' which promises that a true identity-statement could be got by dropping the existential quantifier and correctly specifying x. Similarly, '$\exists j\,(m_n = b_j)$' promises that a true identity-statement could be got by dropping the existential quantifier, and correctly specifying j. Suppose that '$m_n = b_m$' is proposed as a candidate for being this true identity-statement, where 'b_m' is a denoting phrase somewhat analogous to the one for Westminster Abbey we imagined earlier: that is, it is prefaced by "The brain which satisfies the following description:" after which follows what is in fact a faithful record of certain processes that took place in my brain during the period between 0715 and 2340 yesterday.

We are assuming, now, that 'm_n' and 'b_m' are both genuine denoting phrases, so that '$m_n {}^5 b_m$' meets the first of our two conditions. Does it meet the second? Is it conceptually possible that what is (denoted and) partially characterized by 'm_n' *is* what is (denoted and) partially characterized by 'b_m'? If '$m_n 5 b_m$' were *true*, every property of what is denoted by 'm_n' would be a property of what is denoted by 'b_m'; or

$$(\forall \Phi) \ (\Phi m_n \leftrightarrow \Phi b_m).$$

But let us now recall some of those peculiar properties of consciousness highlighted by Schlick. Assume that the "day in the life of JW" to which 'm_n' refers was relatively free of bangs, flashes, etc. Then this stretch of experience will contain few elements that are, in Hume's words, "distinguishable and separable." It is not easy to give a verbal characterisation of its general properties. One wants to say that neighboring elements in this experiential flow interfuse and color each other; but one also wants to say that the interfusing leaves no elements to interfuse with one another. This difficulty shows itself in Schlick's statement, quoted earlier, that we "experience temporarily adjacent elements of consciousness not merely as succeeding one another but also as being simultaneous." One sees what he meant: I heard "Ladies-and-gentlemen" *both* as one contemporaneous unit and as a short temporal sequence. One understands why Schlick called the interconnectedness *indescribable*.

Schlick himself recognized that this interconnectedness posed a problem for his Identity-hypothesis (though he seems to have regarded it as less threatening than that posed by simple sensations). He wrote:

> Mental qualities have that special relationship which, as the interconnection of consciousness, has so often occupied us. And in this way they are distinguished from all other qualities . . . Does this not represent a dualism . . . ?[18]

He met this objection with the cheerful prophecy that science will eventually come up with physiological correlates for the unity of consciousness. To this I will only say that *if* physiology were ever to show that the abovementioned properties of consciousness are *also* properties of the brain, then the brain would be utterly different from the brain as described by contemporary physiology and, indeed, from *any* physical system so far known to us.

Identity-theorists drew encouragement from Frege's "The Morning Star is the Evening Star," which showed that a contingent and even surprising statement of identity may nevertheless be true. Yes, but a star that is the last to become invisible in the morning is the sort of thing that could be a star that is the first to become visible in the evening. To claim that certain cortical processes *are* conscious experience seems to me like claiming that the Morning Star is the evening stillness.

Notes

1. I came to see the Identity-hypothesis in this light after discussion with Ted Honderich. I am grateful to David Armstrong for his patient criticism of an earlier version of this essay.
2. I have argued for it elsewhere, in Part V of my "Three Views Concerning Human Freedom" (R.S. Peters, ed: *Nature and Conduct*, London: Macmillan, 1975).
3. Moritz Schlick, *Allgemeine Erkenntislehre*, 1918; revised edition 1925. Now translated by A.E. Blumberg as *General Theory of Knowledge*, with an introduction by A.E. Blumberg and H. Feigl (Wien-New York: Springer-Verlag, 1974). I have reviewed this work in the *British Journal of Philosophical Science*, 28 December 1977.
4. There are some passing references to Schlick in H. Feigl, *The "Mental" and the "Physical."* I have found no other references to him in the contemporary literature, which often gives the impression that the Identity-theory was first invented in Australia in the late 1950s.
5. See D.M. Armstrong, *A Materialist Theory of Mind*, (London: Routledge, 1968, especially 92 f).
6. See Grover Maxwell, "Rigid Designators and Mind-Brain Identity" in C. Wade Salvage (ed): Perception and Cognition: Issues in the Foundations of Psychology; *Minnesota Studies in the Philosophy of Science*, Vol. IX, (Minnesota: University of Minnesota Press, 1978).
7. *General Theory of Knowledge*, p. 299.
8. Ibid., p. 310.
9. Ibid., pp. 320-1.
10. *Treatise* (ed. Selby-Bigge), p. 634.
11. Ibid., p. 123.
12. Ibid., p. 125.
13. Ibid., p. 126.
14. Ibid., p. 127.
15. J.C. Eccles, *Facing Reality* (New York: Springer-Verlag, 1973) p. 71.
16. *General Theory of Knowledge*, p. 320.
17. Ibid., pp. 300-1.
18. Ibid., p. 332.

4.
Unity of Consciousness and Mind-Brain Identity

Grover Maxwell

Iam here to *defend* the mind-brain identity thesis as a thesis of strict identity; by "identical" I mean *one and the same thing* or *one and the same event*, such that the Leibniz law is at least a necessary condition for identity to hold. One other preliminary remark: Professor Watkins and I have a remarkable amount of agreement; in fact we start from virtually the same premises but, unfortunately, reach contradictory conclusions. Now this is not to impugn John's abilities as a logician; rather, I think that there is a suppressed premise operating in his argument, and I'll just say briefly what I think it is. It's something to the effect that the brain really *is* pretty much like the picture we get from common sense plus the picture we get from people like Karl (Pribram), Sir John Eccles, and other brain physiologists, and eventually what we get from physics. I think this suppressed premise entails that, if the identity theory implies that the brain is different from this, then the identity theory is in serious trouble. I shall challenge this premise, and now I shall try to clarify somewhat the way in which I do it. I like to tell of the time when I heard Benson Mates remark that it makes about as much sense to try to identify a billy goat with a quadratic equation as it does to try to identify a mental state with a brain state. In a perhaps less colorful but suitably more elegant and reasoned approach, Watkins reaches a similar conclusion. Now I have a great deal of sympathy *and* empathy with these sentiments of Watkins, Mates, Sir John and many others, including myself at times.

The difficulty that Watkins poses for the mind-brain identity is an ingenious, highly developed instance of the more general argument, the argument that is by far the most cogent against the identity hypothesis. Let me put it briefly and crudely: Premise 1: we know from direct observation, from common sense, and from physics, chemistry, neuro-physiology, etc., *what* the brain *is*, what it is *like*, what its *properties, states*, and *processes are*, etc. Premise 2: we also know from common sense, from direct acquaintance, and perhaps from the science of psychology *what* the mind or mental states or mental events *are*, and what *they* are *like*. Intermediate conclusion: this knowledge entails that mental events have properties that brain events lack, and conversely. Conclusion: it follows from the Leibniz law, to say nothing of good old everyday horse sense, that mental events cannot be brain events.

Traditionally materialists have countered this argument by denying premise 2. They hold that our knowledge of the mental is so defective that it can be pretty much disregarded, indeed that, in the sense advocated by mentalists, there is no such thing as the mind or the mental, no such thing as mental events, etc. Rightly, Watkins rejects this. I applaud his appreciation of the fact that Schlick does the same. Such a rejection, however, entails that the identity theorist must deny premise 1; that is the identity theorist must deny that we know enough about brain events to be sure that they can't be mental events. Now this already strongly suggests Professor Watkins' contention that, if the identity hypothesis were true, then the brain would be utterly different from the brain as described by contemporary physiology, and indeed different from any physical system so far known to us. And this is already the case before we consider the difficulty Watkins raises about the unity of consciousness. For the identity theorist must contend that among the constitutents of the brain are pains, tickles, joys and sorrows, beliefs that transcend $2^2 2^5 4$, etc., in all of their qualitative, mentalistic richness. Surely a brain that numbers such entities among its constituents *is* utterly different from the brain and from all other physical systems as they are ordinarily conceived, even, for *most* of us, when the results of contemporary physiology are taken into account.

Now as Professor Watkins knows, Schlick not only recognized this, he emphasized and insisted upon it. More specifically, he insisted that contemporary scientific knowledge virtually forces us to change drastically our beliefs about the nature of the brain, and about all physical systems, and that this is independent of the mind-brain identity thesis. Scientific knowledge forces us to change our customary *interpretation* of *scientific knowledge itself*, and this is, moreover, independently urged upon us prior to consideration of mind-brain identity. Moreover, this holds with full force for the picture of the brain that *seems* to result from contemporary physiology.

The general thesis that Schlick emphasizes (along with the late Bertrand Russell) may be put as follows: physical science provides us with knowledge about the structural properties of physical systems, but it leaves us entirely ignorant as to what the intrinsic or the qualitative properties of these systems are. In particular, physiology leaves us entirely ignorant as to what the intrinsic properties of the brain are, and thus ignorant as to the intrinsic nature of the brain events. Regarding any specific brain event, physiology tells us no more than where it is located in that portion of the spatio-temporal, causal network that we ordinarily call the brain. This is utterly different from our ordinary conception of the brain, which misguidedly involves intrinsic properties, even when it seems to take physiology and physics into account. When we correct this and realize that our best knowledge to date, the knowledge from physiology, physics, etc., leaves the intrinsic nature of brain events entirely unspecified, the way is entirely open for speculating that some brain events just are our joys, sorrows, pains, thoughts, etc., in all of their qualitative and mentalistic richness. So Watkins is mistaken, I believe, in intimating that such a speculation is wrong just because it entails that the brain is utterly different from what we and physiologists ordinarily believe it to be, since reflection on the nature of scientific results *from* physiology, physics, etc., suggests very strongly that the brain *is indeed* very different from what our ordinary beliefs entail.

However, the difficulty he poses concerning the unity of consciousness remains a genuine and acute one for the identity theorist, for it becomes apparent upon reflection that some of the differences between mental events involving the unity of consciousness on the one hand, and brain events on the other, are differences in structure rather than differences in intrinsic properties. Specifically his arguments are that, for example, the casual structure of our auditory experience involved in hearing and understanding a phrase such as "Her Majesty the Queen," is very different from the spatio-temporal, causal structure of events treated by physics, physiology, etc. I want to suggest two possible ways to deal with this. The first, if only it would work, would be far simpler. I'm going to abbreviate this very much. It would be to resort to something like short-term memory traces, say something like a reverberating circuit or synoptic microstructure activity. For example, at a given instance the auditory trace on the cortex might have a structure isomorphic to the following:

. . . HER MAJES . . . etc.

Now the size of the letters is supposed to correspond structurally to the intensity of the trace on the cortex, and their order corresponds to an order that is exemplified in the auditory space of the sensorium, or whatever you want to call it. Although such an order is sensed at an instant, it is interpreted at that instant by a scanning mechanism, say in another part of the brain, as temporal succession analogously to our instantaneous visual perception of the symbol, "ICUS," in which you see "ICUS" in an instant and *at that instant* you perceive that "I" precedes "S" in your visual space.

Now even if my account of this less drastic approach is intelligible, I'm not very optimistic about its success. For reasons that include Watkins' unity of consciousness objection, as well as other ones besides, I think it is likely that the existence of the genuinely mental events that both Watkins and I champion necessitates the existence of spatio-temporal, causal structures quite different from those with which contemporary physical science operates. Far from reacting to this with despair, I find it encouraging and exciting, both as an identity theorist and as a student of the physical sciences. For one thing, I am far from satisfied with the current state of physics. In spite of many impressive accomplishments, quantum theory seems to me to be largely a conceptual and scientific mess. Our other current fundamental theory, general relativity, also leaves much to be desired. And finally, I believe that it is generally agreed that all attempts to integrate fully quantum theory and general relativity with each other have been rather abject failures. Perhaps a radically new space-time theory is just what physics needs at this time. I do not find it too fanciful, even, to contemplate that neurophysiologists and bridge scientists, such as neuro-psychologists and psychophysiologists, in their attempts to im-plement an identity theory, may be led to propose bold new theories of spatio-temporal, causal relationships, theories that may alter fundamentally and irrevocably the course of *all* physical theory. In any event, I have no doubt that neuroscientists must make such attempts and not be too intimidated by current physical theory. It would be a happy circumstance if physicists, philosophers and others were to join them in such attempts.

5.
A Critical Appraisal of Brain-Mind Theories

Sir John Eccles

From Greek times to the present an enormous intellectual effort has been made in the attempt to understand how the inner illumination which we may refer to as a conscious state is related to the material world. At first this internal world was restricted to the body of the experiencing subject, so defining the body-mind problem. Now, on the basis of our brain science we can refer to it as the brain-mind problem. The prevailing philosophy of materialism or physicalism offers four more or less independent theories on the brain-mind problem. Three of the theories admit the existence of states of consciousness, but relegate it to an impotent role, hence they are classified as materialistic. A brief outline of each will be followed by their critical examination.

Materialist Theories of the Brain-Mind Problem

1. Radical Materialism. There is a denial of the existence of conscious processes and mental states. Radical behaviorism provides a complete explanation of behavior including verbal behavior and the dispositional states that lead to this. I do not think that many neuroscientists hold such an extreme view. It is however attractive to many philosophers because of its simplicity and because it eliminates not only the brain-mind problem, but also the problem of the origin of mind. The cosmos is reduced to the pristine simplicity that it had before the origin of life. While this may appeal to reductionist philosophers, neuroscientists must find this extreme reductionism absurd, so it will not be further discussed.

2. Panpsychism. This is a very ancient theory developed by the earliest Greek philosophers, who proposed that "soul is mingled with everything in the whole universe." Such philosophers as Spinoza and Leibniz espoused various forms of panpsychism. Essentially their belief was that all things had an inner psychical aspect and were material in their outer aspect. Panpsychism has even attracted modern biologists such as Waddington and Rensch because it offers such an attractive solution to the problem of the evolutionary origin of consciousness, namely that consciousness was associated with all matter in some protopsychic state and was merely developed with the increasing complexity of the brain to appear as the self-consciousness associated with the human brain. However, modern physics does not admit memory or identity to elementary particles—electrons, protons, neutrons —hence the panpsychist doctrine of the "protoconsciousness" of such particles must be rejected.

3. Epiphenomenalism. Epiphenomenalism differs from panpsychism in that mental states are attributed only to animals that exhibit mindlike behavior, such as learning and reacting intelligently and purposively. All varieties of epiphenomenalism have as a central tenet the thesis that the mental processes are completely ineffective in controlling behavior. The neural machinery works without any influence from consciousness, just as, according to T.H. Huxley, the work of a steam locomotive is uninfluenced by the sound of the steam whistle! Yet it is proposed that at a certain stage of evolution these ineffective mental states emerged and were then greatly developed in the evolutionary process to the full human self-consciousness.

4. The psycho-physical identity theory or the central state theory. Like panpsychism this theory was first developed by Greek philosophers and the two theories have often been linked, as for example by Spinoza and Rensch. The most subtle and acceptable form of the theory has been given by Feigl. Several analogies have been used in illustrating the postulated identity, but all are unsatisfactory because both components are in the materialist mode. For example there is the much overworked analogy: evening star, morning star achieving identity in the planet Venus. Other analogies are: cloud and fog, achieving identity in water droplets of the atmosphere; or a flash of lightning = electric discharge; or genes = DNA. Nevertheless there are attractive and important features in the identity theory. Mental processes are regarded as real or things in themselves. They are conjectured to be a property of a very small and select group of material objects, namely neural events in the brain, and probably in special regions of the brain. The conscious experiences are known within, *knowledge by acquaintance*, whereas the "identical" physical events are known from without by description, *knowledge by description*, of the neural events in the brain. These events described by the neuroscientist turn out to be the experiences consciously perceived. Thus the key postulate is essentially a parallelism or an inner and outer aspect.

Neuroscientists find the identity theory attractive because it gives the future to them. It is admitted that our present understanding of the brain is quite inadequate to provide more than a crude explanation of how the brain provides all the richness and wonderful variety of perceptual experiences, or how the mental events or thoughts can have the immense range and fruitfulness that our imaginative insights achieve in their action on the world. However, all this is taken care of by the theory that Popper has named *promissory materialism*. This theory derives from the great successes of the neurosciences, which undoubtedly are disclosing more and more of what is happening in the brain in perception, in the control of movement and in states of consciousness and unconsciousness. The aim of these research programs is to give a more and more complete and coherent account of the manner in which the total performance and experience of an animal and of a human being are explicable by the action of the neural machinery of the brain. According to promissory materialism the scientific advance will progressively restrict the phenomena that appear to require mental terms for their explanation so that in the fullness of time everything will be describable in the materialist terms of the neurosciences. The victory of materialism over mentalism will be complete. I regard this theory as being without foundation. The more we discover scientifically about the brain, the more clearly do we distinguish between the brain events and the mental phenomena, and the more wonderful do the mental phenomena become. Promissory materialism is simply a religious belief held by dogmatic materialists who often confuse their religion with their science. It has all the features of a Messianic prophecy, with the promise of a future freed of all problems—a kind of Nirvana for our unfortunate successors. In contrast the true scientific attitude is that scientific problems are unending in providing challenges to attain an even wider and deeper understanding of nature and man.

General Discussion of the Four Materialist Theories in Relation to Dualist-Interactionism

A simple formulation of the similarities and differences may be given on the basis of Popper's terminology:

World 1 is the whole physical world, the world of matter-energy;

World 2 is the world of mental phenomena, the subjective states.

For *Radical Materialism* all is World 1, World 2 does not exist.

For *Panpsychism* all is World 1-2, neither World 1 nor World 2 has any independent existence.

For *Epiphenomenalism* World 1 has two components: World 1_p, all the world of physics without mental states; and World 1_M, the world of physics with mental states as an epiphenomenon. So it may be written that: World 1 = World 1_p + World 1_M, where World $1_M \rightarrow$ World 2.

For *Identity theory* World 1 = World 1_p + World 1_M and World 1_M = World 2 by virtue of the identity relationship.

For *Dualist interactionism* World 1 and World 2 are independent entities and it is proposed that in special sites in the brain, the liaison brain (LB), there is reciprocal interaction. World 1_{LB} = World 2 where World 1_{LB} is the part of World 1 that forms the liaison brain.

I propose now to consider the biological implications of the three materialist theories that admit the existence of consciousness or mental states (World 2). Despite the differences in detail with respect to the relationship of World 2 to World 1, all are in agreement that the physical events in the brain (World 1) are alone causally effective in bringing about actions. In panpsychism the mental accompaniments of brain events are given no more causal effectiveness than in epiphenomenalism. They are merely the necessary concomitants of the on-going brain activities. At first it seems otherwise with the identity theory where World 1_M can interact with World 1_p because both are components of the neural machinery in the brain. Thus we have:

World $1_p \rightleftharpoons$ World 1_M and World $1_M =$ World 2.

Nevertheless the performance of the brain in controlling behavior is entirely within the physical structures of the brain. No causal effectiveness of World 2 is admitted other than that of pertaining to World 1_M. Thus the closedness of World 1 is as absolute as with panpsychism or epiphenomenalism.

These three theories assert the casual ineffectiveness of World 2 and hence fail completely to account for the biological evolution of World 2, which is an undeniable fact. There is first its emergence and then its progressive development with the growing complexity of the brain. In accord with evolutionary theory only those structures and processes that significantly aid in survival are developed in natural selection. If World 2 is impotent, its development cannot be accounted for by evolutionary theory. It has not been recognized by the proponents of panpsychism, epiphenomenalism and the identity theory that they are advocating a theory that is in contradiction with the theory of biological evolution. According to that theory mental states and consciousness (World 2) could have evolved and developed only if they were *casually effective* in bringing about changes in neural happenings in the brain with the consequent changes in behavior. That can occur only if World 1 of the brain is open to influences from the mental events of World 2, which is the basic postulate of the dualist-interactionist theory.

The Dualist-Interactionist Theory

This theory is the most ancient formulation of the mind-body problem, being in some form generally accepted by Greek thinkers from Homer onwards. It was developed by Descartes who attempted to define a detailed mode of operation that led to it being rejected in favor of some form of parallelism. In its modern form it is distinguished from all parallelistic theories precisely by the requirement of the openness of World 1 to World 2 events. As formulated above:

World $1_{LB} \rightleftharpoons$ World 2, World 1_{LB} being the liaison brain.

Since World 1_{LB} is some part of the brain, it is of course in an intimate and intense reciprocal interaction with the rest of the brain, but, over and above that, it is open to the mental influences of World 2, which are of a non-physical kind. The casual effectiveness of these mental influences is apparent in countless actions of everyday life where thoughts become expressed as actions or in the recalls of memory on demand. It is reassuring to find that the causal effectiveness of mental states can be deduced from evolutionary theory.

The self-conscious mind is conceived to be an independent entity, a World 2 existence, which has a status in reality equivalent to that of the brain with its World 1 existence. This is a strong dualism.

A brief outline of the hypothesis may be given as follows. The self-conscious mind is actively engaged in reading out from the multitude of active centers at the highest level of brain activity, namely the liaison modules that are largely in the dominant cerebral hemisphere. The self-conscious mind selects from these modules according to attention and interest, and from moment to moment integrates its selection to give unity even to the most transient experiences. Furthermore the self-conscious mind acts upon these neural centers modifying the dynamic spatiotemporal patterns of the neural events. Thus it is proposed that the self-conscious mind exercises a superior interpretative and controlling role upon the neural events.

A key component of the hypothesis is that the unity of conscious experience is provided by the self-conscious mind and not by the neural machinery of the liaison areas of the cerebral hemisphere. Hitherto it has been impossible to develop any neurophysiological theory that explains how a diversity of brain events comes to be synthesized so that there is a unified conscious experience of a global or gestalt character. The brain events remain disparate, being essentially the individual actions of countless neurones that are built into complex circuits and so participate in the spatiotemporal patterns of activity. This is the case even for the most specialized neurones so far detected, the feature detection neurones of the inferotemporal lobe of primates. The present hypothesis regards the neuronal machinery as a multiplex of radiating and receiving structures: the experienced unity comes, not from a neurophysiological synthesis, but from the proposed integrating character of the self-conscious mind. It is conjectured that in the first place the self-conscious mind was developed in order to give this unity of the self in all of its conscious experiences and actions.

Notes

1. D.M. Armstrong, *A Materialist Theory of the Mind* (London: Routledge, 1968).

2. H.B. Barlow, *Perception* (England: Cambridge University Press, 1972) pp. 1, 371-94.

3. J.C. Eccles, *Cerebral Correlates of Conscious Experience*, P. Buser and A. Rougeul-Buser, eds. (Amsterdam: Elsevier, 1978).

4. H. Feigl, *The "Mental" and the "Physical"* (Minneapolis: University of Minnesota Press, 1967).

5. E. Laszlo, *Introduction to Systems Philosophy* (London and New York: Gordon and Breach, 1972).

6. S.C. Pepper, *Dimensions of Mind*, Sidney Hook, ed. (London: Collier-Macmillan Ltd., 1960).

7. U.T. Place. 1956. *British Journal of Psychology*, pp. 44-47.

8. E.P. Polten, *A Critique of the Psycho-physical Identity Theory* (The Hague: Moulton Publishers, 1973).

9. K.R. Popper and J.C. Eccles, *The Self and its Brain* (Heidelberg, London and New York: Springer-Verlag, 1977).

10. W.V.O. Quine, *World and Object* (Massachusetts: M.I.T. Press, 1960).

11. B. Rensch, *Biophilosophy* (New York: Columbia University Press, 1971).

12. M. Schlick, *General Theory of Knowledge* (Heidelberg, London and New York: Springer-Verlag, 1974).

13. J.J.C. Smart, *Philosophy of Mind*, V.C. Chappell ed. (Englewood Cliffs: Prentice-Hall, 1962).

14. J. Szentagothai. 1975. *Brain Research*, 95, pp. 475-496.

15. C.H. Waddington, *The Nature of Life* (London: Allen & Unwin, 1961).

But where does this occur?
It can't just happen in space
Emergent principle of interacting networks?
So that examining individual neurons
destroys it?
Specific mind events - attention, preparation
apparently correlate with specific patterns
in an EEG

Commentary

Hardin B. Jones

Sir John Eccles has given examples of the differences between the cerebral hemispheres with regard to the location of self. It provides a basis for understanding mind-brain relationships. I wish to extend the examples.

Some forms of mental impairment are not perceived by the person affected. He needs the very part of the brain now suppressed in order to realize the deletion. Some effects of drugs are of this sort. The active ingredient of cannabis accumulates in the body and in the brain. This explains the progressive changes in the personality and behavior of the marijuana smoker, and the point is that the user has little or no insight to the altered mental function even if it is so severe that he becomes indolent. During months of abstinence, however, the former user becomes aware of many steps in recovery. This process may last several years in heavily affected persons.

Persons using opiates gradually develop faulty memory and a curious defect in mental process that denies them comprehension of the significance of many of the facts available. This is particularly true of the deductions that would allow the opiate user to realize the threat of harm or to know the consequence of an act. These changes from taking opiates occur prior to addiction and are reversed only slowly during months of abstinence.

When enough cocaine has been taken to induce euphoria, the sensation is often reported by the observer as a sensation of clear-headedness. This is illusion, for the person is usually hallucinating at the same time. Also from animal studies it has been shown that although a state of hyperactivity is induced by administration of cocaine the metabolism of the

59

brain is not increased, rather it is decreased approximately by one-third.

These examples suggest that the self of the mind is complex; perhaps self is divisible into many subparts. For a more complete discussion of the effects of drugs on the mind see *Sensual Drugs* by Hardin and Helen Jones, Cambridge University Press, 1977.

6.

The Mind/Brain Issue As a Scientific Problem

Karl H. Pribram

ohn Eccles, in his opening address, noted that the Mind/ Brain problem is at the center of a revolution *necessitated* by the relatively recent discoveries of modern physics. However, as Daniel Robinson has reviewed for us, philosophers have been concerned with this problem for some time and have provided us with a variety of answers which are encapsulated by the labels dualism and monism. Dualistic theories are ordinarily distinguished as parallelist or interactionist and monism has engendered multiple aspects and identity proposals. Philosophers have also stated, and this view was affirmed here by Robinson and Watkins, that scientific experiment and observation will yield little, if any, resolution of the question as to which of the philosophical positions is the correct one. These thoughtful scholars suggest that what is needed is more philosophical analysis, or perhaps the acceptance of one viewpoint because of its overwhelming logical persuasion.

As a scientist I cannot accept either the premise that scientific experiment and observation are irrelevant to an issue of such fundamental import nor the view that therefore we should continue the analysis much as philosophers have done for almost three millenia.

When in science a question arises that appears to be unresearchable the scientist asks whether that question has been properly phrased. As Medawar has stated so succinctly "science [in common with politics] is the art of the possible." Ordinarily, problems that appear to be resistant to research are so either because the appropriate technical (and that includes analytical techniques such as forms of mathematics) resources have as yet not been invented or because the question has not been broken down into meaningful (i.e., precisely interrelated) subquestions.

Scientists using the techniques of behavioral psychology, information engineering and brain physiology are addressing problems on the interface between brain and mind. Thus, the difficulty with the Mind/Brain issue appears to be conceptual rather than technical (as our philosophical contributors suggest). But rather than continue the century old debate as to which philosophical position is correct, I will approach the problem from a different vantage.

The logical possibility exists that the Mind/Brain issue consists not of one global problem but a set of specific and interrelated questions. If that should prove the case, then experimental observations might well become relevant to one or another of these questions. Further, it could turn out that each of the more global philosophical "positions" is correct with respect to one or another of these specific questions.

Using this approach it is possible to discern at least three very different questions that compose the Mind/Brain issue. These questions are: 1) how to characterize existential reality 2) how to characterize the transactions between an organism and its environment and 3) how to characterize the organization of the universe (including the biological universe).

Philosophical inquiry has approached the first question, the nature of existential reality through introspection. Scientists have approached the same question by making experiments and observations on the physical universe. Both introspection and physical science have yielded the same result: one must take into account both the observer and the observed. As an example, in philosophy Brentano characterized the essence of self-report to be the ability to distinguish between perceiver and the perceived and between intent and act. This principle is usually referred to as "intentionality." In physics Heisenberg and Wigner,[1] among others, have clearly stated that the science of physics deals primarily with probability correlations among *observations*, and that the referents of those observations must be inferred.

Thus both philosophy and science arrive at an existential

dualism. The scientist investigating the material universe is thrown back upon his own observation as critical; the introspective philosopher finds "self" only when he can distinguish a difference between intention and that which is intended.

Questions as to the "existence" of each of these "realities" and whether the one can be "reduced" to the other are subsidiary questions to which I shall return shortly. For the moment it is sufficient to understand that dualism is composed of a duality in which neither the material nor the mental can ultimately be examined (at least at present) without recourse to the other.

Are there any observations or experiments that are relevant to this issue? I believe there are. One such question concerns the evolution of intentionality. Are apes self–aware? If so, are monkeys? Other mammals? What will the results of answers to these questions have on our existential experience of intentionality? Will the centrality of intentionality to the Mind side of the Mind/Brain issue be jeopardized if animals other than man can be shown to possess intent?

Another relevant experimental observation concerns the specialization of function of the hemispheres of the brain, as Eccles[2] has repeatedly pointed out. If both hemispheres display intentionality and their behavioral output can be separated, are there then two selves? And if there are, does that not mean that a two hemispheres-two minds correlation becomes established? And if not, then the quest for what brain process does correlate continues and doesn't it make a difference to the Mind/Brain issue whether total brain hemisphere processes or for instance linguistic processes correlate with mental processes? Aren't precise definitions of Mind dependent on such observations?

It is, of course, with just such precise definitions that questions about the Mind/Brain issue must be asked. So far we have asked about the existence of Mind and Brain—their reality in experience. Mind so defined becomes identified with intentional being, with "self"—self-awareness, self–consciousness. Being, awareness and consciousness can, however, be conceived either as states (relatively enduring configurations) or as functions (relationships among relatively enduring configurations). Two very different theoretical frames are derived depending on which conception is pursued.

Gilbert Ryle first defined mind in terms of minding, a function. Minding is behavior. Minding is paying attention. And there is a considerable body of scientific knowledge concerning behavior and attention. The consequences of behavior (technically these are called acts when they rearrange environmental configurations and reinforcements when they rearrange organismic states,[3] and of paying attention (or not paying attention) are well documented scientifically. When these consequences are framed within the Mind/Body issue they lead to an interactionist view.

Popper and Eccles in their recently published book "The Self and its Brain" (1977) develop the case for such an interactionist viewpoint. Unfortunately, they do not clearly distinguish between Mind as state and Mind as function so that the thrust of their argument often loses force and the experiments described by Eccles do not address the specific problem to which they are appropriate.

It should not be surprising that Popper, as one of the most influential heirs of Mach's emphasis on sensory experience and the consequent positivism of the Vienna Circle, espouses a position in which Mind as function—as minding—acts upon the physical universe which in turn influences Mind as state through the senses. But note also that other equally perspicacious philosophers of the Vienna Circle such as Feigl[4] could bring to flower an identity position from the same roots.

Perhaps this difference between philosophical views stems from the confounding of Mind as state and Mind as function already noted. If emphasis is placed on minding as function, its interactive properties become paramount. If, on the other hand, emphasis is placed on Mind as state, correspondences, identities between states (configurations) will be sought. In biology and physics, Helmholtz[5] and Hertz,[6] for example, looked for such correspondences, e.g., between the physical stimulus as described by instruments, and the resulting experience as described by verbal response. Hertz used the terms *Bild*, image, and *Darstellung*, representation, as a construction or model of reality which is best described in mathematical terms. Whereas Machian functionalism leads to interactions by way of the senses and behavior, Helmholtz and Hertz's structuralism leads to modelling, a cognitive constructional activity which searches for identities.

Popper combines these historical traditions by making his third world (Mind as function) the medium for interaction between Brain (World 1) and Mind as state (World 2). But he fails to point out, as does Hertz, that interaction occurs only to the extent that World 3 identifies World 1 with World 2—i.e., the limits of interaction are described by the limits of the *identity* between model and what is being modelled ("reality").

Further, by creating World 3 as apart from World 2, World 2 the mental world, becomes restricted to the sensory world of Mach, from which cognitive activity is derivative (Mach) rather than integral (as proposed by Kant.[7] Neuropsychological research[8] has indicated that the Kantian view must at least be seriously considered.

Max Jammer, in this conference, has given a superb account of these differences between Mach's functionalism and the scientific approach developed by Helmholtz and Hertz. Toulmin also gives a detailed account of these developments.[9] Feigl's views and those derived from them such as Grover Maxwell's thoughtful and thought provoking paper presented at this conference appear to me to be kin to the structural approach. "Multiple aspects" of some partially perceived identity are not altogether different from the "models" of reality espoused by Hertz.

I am inclined to accept this structuralist approach to the Mind/Brain problem because it can subsume the others and bring to bear additional scientific evidence. The concept "structure" in this sense is not to be confused with morphology or anatomical structure. Structure here means the structure of process, the meaning used by Hertz, Levi-Strauss[10] and by Merleau-Ponty."[11] Process involves one state becoming another. Functional interactions are thus encompassed.

A structural approach to the Mind/Brain issue discerns systems of states some of which are hierarchically related, others are processed in parallel, while still others interact to produce new states. Examples of such systems are information processing devices. There is a hierarchy of configurations—at the lowest level are electrical circuits which are organized into flip-flops, then into "and" "or" gates and "nand" and "nor" configurations. From these more complex computational elements are constructed. These are then combined into the hardware "brains" that we call computers. To operate, i.e., to function, these "brains" must interact with an appropriate environment through input-output devices (hardware sense organs and effectors). Without such devices the computer does not function, nor does it function without programs which constitute its appropriate interactive environment. One might say that without programs computers won't mind. They won't attend, they won't change their configurations, their states. Programs and hardware are certainly different in function and realization—perhaps as different as Mind and Brain.

Still there are identities, as well. There is a truism in the information sciences that anything that can be realized in a program can be constructed in hardware—and vice-versa.

What is it that shares this identity? It is called the "structure" of the process. It is this structure which we recognize functional program and functioning computer to have in common. It is the same commonality as that which characterizes the structure of a symphony which we recognize whether it is realized as an experience in the concert hall or as the score in sheet music. A variety of realizations—score, tape, disc, performance, shares an identity in structure which we can experience in appropriate circumstances.

The structural approach therefore does not deny an apparent dualism in Mind/Brain. It does, however, suggest that a better description might be that of a duality (a set of symmetry relationships) which has certain properties in common. It can explain the apparent dualism in terms of a hierarchy of knowledge systems (Sociology, Psychology, Physiology, Chemistry, Physics) which, when explored in a reductive direction, yields ever more material descriptions until the limit is reached in microphysics where such descriptions become almost totally mathematical—i.e., descriptions of relationships among observations rather than of relationships among observables. (There is therefore an ultimate paradoxical circularity to the hierarchy). When, by contrast, the explorations are performed in an upward direction in the hierarchy, conventions must be established in order that the exploration may proceed. The theories of relativity established the role of such conventions in physics, the periodic table based on atomic number is such a convention in chemistry, and *mental* language (consensually, i.e., socially validated) provides this convention for psychology.[12]

Note that with this view, intentionality is derived by looking upward in a hierarchy which is comprised of the biological organism is his eco-system. The convention becomes established that the organism can distinguish between himself and his environment and that this distinction characterizes mental life, or mind. Other conventions adopt other distinctions. For example, the functional approach is characterized by the convention that mind is to behaving biological *bodies* as force is to *masses* in motion (i.e., behaving).

It is this conventional aspect—the fact that one must choose a frame within which exploration proceeds—that makes plausible the varieties of philosophical approaches to the Mind/Body issue. I have tried here to make explicit which frame, which convention, proscribes which philosophical position. I have also therefore attempted to show that each position has merit and to discern that merit. In short, the Mind/Body issue appears to me to yield to a set of *complementary* theories, each of which has explanatory power and limits.

Unity is therefore to be achieved when the relationships between the complements that characterize the theories are clarified. Ultimately understanding the complementarities may devolve on understanding what goes on at the limits of the theories. Thus, does the fact that microphysical theory is a description of observations rather than of observables mean that "ultimately" the universe is made up of observations, i.e., Mind, or does it mean that we simply cannot, in this instance, use the ordinary neurophysiological mechanisms of "projection"[13] to construct an apparent physical reality as we normally do for the mechanistic universe? As a scientist I believe it is this type of question that can now supplant the earlier philosophical analyses. As a scientist, also, I believe that experiment and observation will have a high yield of contributions to make in answer to such specific questions.

Notes

1. E.P. Wigner, "Epistemology of Quantum Mechanics: Its Appraisal and Demands," in M. Grene, ed. *The Anatomy of Knowledge* (London: Routledge and Kegan Paul, 1969).

2. J.C. Eccles, *Facing Reality* (Heidelberg, Berlin and New York: Springer-Verlag, 1970).

3. K.H. Pribram, *Languages of the Brain: Experimental Paradoxes and Principles in Neuropsychology* (Englewood Cliffs: Prentice-Hall, 1971).

4. H. Feigl, Mind and Body, not a pseudo problem. In S. Hook, ed. *Dimension of Mind* (New York: Collier Books, 1960).

5. H. von Helmholtz, *Lehre von den Tonempfindungen* (Braunschweig: Vieweg, 1863).

6. H. Hertz, *The Principles of Mechanics Presented in a New Form*, translated by D.E. Jones and J.T. Walley, with Preface by H. von Helmholtz and Introduction by Robert Cohen (New York: Dover, 1956).

7. I. Kant, *Critique and Pure Reason*, translated by N. Kemp Smith (New York: Macmillan, 1963).

8. K.H. Pribram, *Languages of the Brain*, Chap. 17.

9. A. Janik and S. Toulmin, *Wittgenstein's Vienna* (New York: Simon & Schuster, 1973).

10. C. Levi-Strauss, *Structural Anthropology* (New York: Basic Books, 1963).

11. M. Merleau-Ponty, *The Structure of Behavior* (Boston: Beacon Press, 1963).

12. K.H. Pribram, Proposal for a structural pragmatism: some neurophysical considerations of problems in philosophy. In B. Wolman and E. Nagle, eds. *Scientific Psychology: Principles and Approaches* (New York: Basic Books, 1965), pp. 426-59.

13. G. von Bekesy, *Sensory Inhibition* (New Jersey: Princeton University Press, 1967).

7.

Persons in Recent Thought

H.D. Lewis

he topic of this paper is a large one indeed. It is, however, in my view, altogether central to our main concerns today. It is therefore appropriate to direct attention to the main issues involved in our thought and about persons and outline what I take myself to be most important in the way we should think about persons.

First of all, there is the long debate about dualist and monist views of persons. Are we two things, or perhaps two streams of events, in some peculiar relation, or is there just the one type of reality which may be viewed in some respect mental and in another material or physical—or perhaps even more simply just one mode of being, as far as we are concerned and perhaps the entire universe?

All these views have been held. Indeed, they have a long and fairly continuous history from as early as we have records of reflective and speculative thought—and they figure in diverse cultures. The most popular form of monistic view—that is the doctrine that there is only one type of being—in our times is materialism. All reality must be thought to be material or physical, including our thoughts and purposes. But while this is a highly fashionable doctrine in our times we do well to remember that this has come about by a very massive swing of opinion early in this century. The philosophical thinking, and with it related attitudes, which dominated almost every aspect of thought, not only in the English-speaking world but elsewhere including the Orient, at the turn of the century and for some decades before that, was idealism. In an astonishing variety of ways, idealism proclaimed the view that in one way or another all reality was thought or mental, usually along the lines of the many variations on the Hegelian theme of the one absolute being appearing in many forms. "The real is the rational" was the famous text, and for many this was understood to mean that all existence is mental or some kind of experience. The confidence with which this view was held at one time, the strong belief that all future philosophy must be some variation on it, may seem astounding today, but it is salutary to recall it when we note the surprising assurance with which some other fashionable views have since been held.

There are other forms of idealism, some to my mind more attractive than post-Hegelian idealism, though we have much to learn from the latter and much though we greatly appreciate the revival of Hegelian studies pioneered by John Findlay, H.B. Acton, W.B. Walsh, T.M. Knox and a host of others in many countries. There is the idealism of Berkeley and the monadology of Leibniz, to name some of the obvious examples, and some forms at least of recent phenomenalism.

The fashionable monism today is some form of materialism, although it was not from that quarter, but from the very different realism of Cook Wilson and G.E. Moore, that the initial drastic inroads were made on nineteenth century idealism. There are many forms of materialism, and not all exponents of it favor the term, but they are all agreed in maintaining that there can be no mental existence which is altogether distinct from physical reality or wholly real in its own right.

The more outright form of this is what is usually known as "old-fashioned" materialism. This took the extraordinary line of maintaining that all that we are apt to take as distinct mental reality, thoughts, sensations, etc., as states or processes in our bodies conditioned solely by material events in the world around us. Thought itself compromises just movements in our vocal chords and hopes and fears are tensions in our breasts or stomach. It is a constant source of wonder to me that highly intelligent people should have adhered seriously to this view. Yet at one time it was strongly held, not only by ingenious behaviorists like J.B. Watson but also as a cardinal feature of communist philosophy.

My own reaction here is a very simple one. If nothing exists other than these dispositons of our bodies, almost everything to which we attach importance loses its significance. The attitudes of many highly intelligent adherents to strictly materialist communist philosophy, which is not the same thing as saying that material needs are basic or decisive in human responses—a more modest though still very questionable form of materialism—are often ambivalent. They stress the advantages which, in their views at least, follow from communist systems, better living conditions, better education, art and music. But even if all this could be established, what would it matter if this new happiness or more creative existence could be reduced to purely physical states.

The materialist in more recent times is more subtle. He insists that he holds nothing to bring into question or discredit the obvious facts of everyday existence, that we do think and purpose and feel pain and other sensations. What he claims is somehow to dissolve the difference, in Gilbert Ryle's famous terms, between the dualist and the materialist account of thought and existence,. Ryle, with his exacting standards in thought and expression, would not want to say that we never think and that it does not matter how sound and clear is our thought and its expression. He could not have been one of the most famous editors of our time if he held such a view. At the same time, when we look carefully at what Ryle, and his many followers, actually hold it is very hard to see what difference, in essentials, there is between their ingeniously held positions and the simpler less ambiguous materialism of J.B. Watson. So strongly entrenched in some quarters is the "corporealist" view of persons that many do not seem to think it necessary even to argue for it, and such people include some of the ablest and most scholarly writers. Thus Mr. Jonathan Barnes, of Oriel College, Oxford, after one of the most learned and incisive surveys of the many ingenious forms of the famous "ontological argument"[1], disposes, in direct consideration, of the idea of God on the ground that "Gods are persons" and it is "becoming increasingly clear that persons are essentially corporeal"[2]. All the same, however ingenious the defenses, or however firm and widespread the conviction, nothing seems more certain to me, as a matter of obvious immediate experience, than that thoughts, purposes, sensations, etc., have a character as experience which is quite radically different in essential nature, a quite different mode of being altogether, from all corporeal or physical or observable reality. I also hold that recognition, of what seems here a simple fact of common sense and immediate apprehension, is vital for all good sense in the treatment of all other major issues and our basic attitudes. In practice, it all may seem to make little difference. Corporealists live and argue like the rest of us, but in the long run I cannot but believe that failure to recognize the distinctness of mental states and processes will lead to an impoverishment and enervation of all our distinctive activities and the very will to live as civilized communities.

There is one point that needs to be very much stressed here. The essential appeal in these matters must be to the immediate awareness we have of what it is like to have thoughts or sensations. Defenders of materialism are apt to confront us with the need for argument, and they vigorously reject the view that we can appeal to "private access" or "private detection"[3]. We must not be dogmatic and merely lay down the law, we must provide a proper argument. This is the ploy, disconcerting enough in its way, to which Mr. Roger Squires has recourse in his very gifted and spirited defense of materialism in the paper from which I have just quoted. But this is the issue which I have also discussed at length in my own paper "Ultimates and a Way of Looking." In this paper, as in other essays in this volume, I insist that philosophers must be prepared to recognize the limits of argument. It is hard for us to do so, for at once we seem to be opening the door to dogmatism and blind assertion—what is philosophy without argument? Nonetheless I think Wittgenstein, with whom I do not often agree, was altogether right in insisting that "philosophers must know when to stop." There is a point beyond which further argument is not possible, and there are certain "given" features of experience, however baffling, which we must simply recognize as being the case. This is a delicate and tricky issue which I cannot discuss as carefully here as I have done in my book. It seems to me all the same of quite crucial importance for good sense in philosophy, and, however easily abused, indispensable for a sound understanding of ourselves and the world around us. We have to cultivate the sense of when we have reached this kind of ultimate, and the flair for this appears to be one of the major requirements of sound philosophy.

In my own writings on these subjects, in *The Elusive Mind* and *The Self and Immortality* for example, I have tried to come closely to terms with an array of formidable arguments from Ryle, Passmore, Hampshire and others, but in the last analysis, when all the ground has been cleared in this way, we come down to our claim to recognize, or fail to recognize, the inherent distinctness of mental existence, for man and brute, and the radical difference between it and the reality about which we learn in sensible observation. If this appeal to what we seem to find to be the case is denied us, there is nowhere else to which we may turn. I can only invite those who disagree to think again or look again. When Ryle, for example, declares that the surgeon's skill lies in his hands making the correct movement, I cannot but remain convinced that something vital is left out here from the total picture. Nor will dispositions supply the defect. There is something going on *all the time* besides the work of the "skilled hands" as such. And there I must leave this matter as far as this short paper is concerned.

There are not in fact many who would persist today in denying that mental processes are inherently different from physical ones, and that we have in this way an "inner life" to which we have some sort of immediate access. So far the battle has swung round fairly firmly in favor of the dualist. But this is only half the battle. Two main things in particular may be maintained. Firstly, it will be argued that while mental states and processes are not strictly reducible to states of the body, they are conditioned throughout or at least essentially dependent on physical states, ultimately the brain. That there is peculiarly close dependence on the body will not, I think, be in serious dispute. Any change in my bodily state, most of all some serious malfunctioning, immediately brings about a corresponding change in my state of mind, a fever or brain damage seriously disrupts my thinking and experience in general. These obvious facts of experience need not be amplified. But it does not at all follow, as some suppose, that the state of the body is the sole determinant of my mental states. Sensitivity and understanding prescribe their own course and reactions, subject, normally at least, to physical conditions. I answer the telephone because I *hear* and *understand* what is said. To deny the influence of our own apprehension of meaning in the course of our activities is again to run against the plain evidence of normal experience.

A more plausible position is to hold that, in view of the close correlation of mental and physical events, it cannot be allowed that mind can function at all without its bodily correlate. This does not seem to me, however, in any way inevitable. Under present conditions of existence the dependence on the body is close, but that does not preclude the possibility of mental existence without the present physical correlates. How this may be conceived, and how communication, etc., would be possible is one of the main topics of my book. *The Self and Immortality.*

There is, however, a second major submission which the critics of dualism are apt to make, and this is the one to which most importance would be ascribed today. It is the real crux in these matters in the present state of the discussion. This is the question of ownership of experience and continued identity. Critics of my own view (see my forthcoming *Persons and Life After Death—Essays by Hywel Lewis and his Critics*, Macmillian), are apt to stress especially the difficulty of accounting for personal identity without bodily continuity. In my own replies the following points are made.

Firstly, I accept the substance of the Kantian argument that our awareness of an objective world around us presupposes a subject which transcends our passing experience and gives us a unified world which we can understand, and within limits change. But I take the argument further than this and maintain that the Kantian argument itself would be very hard to understand without some more direct awareness of oneself as subject and agent. My second main contention then is that, at any time, everyone is aware of himself as the being that he is, unique and irreducible. This is very different from the more specific knowledge that I have of myself as the particular kind of person that I am, my likes and dislikes, my aptitudes, skills and dispositions, etc. I am better placed in many ways to know these than my friends, but in some ways they may know me better at this level (and so might a psychiatrist if I consulted him). But all these properties characterize me, and no other, and it is this *me* (*being me* is Professor Roderick Chisholm's recent phrase) that I know, so I claim, immediately as the being that I am essentially and which at this level cannot be characterized further. Self-awareness in this sense is one of the *ultimates* to which I give prominence in my forthcoming book.

But there remains the question of continued identity. How do I know that the distinct being I am now is the same as the being who came into this room and started to write an hour ago? Very briefly, and this is the third point I am noting now, the Kantian argument will take us a long way here. But I supplement and strengthen it by recourse to what I have elsewhere called "strict memory." Most that we may be said to remember about ourselves and the world around us, depends on elaborate evidence and extends well beyond the sphere of our own immediate experience —sometimes to remote times—for instance I remember that Plato lived from 427 to 347 B.C. But I do not strictly remember this—I was not alive at the time; I do not remember the battle of Arginusiae because I was not there. But I remember coming into this room in a sense which would not be intelligible if I had not actually done this myself. My claim is that there are cases where we do directly, and independently of supporting evidence, remember such things as coming into the room, visiting places in Israel a few weeks ago and some things very early in my life. If this is so, then the being that I know myself to be, having these experiences now, just has to be the being who experienced other things and did certain things in the past, however much I may have changed in other ways, physical appearances, skills and interests, etc. This does not apply to all that has happened to me or which I have done. I am very far from strictly remembering all my life. But if there are cases, and I think they are extensive, when we strictly remember our past, then we have very firm assurance of continued identity around which we may build the other things we know less directly about ourselves. The question of the fallibility of memory presents difficulties with which I have tried to cope elsewhere.

We have thus, in outline here, the notion of persons as essentially non-corporeal and continuing as the distinct beings that they are, ultimate and irreducible, through changes of circumstances and fortune, including physical appearance. Such persons do not of necessity outlive the destruction of the body; they are no more inevitably immortal or indestructible than other finite existences. God alone exists by necessity of his nature. But there is no inherent reason why we should not exist and be the same persons essentially without the present body—or indeed any body at all. I have indicated elsewhere[5] what reasons I think there are for believing that we shall so exist.

Personal identity, in this view is absolute and not relative. This contrasts sharply with positions, like those of post-Helgelian idealists like T.H. Green and Bosanquet, who find the identity of persons in partial continuity of characteristics and circumstances. If a tree is cut down into logs and burned, the ashes (or what grows out of them) would not be regarded as the same entity as the tree. Just where we draw the line is arbitrary in the last resort, though not independent of continuities in the course of events. Location and spatial contiguities play an important part here. A suit that is so patched over that none of the original material remains might still be said to be the same suit. But this is relative and arbitrary. In the case of persons the identity is strict and not partial, however completely we may change. A man who is converted and abandons erring or evil ways is the same being as the one he was before, although we may say at another level, or for rough and ready purposes, that he is "not the same person" anymore. This is where I differ radically from an idealist, like Bosanquet at one extreme, and many fashionable thinkers of today at the other, for they would say that after a lapse of time I cease to be responsible for what I did long ago—or at least my responsibility is much diminished—because it is not the present "I" who did what I am to be praised or blamed for in the past—I am no longer the same person. My submission is that I am essentially the same person through all changes of circumstance and fortune and in all my actions.

This distinct being that I am is normally dependent on physical conditions, and the experiences that I have are extensively, though by no means wholly, conditioned by physical factors, especially the state of my brain, but it also acts upon the world around us, normally and perhaps always through the brain and the body—causation at a distance, if it happens, as some maintain, would make an exception. What we have therefore is an essentially mental entity, which has a unique and final identity, which is nonetheless in continuous interaction with the physical world, mainly at least through one's own body. The relation with the body is peculiarly close, as I have also stressed (see the chapter in "The Importance of the Body" in *The Self and Immortality*), but we are not essentially corporeal beings, however much we may for rough and ready purposes, identify ourselves as or through our bodies.

This is an essentially Cartesian position, with antecedents from Socrates through Plato and Augustine and Kant and many others, in Eastern as in Western thought. To establish it seems to me of first importance for all our major concerns and issues today.

I had meant to take up most of my address on the implications of holding this notion of the distinct and ultimate identity of persons. In the little that remains to me I can only make the briefest reference to what I take to be the significance for us of this doctrine today. Some of the matters of the greatest importance here have been reflected in some things, matters I have already discussed. For example, the question of moral responsibility. In terms of the view I have advanced it is possible to conceive of *some* of our actions as being cases of genuinely open choice where our actions as being cases of genuinely open choice where our action is in no sense at all determined. To reinstate the sense of our own ultimate and unquestioned responsibility is, in my view, a matter of the utmost importance—and on this I have also ventured to say much in other writings.

Then there is the question of life after death and the genuineness of our identity in any postmortem existence which we may have reason to expect. Many aspects of personal relationships, and the values which center upon them, are affected in the same way—to recognize the "other" as genuinely other and have due regard to what Bertrand Russell, in somewhat surprising terms for him, described as "our somber solitude, the genuine inner existence and essential privacy of everyone, is one of the major conditions of healthy personal and social relations."

Likewise, in religion, much that is travestied and distorted in traditional doctrine, like the notion which some have seriously held, of an angry God who sentences sinners to eternal torment, comes to be seen in its right meaning and context when we reflect on the consequences for our inner existence and solitude of much that we actually do. There is no need for trivializing or attenuation of traditional doctrine but the terms of it have to be thought out afresh and its meaning, in times past as today, properly appreciated on the basis of a sound understanding of what makes us the creatures we actually are. So also, for the vexed question of mysticism, and the claims often made for it. There is no doubt of the profound spiritual experience reflected in mystical writings and the lives of the mystics. But the sense in which this involves the extinction of the self is a further moot point. There are few things more central in contemporary religious and metaphysical thinking than this matter of the possible fusion of person as against the view that, even in the finest and holiest relationships, each remains the person he is and no other. The real divide, in the great religions, begins here, and if we are to find what I have elsewhere called "the points of convergence" in modern thought and civilized existence, we must face this basic question of how we are to think of individual existence. This is where it is hardest to find agreement, and it is for this reason above all that I direct attention to it in this paper. My view is that nothing important is lost, for any of the great religions, if the finality of the distinctness of persons is allowed. On the contrary, it is in the light of this, I would contend, that we can properly grasp what is vital in the main traditions, appreciate differences where they remain, and rethink our way to the appreciation of the most creative ways in which religious traditions may correct and enrich one another. This seems to me the most urgent concern for our times, and I regret that exposition of my own stance, for those not familiar with it, has been allowed to take up most of my time here. In the discussion we can perhaps advert more to these implications and significance of the issues I have raised and the view of them I have outlined.

Notes

1. Jonathan Barnes, *The Onotological Argument* (New York: Macmillan, 1972).
2. Jonathan Barnes, *The Onotological Argument*, p. 84.
3. Cf. Roger Squires in "Zombies vs. Materialists" in *Proceedings of the Aristotelian Society* supp. vol. XLVIII, pp. 162-63.
4. H.D. Lewis, *Persons and Survival in Death* (New York: Macmillan, 1978).
5. H.D. Lewis, *Persons and Survival in Death*.

Commentary

Mary Carman Rose

℘sycho-physical dualism which Professor Lewis wisely associates with the thought of Socrates, Plato, Augustine, Descartes, and Kant has had few explicit defenders in twentieth century Western philosophical thought. Hence, our thanks are due to Lewis for his unequivocal attempts to draw our attention to this position. Those of us who are dualists will certainly be grateful to Lewis. But those who are not dualists ought to be grateful to Lewis also. For we hear so little in defense of dualism these days that those who oppose it are in danger of forgetting what it is they are opposing. Also valuable is Lewis' brief noting of metaphysical materialism and idealism as positions opposed to dualism. Lewis argues fairly and cogently with his materialist opponents. And perhaps on their part materialists have argued honestly according to their rights; though I agree with Lewis that they have not argued wisely from their own and others' experience as persons.

There are, however, others whose opposition to psycho-physical dualism is to some extent covert. That is, their arguments pertaining to personhood and embodiment are enthymemes, and their conclusions depend on premises that are not explicitly examined nor even articulated. Two such thinkers Lewis mentions—i.e., Ryle and Wittgenstein. An academic generation which sometimes pays too little attention to courtesy will do well to think highly of Lewis' generosity to these thinkers. Clarity and courtesy are compatible, however, and philosophical advance requires the assessment of covert premises. I suggest that Ryle's insufficiently examined premise is that what cannot be said in behavioristic or operational language has no role in the study of mind. And Wittgenstein seems to be arguing always from the premise that what words pertaining to mind, personhood, and

79

embodiment mean to him will mean the same to all of us and that where he finds "muddles" in these words all of us will.

There are, however, opponents of dualism whose arguments against that position are more formidable because they are more nearly totally covert. These involve Husseralian phenomenology; Heideggarian ontology; and secular existentialism as practiced by Sartre, Camus and Merleau-Ponty. Husseralian phenomenology does not encompass all data pertaining to personhood and embodiment because of its assumption that all concepts, intentionalities, and data which pertain to these topics are fully open to inspection and can be fully explicated and articulated by the thinker who has been trained exclusively along Husseralian lines. Clearly, however, on the one hand, many aspects of mind-body inter-relations are not open to direct inspection and, on the other hand, the spiritual development of the investigator determines what he will find in his own experience as a person and embodied consciousness and how he will interpret the reports of others concerning their experiences. *Mutatis mutandis* similar criticisms are to be made of Heidegger's "fundamental ontology" with its insufficiently examined assumption that "being is unconcealed"—e.g., the being of mind and of its *de facto* dependencies on and various apparent independencies of body. *A fortiori* this is true of the secular existentialists' deliberately idiosyncratic decisions, discoveries, and interpretations of their own experiences as persons and embodied consciousness. Further, Lewis himself is implicitly contributing to a phenomenology of personhood and embodiment. This is clear, for example, in his concern with the content and import of certain given features of experience. Five conclusions may be drawn from the data pertaining to personhood and embodiment which are provided by Lewis and all the others.

First, the data pertaining to personhood and embodiment in the life of any one individual and his mode of interpreting these data depend to some extent on his world view and convictions concerning human ethico-religious potentialities and the human predicament. Thus, Lewis wisely draws our attention to Eastern views on personhood. And some experiences of personhood and embodiment as known to Buddhism, Hinduism, and Zen Buddhism will support Lewis' observations and conclusions. On the other hand, perhaps the Indian thinker for whom reincarnation is a fact will not agree with Lewis' understanding of "strict memory" as essential to the continuity of the person. Second, persons with different world views will differ in their conclusions concerning the phenomenology of personhood and embodiment. Third, persons with different world views will come to some of the same phenomenological conclusions if they share some experiences, commitments, and hopes. Thus, Lewis finds common ground with Bertrand Russell on the importance of the individual's "essential privacy" and "genuine inner existence."

Fourth, it is not only the investigator's intellectual integrity and training which have necessary investigative roles in his inquiry concerning personhood and embodiment. His spiritual or ethico-religious development, experiences, convictions, and commitments also have investigative roles in this enquiry. Fifth, there is necessarily a coherence among the individual's experiences and interpretation of embodiment and his world view. This means, as I indicated above, that his experiences and interpretations of the many facets of his own being are in part at least determined by his world view. It also means that his experiences reinforce, illumine, and lead to the further development of his views concerning man, reality, and the relations between them. Further, I wish to emphasize the fact that I am not here drawing attention to coherence among various aspects of philosophical thought as a possible ideal of philisophical work. That is another topic altogether. Rather, I am drawing attention to the *de facto* limitation or support given to an individual interpretation of personhood and embodiment by his metaphysical, ontological, axiological, and epistemological convictions.

Because of the coherence among beliefs, commitments, and aspirations which inform any situation where an individual reflects on personhood and embodiment I am uneasy about Lewis' appeal to Wittgenstein. To be sure, in some philosophical contexts it is wise to stress resemblances among thinkers who are in some ways very different in their interpretations of philosophical work, philosophical commitments, modes of inquiry, and conclusions. Yet it is important to be cautious in this philosophical generosity and cooperativeness. For two thinkers who are diametrically opposed may use the same words although, because of the fundamental differences in their philosophical views, their respective uses of these words may have very different meanings. In fact, the introduction on the basis of a superficial similarity of meaning of a philosophical dictum which is fundamentally alien to the view into which it is introduced may be dangerous or even destructive to the latter.

Such, I suggest, is the case with the manner in which Lewis has introduced Wittgenstein's thought into his own defense of dualism. I take it that Lewis is referring to Wittgenstein's famous dictum, "Whereof we cannot speak let us be silent." Of course, virtually all aspects of Wittgenstein's thoughts are controversial. Yet I think there is ample ground for concluding that when, as Lewis expresses it, Wittgenstein says, "philosophers must know when to stop," Wittgenstein is working in the tradition of Gorgias rather than in that of Socrates.

Further, the Sophist and the Socratic traditions are diametrically opposed. Gorgias is speaking from the point of view for which it is useless to seek knowledge of an objective order—e.g., to seek facts concerning mind-body relations, personal survival of physical death, or the fundamental universal nature of personhood. This is not the tradition of Socrates, Plato, Augustine, or Descartes. And while Kant introduces a fundamental agnosticism in respect to the ontological and metaphysical aspects of these topics, his ethico-religious thought which draws attention to the universally human spiritual needs, potentialities, and legitimate hopes is very definitely in their tradition.

Yet these two traditions share dicta to which they give opposed interpretations—e.g., Protagoras' reinterpretation of "Man is the measure of all things." Another example is Wittgenstein's "Whereof we cannot speak let us be silent" which Lewis introduced into his own inquiry. When used in any defense of dualism, however, it must be given a meaning consistent with the spirit of Socratic inquiry. Perhaps in this role it is a new form of the Socratic admonition to be aware of the limits of our knowledge. Thus the dualist who believes that he is not identical with his body and that he will survive physical death not only may, but must, remind the materialist, metaphysical naturalist, and secular existentialist and phenomenologist that their experiences of personhood and embodiment are not the measure of all human experiences which pertain to these. The presence in our midst of representatives of all the great world religions who know at first hand the existential import of the hope for survival provides ample evidence for this last statement. And at the very least this evidence also establishes the import for philosophical study of personhood and embodiment of the thinker's spiritual commitment and aspiration which provide him with data and insights that he can achieve in no other way.

Part II

Cerebral Correlates of Consciousness

8.
The Human Brain and the Human Person

Sir John Eccles

The theme of this address relates to the mysterious experience that each of us continually has of being a person with a self-consciousness—not just conscious, but knowing that you know. In defining "person" I will quote two admirable statements by Immanuel Kant: "A person is a subject who is responsible for his actions;" and "A person is something that is conscious at different times of the numerical identity of its self." These statements are minimal and basic, and they could be enormously expanded.[1] For example, Popper and I have just published a 600-page book on *The Self and Its Brain.*

We are now able to go much further than Kant in defining the relation of the person to its brain. We are apt to regard the person as identical with the ensemble of face, body, limbs, etc., that constitutes each of us. This is easily shown to be a mistake. Amputation of limbs and losses of eyes, for example, though crippling, leave the human person with its essential identity. This is also the case with removal of internal organs. Many can be excised in whole or in part. The human person survives unchanged after kidney transplants or even heart transplants. You may ask what happens with brain transplants. Mercifully, this is not feasible surgically, but even now it would be possible to successfully accomplish a head transplant. Who can doubt that the person "owning" the transplanted head would now "own" the acquired body and not vice versa!? We can hope that with human persons this will remain a Gedanken experiment, but it has already been successfully done in mammals by Professor White (Chapter 9). We can recognize that all structures of the head extraneous to the brain are not involved in this transplanted ownership. For example, eyes, nose, jaws, scalp, etc., are no more concerned with ownership than are other parts of the body. We can therefore conclude that it is the brain and the brain alone that provides the material basis of our personhood.

But when we come to consider the brain as the seat of the conscious personhood, however, we can also recognize that large parts of the brain are not essential. For example, removal of the cerebellum gravely incapacitates movement, but the person is not otherwise affected. It is quite different with the main part of the brain, the cerebral hemispheres. They are very intimately related to the consciousness of the person, but not equally. In more than 95% of persons there is dominance of the left hemisphere, which is the speaking hemisphere (Fig. 8-1). Except in infants its removal results in a most severe destruction of the human person, but not annihilation. On the other hand, removal of the minor hemisphere (usually the right) is attended with loss of movement on the left side (hemiplegia) and blindness on the left side (hemianopia), but the person is otherwise not gravely disturbed. Damage to other parts of the brain can also greatly disturb the human personhood, possibly by the removal of the neural inputs that normally generate the necessary background activity of the cerebral hemispheres. A tragic example of this is shown by the vigil coma that often follows severe head injury in accidents. The subject remains in deep unconsciousness even though the cerebral hemispheres themselves have not been damaged. Damage at lower levels of the brain, for example of the reticular activating system, causes the cerebral hemispheres to be inactive and so to be functionally dead. This terrible state can go on for months. Sometimes there is a slow and often imperfect awakening some weeks after the accident, but often this never occurs. The electroencephalograms show an almost complete silence, which indicates little or no activity in the cerebral cortex. In other cases the cerebral cortex may be so severely damaged that the diagnosis of brain death can be sustained, as for example following a long interruption of the heart beat. The person is literally dead though the rest of the body and its organs can function indefinitely when respiration is provided by an iron lung.

So to sum up the evidence, we can say that the human person is intimately associated with its brain, probably exclusively with the cerebral hemispheres, and is not at all directly associated with all the remainder of its body. The association that you experience of limbs, face, eyes, etc., is dependent on the communication by nerve pathways to the brain, where the experience is generated.

Let us now briefly consider how a human embryo and baby eventually become a human person. The route is one that all of us have traversed, but much is unremembered. A baby is born with a brain that is very fully formed in all its detailed structure, but of course it has yet to grow to the full adult size of about 1.4 kg. The

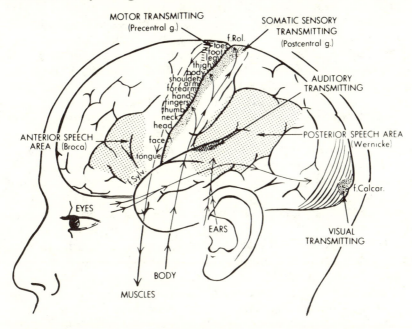

Figure 8-1: Motor and sensory transmitting areas of the cerebral cortex. The approximate map of the motor transmitting areas is shown in the precentral gyrus, while the somatic sensory receiving areas are in a similar map in the postcentral gyrus. Other Primary sensory areas shown are the visual and auditory, but they are largely in areas screened from this lateral view. The frontal, parietal, occipital and temporal lobes are indicated. Also shown are the speech areas of Broca and Wernicke.

nerve cells and the unitary components of the brain have almost all been made. All the major lines of communication from the periphery and from one part of the brain to another have been grown ready for use. Much before birth the brain has been causing the movements sensed by the mother. And even before birth the child can respond to sounds. Its hearing system is already functioning well by birth, which is far earlier than the vision system. It is remarkable that by seven days after birth a baby has learned to distinguish its mother's voice from other voices, just as happens with lambs. Then follows a long period of learning to see and to move in a controlled manner.

As we all know, even in the first months of life a baby is continually practicing its vocal organs and so is beginning to learn this most complex of all motor coordinations. Movements of larynx, palate, tongue and lips have to be coordinated and blended with respiratory movements. These exercises form another variety of motor learning, but now the feedback is from hearing and is at first imitative of sounds heard. This leads on to the simplest types of words like "dada," "papa," and "mama" that are produced at about one year. It is important to realize that speech is dependent on feedback from hearing the spoken words. The deaf are mute. In linguistic development recognition outstrips expression. The child has a veritable word hunger, asking for names and practicing incessantly even when alone. It dares to make mistakes evolving from its own rules, as for example with the irregular plural of nouns. Language does not come about by simple imitation. The child abstracts regularities and relations from what it hears and applies these principles in building up its linguistic expressions.

To be able to speak given even minimal exposure to speech is part of our biological heritage. This endowment has a genetic foundation, but one cannot speak of genes for language. On the other hand the genes do provide the instructions for the building of the special areas of the cerebral cortex concerned with language (Fig. 1), as well as all the subsidiary structures concerned in vocalization.

The 3 World philosophy of Popper (c.f. Chapter 5) forms the basis of my further exploration of the way in which a human baby becomes a human person. All of the material world, including human brains, is in the matter-energy World 1. World 2 is the world of all conscious experiences (c.f. Fig. 8-2) and World 3 is the world of culture including, especially, language. At birth the human baby has a human brain, but its World 2 experiences are very rudimentary and World 3 is unknown to it. The baby, and even a human embryo must be regarded as a human being, but not as a human person.

The emergence and development of self-consciousness (World 2) by continued interaction with World 3 is an utterly mysterious process. This process can be likened to a double structure (Fig. 8-3) that ascends and grows by the effective cross-linkage. The vertical arrow shows the passage of time from the earliest experiences of the child up to the full human development. From each World 2 position an arrow leads through the World 3 at that level up to a higher, larger level which illustrates symbolically a growth in the culture of that individual. Reciprocally the World 3 re-

BRAIN⇌MIND INTERACTION

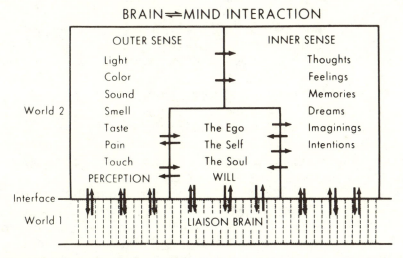

Figure 8-2: Information flow diagram for brain-mind interaction. The three components of World 2: outer sense, inner sense and the ego or self are diagrammed with their connectivities. Also shown are the lines of communication across the interface between World 1 and World 2, that is from the liaison brain to and from these World 2 components. The liaison brain has the columnar arrangement indicated (cf. Fig. 8-6). It must be imagined that the area of the liaison brain is enormous with open modules (cf. Fig. 8-7) probably numbering up to 1 million and not just the 40 here depicted.

sources of the shelf act back to give a higher, expanded level of consciousness of that self (World 2). And so each of us has developed progressively in self-creation. The more the World 3 resources of the individual, the more does it gain in the self-consciousness of World 2. What we are is dependent on the World 3 that we have been immersed in and how effectively we have utilized our opportunities to make the most of our brain potentialities. The brain is necessary but not sufficient for World 2 existence and experience, as is indicated in Fig. 8-2, which is a dualist-interactionist diagram showing by arrows the flow of information across the interface between the brain in World 1 and the conscious self in World 2.

There is a recent tragic case illustrative of Fig. 8-3. A child, Genie, was deprived of all World 3 influences by her psychotic father. She was penned in isolation in a small room, never spoken to and minimally serviced from the age of 20 months up to 13 years and 8 months. On release from this terrible deprivation she was of course a human being, but not a human person. She was at the bottom rung of the ladder in Fig. 8-3. Since then with the dedicated help of Dr. Susan Curtiss she has been slowly climbing up that ladder of personhood for the last 8 years. The linguistic deprivation seriously damaged her left hemisphere, but the right hemisphere stands in for a much depleted language performance. Yet, despite this terribly delayed immersion in World 3, Genie has become a human person with self-consciousness, emotions, and excellent performance in manual dexterity and in visual recognition.[3] We can recognize the necessity of World 3 for the development of the human person. The brain is built by genetic instructions (Nature), but development to human personhood is dependent on the World 3 environment (Nurture). With Genie there was a gap of over 13 years between Nature and Nurture.

It may seem that a complete explanation of the development of the human person can be given in terms of the human brain. It is built anatomically by genetic instructions and subsequently developed functionally by learning from the environmental influences. A purely materialist explanation would seem to suffice with the conscious experiences as a derivative from brain functioning. However, it is a mistake to think that the brain does everything and that our conscious experiences are simply a reflection of brain activities, which is a common philosophical view. If that

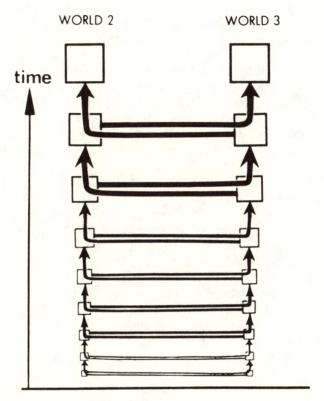

Figure 8-3: Diagramatic representation of the postulated interrelationship of the developments of self-consciousness (World 2) and of culture (World 3) in time as shown by the arrows. See full description in text.

were so, our conscious selves would be no more than passive spectators of the performances carried out by the neuronal machinery of the brain. Our beliefs that we can really make decisions and that we have some control over our actions would be nothing but illusions. There are of course all sorts of subtle cover-ups by philosophers from such a stark exposition, but they do not face up to the issue. In fact all people, even materialist philosophers, behave as if they had at least some responsibility for their own actions. It seems that their philosophy is for "the other people, not for themselves," as Schopenhauer wittily stated.

These considerations lead me to the alternative hypothesis of dualist-interactionism (c.f. Chapter 18), that has been expanded at length in *The Self and The Brain.* It is really the commonsense view, namely that we are a combination of two things or entities: our brains on the one hand; and our conscious selves on the other. The self is central to the totality of our conscious experiences as persons through our whole waking life. We link it in memory from our earliest conscious experiences. The self lapses during sleep, except for dreams, and recovers for the next day by the continuity of memory. But for memory we as experiencing persons would not exist. Thus we have the extraordinary problem that was first recognized by Descartes: how can the conscious mind and the brain interact?

Let us look at this question by considering what is involved in vision. When we sense an object visually, the upside down retinal image is conveyed to the brain by the Morse code-like signals of nerve impulses, dots only, in the million lines of each optic nerve and in the brain there is an enormous expansion (Fig. 8-4). In the initial stage hundreds of millions of cortical nerve cells are involved, and even more in the further stages of brain response to the image of the retina. But never in the brain is the retinal image reconstituted. What we have is the immense and complicated coded information about lines and angles and location, which is all that the machinery of the brain can do. The fully evolved coded response of the brain is read out by the mind to give the visual experience from moment to moment with all the qualities of light and color and form and contour. More wonderfully this experience gives meaning—the perceived world that we recognize with objects and distances and movements. The mind is not passive in this transaction, but is selecting and interpreting the immense mass of information that is provided by the brain in coded form.

We are of course far from understanding how this miraculous transformation can occur. It is important to realize that in the world that we sense with vision there are none of the properties that we experience, even light and color. All that the world has for our sensing are patterns of electromagnetic radiation of various frequencies and intensities. The vivid pictures of the world that we experience are actually created in the mind.

This generalization is also true of our other senses,—hearing, touch, smell and taste,—which all have counterparts in the material world. It is otherwise with the sense of pain for which there is no physical or chemical counterpart. Pain is signalled to the brain by very simple sense organs that are sensitive to injury. Again after much complication by the neural machinery of the brain, the messages come to the cerebral cortex where eventually they are transmitted to the experience of pain. This is a unique creation by the mind with the extreme range from unpleasantness to agony.

Other ranges of conscious experiences are independent of signalling by sense organs and are listed in Fig. 8-2 under Inner Sense. They are more subtle and even more uniquely private to us and so are denoted by rather vague descriptive words such as feelings, thoughts, imaginings, intentions, dreams, and memories. Yet they have counterparts in brain actions. Changes in the electrical potentials in the brain accompany dreams and mental tasks such as mental arithmetic or the attempt to recall a memory. Also, the willing of a simple movement such as the bending of a finger generates electrical potentials that begin in the brain almost one second before the movement occurs.

It is useful to think of the brain as an instrument, our instrument, that has been our lifelong servant and companion. The brain provides us, as conscious persons, with the lines of communication from and to the material world (World 1) which comprises both our bodies and the external world. It does this by receiving information by the immense sensory system of millions of nerve fibres that fire impulses into the brain where it is processed into the coded patterns of information that we read out from moment to moment in deriving all our experiences—our percepts, thoughts, ideas, memories. But we as experiencing persons do not slavishly accept all that is provided for us by our instrument, the neuronal machine of our sensory system and of our brain. We select from all that is given according to interest and attention, and we modify the actions of the neuronal machinery, for example, to initiate some willed movement or in order to recall a memory or to concentrate our attention.[4]

How then can we develop ideas with respect to the mode of operation of the brain? How can it provide the immense range of coded information that can be selected from by the mind in its activity of reading out conscious experiences? It is now possible to give much more informative answers because of very recent work on the essential mode of operation of the neocortex. By the use of radiotracer techniques[5] it has been shown that the great brain mantle, the neocortex, is built up of units or modules.[6] The total human neocortex has an area of about 2500 cm.[2] and is about 3 mm. thick. It contains about ten thousand million nerve cells. These are arranged in small ensembles in the form of a column or module, that runs through the whole thickness of the cortex, three millimeters across. It is a functional unit because of its selective communication with other modules of the neocortex (Fig. 8-5). The projection is seen to be in a completely overlapping manner and not diffusely.

This modular organization has provided a most valuable simplification of the enterprise of trying to understand how this tremendously complex structure worked. The potential performance of ten thousand million individual units is beyond all comprehension. The arrangement in modules of about 2500 nerve cells reduces the number of functional units of the neocortex to about 4 million. These modules have a complex internal operation that is still very little understood, but the structural arrangements have been now fairly well defined by Szentagothai (Fig. 8-6). The remarkable new discovery is that the modules act as communication units. Each one gives out at least 500 nerve fibres to other modules, but this output is strictly channelled to a few (Fig. 8-5), perhaps 20 other modules. On the basis of this communication system of each module receiving from 20 and giving to 20, it can be imagined how a sensory input, visual for example, could be rapidly (in a fraction of a second) evolved to a spatio-temporal pattern of active modules that will uniquely encode the information provided by that sensory input, as is shown for one instant in the greatly simplified diagram of Fig. 8-7. It is postulated that such scintillating spatio-temporal patterns are read out by the mind in its performance of providing a unique perceptual experience.

It can, however, be questioned if the four million modules of the neocortex are adequate to generate the spatio-temporal patterns

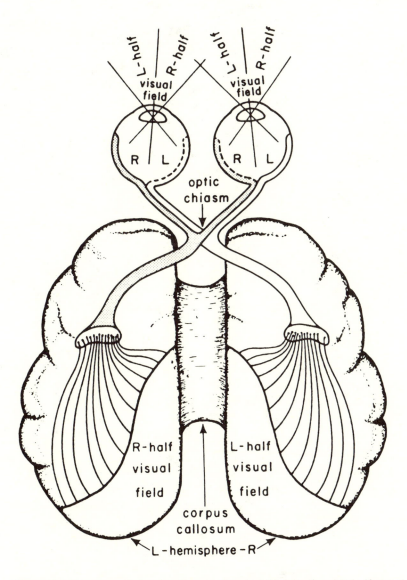

Figure 8-4: Diagram of visual pathways showing the L-half and R-half visual fields with the retinal images and the partial crossing in the optic chisma so that the right-half of the visual field of each eye goes to left visual cortex, after relay in the lateral geniculate body (LGB), and correspondingly for left visual field to right visual cortex.

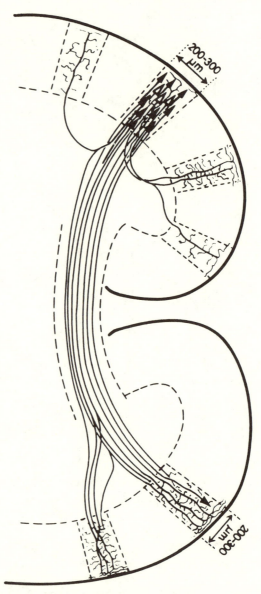

Figure 8-5: The general principle of cortico-cortical connectivity is shown diagrammatically in the two hemispheres of the brain. The connections are established in highly specific patterns between vertical columns of 200-300 um diameter in both hemispheres. Ipsilateral connections are derived mainly from cells located in layer III (cells shown at left in outlines), while contralateral connections (cells shown in full black) derive from all layers II-VI. The diagram does not try to show the convergence from afferents originating from different parts of the cortex to the same columns.

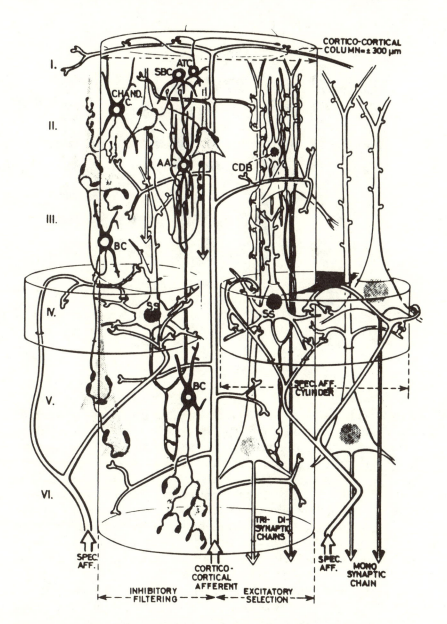

Figure 8-6: Diagram illustrating a single cortico-cortical column and two specific subcortical afferent arborization cylinders. Lamination is indicated on the left margin. The right half of the diagram indicates impulse processing over excitatory neurone chains, while the left half shows various types of inhibitory interneurones (in full black). Further explanation is in the text.

97

Pattern of open and closed modules

Figure 8-7: Diagrammatic plan of cortical modules as seen from the surface. As described in the text the modules are shown as circles of three kinds, open, closed (solid black) and half open. Further description is in the text. For the human brain this pattern has to be extended about 200 times in each direction.

which encode the total cognitive performance of the human brain—all the sensing, all memories, all linguistic expression, all creativities, all aesthetic experiences—and for our whole life time. The only answer I can give is to refer to the immense potentialities of the 88 keys of a piano. Think of the creative performances, for example, of the great composers, Beethoven and Chopin. They could utilize only four parameters in their creation of music with the 88 keys, each of which has invariant pitch and tonal quality. And a comparable four parameters are utilized in creating the spatio-temporal patterns of activity in the four million modules of the human brain. I will consider these four parameters in turn, pointing out the comparable features.

Firstly, there is intensity. In music this is the loudness of the note, whereas with the module it is the integral of the impulse firing in the output lines from the module. It has to be recognized that in the analogy the keys of the piano have a pitch differentiation, whereas in the brain, the modules or keys have location which is the basis of coded properties that give the kind of perception read out from them, e.g., light or color or sound.

Second, there is the duration of the note or of the impulse firing from a module. *Third,* there is the sequence of the notes which gives a melody with piano music and the temporal pattern of modular activities in the brain. One can imagine that this modular pattern is dispersed over the surface of the brain. (c.f. Fig. 8-7). *Fourth,* there is the simultaneous activation of several notes, a chord, or of several modules in the brain. With the chord the maximum number is ten. With the modules it may be thousands.

I think it will be recognized that the enormous generation of musical patterns using the 88 keys of a piano points to a virtually infinite capacity of the four million modules to generate unique spatio-temporal patterns. Moreover it must be realized that, just as with piano keys, these patterns giving the conscious experiences are dependent on the four parameters listed above. We can imagine that the intensities of activation are signalled symbolically by the lighting up of modules. So if we could see the surface of the neocortex, it would present an illuminated pattern of 50 cm. by 50 cm. composed at any moment of modules ¼ mm. across that have all ranges from dark to dim to lighter to brilliant. And this pattern would be changing in a scintillating manner from moment to moment, giving a sparkling spatio-temporal pattern of the four million modules, appearing exactly as on a TV screen. This symbolism gives some idea of the immense task confronting the mind in generating conscious experiences. The dark or dim modules would be neglected. Moreover it is an important feature of the hypothesis of mind-brain interaction that neither the mind nor the brain is passive in the transaction. There must be an active interchange of information across the frontier (Fig. 8-2) between the material brain and the non-material mind. The mind is not in the matter-energy world so there is no energy exchange in the transaction, merely a flow of information. Yet the mind must be able to change the pattern of energy operations in the modules of the brain, else it would be forever impotent.

It is difficult to understand how the self-conscious mind can relate to such an enormous complexity of spatio-temporal modular patterns. This difficulty is mitigated by three considerations. First, we must realize that our self-conscious mind has been learning to accomplish such tasks from our babyhood onwards, a process that is colloquially called "learning to use one's brains." Second, by the process of attention the self-conscious mind selects from the total ensemble of modular patterns those features that are in accord with its present interests. Third, the self-conscious mind is engaged in extracting "meaning" from all that it reads out. This is well illustrated by the many ambiguous figures, for example, a drawing that can be seen either as a staircase or an overhanging cornice (Fig. 8-8). The switch from one interpretation to the other is instantaneous and holistic. There is never any transitional phase in the reading out by the mind of the modular pattern in the brain.

A key component of the hypothesis of brain-mind interaction is that the unity of conscious experience is provided by the self-conscious mind and not by the neuronal machinery of the neocortex. Hitherto, it has been impossible to develop any theory of brain function that would explain how a diversity of brain events comes to be synthesized so that there is a unity of conscious experience. The brain events remain disparate, being essentially the individual actions of countless modules.

I have endeavoured to keep the story of mind-brain interaction as simple as possible. How should we expect to have an easy solution to the greatest problem confronting us? I do not claim to have offered a solution, but rather to have indicated in general outline the way the solution may come. In some mysterious way the human brain evolved with properties of a quite other order from anything else in nature. At the summit of these brain properties I would place initially the interaction with another,

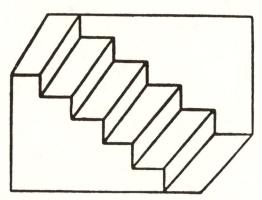

Figure 8-8: Ambiguous figure that can be interpreted either as an ascending staircase or an overhanging cornice.

non-material world (World 2). The coming-to-be of self-conscious-ness is a mystery that concerns each person with its conscious and unique selfhood. And our self-conscious forebears with their creative imagination built the world of culture and civilization that has played a key role in enriching the formation of each of us as human persons with our culture and our values. The coming-to-be of each unique selfhood lies beyond scientific enquiry, as I have argued elsewhere.[7] It is my thesis that we have to recognize that the unique selfhood is the result of a supernatural creation of what in the religious sense is called a soul.

I hope that I have shed some light on the great and mysterious problem of the human brain and the human person. Each person must be primarily considered as a unique self-conscious being that interacts with its environment—especially with other persons—by means of the neuronal machinery of the brain. Beyond the scope of this lecture there is the realm of the human person with all the human values that has been the theme of so much of this conference. I have concentrated on the dualist-interactionist view of this mind-brain transaction, because, as Popper and I have argued, all monist-materialist explanations are mistaken simplifications. I offer no final solution of this age-old problem, but hope that I have indicated the way that deeper understanding may be won. Certainly there will be no cheap solutions of a doctrinaire kind.

Notes

1. K.R. Popper and J.C. Eccles, *The Self and its Brain* (Heidelberg, Berlin and New York: Springer-Verlag, 1977).

2. J.C. Eccles, *The Human Mystery* (Heidelberg, Berlin and New York: Springer International, 1979).

3. S. Curtiss, *A Psycholinguistic Study of a Modern-Day "Wild Child"* (New York: Academic Press, 1977).

4. J.C. Eccles, *The Human Psyche* (Heidelberg, Berlin and New York: Springer International, 1980).

5. P.S. Goldman and W.J.H. Nauta. 1977. Columnar distribution of cortico-cortical fibres in the frontal association, limbic and motor cortex of the developing rhesus monkey. *Brain Research* 122, pp. 393-413.

6. J. Szentagothai. 1978. The neuron network of the cerebral cortex: A functional interpretation. *Proceedings of the British Royal Society*, pp. 219-48.

7. J. C. Eccles, *The Human Psyche*.

9.
The Science of Behavior and The Internal Universe

W. Horsley Gantt

Introduction

At the fourscore year mark my curiosity about the universe having increased rather than diminished, I have the advantage of using the perspective of many years in the background to look forward.

Science began with unity, e.g., Aristotle was not only one of the three great Greek philosophers who dominated thinking down to the Middle Ages, but he was as well an astronomer, a physicist, an anatomist and a biologist.

The Middle Ages saw the foundation of a science with a new outlook, a perspective based upon the experimental method and observation combined with an elaboration of concepts. This foundation was laid especially by Galileo and Newton, with an emphasis on the conceptual side by Francis Bacon and Descartes.

Our interest, however, is centered around John Locke, born in 1723, on account of his emphasis on the relation of the individual to the external environment, his *tabula rasa* upon which experience writes. From him has developed the materialistic point of view in behavior. Hence began the emphasis upon the data brought to us by the sense organs, later greatly amplified by instrumentation. What occurred in the body was likened to what was seen with machines, e.g., the pumping of the blood by the heart and the discovery of the circulation by Harvey to hydrodynamics. Thus, it was apparent that many of the functions of the body obeyed the laws of mechanics.

Behaviorism as we know it today obtained a great stimulus from the discovery of sensory and motor nerves by Bell and Majendie, about the beginning of the 19th century. The Russian physiologist Sechenov in 1863 wrote his "Reflexes of the Brain." This was a bold step to include thinking and mind on a purely reflex basis, denying the reality of a separate subjective life. This was emphasized by Thomas Huxley in his statement, "No psychosis without neurosis," meaning that all thinking was underlayed by detectable neural processes. Thus the 19th century began to think of mind as equivalent to complex physical and chemical changes in matter.

The study of the nervous system as a vehicle for total behavior was founded around the turn of the 20th century. This development diverged along two paths, the study of gross movement, and the quantitative measurement of secretions to a food stimulus, the former being developed by Bekhterev, Thorndike, Watson, and Skinner, the latter by Pavlov. On this divergence there have been built up two schools called the Operant and the latter the Classical-Pavlovian. Operant conditioning has been greatly expanded in America; its emphasis is chiefly on how the external behavior can be "shaped" according to the wishes of the experimenter. This at first made use only of the skeletal movements, but later has included the autonomic nervous system.

An entirely different elaboration was centered around Pavlov, who had received the Nobel Prize in 1903 for his work on the physiology of digestion. His contributions involved chiefly the use of the dog over its life span, viz., the chronic experiment, the use of quantitative measures (units of saliva), the emphasis on the individual rather than on statistical surveys and the recognition of individual differences by his four "temperaments."

The evaluation of the Pavlovian school, including that of his successors, such as Skinner, the electrophysiologists, and others, fluctuates from the extreme optimism that "the behaviorists are the people who have got to save the world; they may win the race with total destruction" to the more cautious statement of Grey Walter: "At the present time there is still not one single principle of mental physiology that can claim the status of a natural law, in the sense that it receives universal acceptance and permits deductive prediction or extrapolation."

Though they may espouse monism, most scientists will recognize that for the subjective phenomena of our life there are no objective representations. A simple test is to try to communicate to anyone the sensation of the color "blue." No matter what you say about its wave length or other measurable physical properties, these do not even approach the subjective feeling. They are of a different order—and never the twain shall meet.

Pavlov said science must be satisfied with its practical achievements—its ability to give us the measurable relationships in physical, objective items. Perhaps the monist should heed the counsel of Planck, not to ask of science questions it cannot answer.

Finally, Pavlov, as well as every student of the nervous system, owes much to Descartes' concept of reflex. Pavlov and Sherrington adhered to this concept either implicitly or explicitly in their epochal researches. The difference between them is that whereas Sherrington did not think that his laboratory methods could give him the ultimate answers to the riddle of our mental life, Pavlov had the adolescent hope that at some future time "the omnipotent scientific method will deliver man from his present gloom, and will purge him from his contemporary shame in the sphere of interhuman relations."

Many other responses and reactions in the organism have been brought within the conditional reflex (CR) methodology since Pavlov. In the Pavlovian Laboratories, we have extended this field to include vestibular reactions of equilibration, respiratory and cardiovascular responses including heart rate and blood pressure as well as responses to stimuli placed within the central nervous system (interoceptors). In the human being we have added to these the psychogalvanic.

To epitomize, four decades of work from my laboratory on the cardiac reactions: (the cardiac component of the CRs are in general parallel to the secretory and motor) there is a quantitative relationship to the intensity of the excitatory CR, a marked difference between the cardiac component of the excitatory and inhibitory CRs, a precise cardiac time reflex, etc. The inhibitory CR is characterized by a slight rise in heart rate with a marked subsequent decrease below normal. Here we have in the cardiac response a measure of inhibition which gives an explanation to the quiescent phase and sleep which Pavlov found resulting from inhibitions.

George Burch and some others in the USA have contributed to this field through a study of vasomotor responses. Burch, in the course of his detailed and painstaking research on the heart and vascular reactions has shown that the latter are definitely modified through experiences of the individual, i.e., they are capable of being conditional reflexes.

The preceding description of the ability of many systems to form CRs involves many stimuli from the external environment. The relative role of the periphery and the center, the external sense organs and the central nervous system, concerned us. To solve this, we considered the elements of the reflex arc, both the conditional reflex arc and the unconditional reflex arc. We successively eliminated the different parts of the conditional reflex arc—the external sense organs, the peripheral nerves, the spinal pathways to the motor area of the brain, and finally the executor organ, viz., the motor movement or the salivary secretion, with the result that the only essential part for conditional reflex function is the central nervous system.

This then puts the importance of the adaptation *within* the central nervous system, diminishing the function of the external environment in the healthy subject. This, of course, does not negate the influence of the external environment in such items as nutrition, etc. It means that many adaptations can be found within the central nervous system.

In directing our attention to the inner universe, we must acknowledge the debt we owe to Claude Bernard for his study of the inner world through which study he was led to the realization that the body maintains a constant chemical composition for its life within. This idea was taken up later by Cannon and made the principle of his "homeostasis." Thus arose an over-emphasis of the ability of the organism—beyond its powers—to regulate its economy and to maintain its equilibrium in an unfavorable environment. In psychiatry it took the form of believing that whatever the individual tended to do represented a healthy, balancing action. The counterpart of this idea was expressed by Pavlov, viz., that the CR was a means of preserving an equilibrium between the individual and its environment. This idea of equilibrium will be discussed later.

In the formation of the conditional reflex we can eliminate the external sense organs (eye, ear, skin) by placing electrodes within the nerves to produce the conditional stimulus. To supplant the unconditional stimulus an electrode may be placed 1) on the posterior nerve root, 2) on the posterior columns of the spinal cord, 3) within the cerebellum, 4) in the motor area of the cortex. In all these regions the movements produced can be conditioned as easily as if the stimulus were applied to the skin receptors. An electric stimulus may be substituted for the conditional stimulus in the silent areas of the cortex. In these instances the unconditional stimulus or the conditional stimulus or both are entirely within the central nervous systems. The efferent end may be eliminated by crushing of the anterior nerve roots within the spinal canal to a limb, training the animal during the period of paralysis and testing him after recovery; the motor reflex appears on the first trial after several months interval required for regeneration of the nerve.

Thus the conditional reflex can be formed and can exist internally without involvement of the external environment! If the nervous system can form conditional reflexes from a stimulus applied within, albeit an artificial one, it is reasonable to assume that it can elaborate conditional reflexes from stimuli arising from origins peculiar to itself.

From the consideration of many approaches to the adaptability of the organism during its life experiences we see that its various functions do not make parallel adaptations; some functions readily become CRs, others are absolutely unconditionable. From this we arrive at the law of *fractional conditioning.* Besides this absolute difference, there are differences of degree relative to the speed of formation of a CR and the durability once formed. To this marked difference, first seen with the cardiac conditional reflex, we get the name of *schizokinesis.*

In the study of the cardiac components of the conditional reflex to food or to pain we saw that the cardiac conditional reflex formed rapidly, usually before the motor or the salivary components and often after one reinforcement by the unconditional stimulus. Not only did it form first, as a rule, but it generally was much more resistant to extinction. Often the cardiac conditional reflex might continue for several years after the motor or the salivary component had been extinguished by active efforts for extinction. The respiratory conditional reflex behaves in this respect more like the cardiac conditional reflex than like the specific salivary or motor components.

The fact that the cardiac conditional reflex may continue while the other components are absent led to the concept of schizokinesis, a split between the more general functions as the respiratory and the cardiovascular and the specific ones. Such a split—a persistence of one activity in the absence of the other—would seem to represent a maladaptation, a kind of built-in lack of integration of the physiological systems.

The existence of the conditional reflex may at times seem to be a liability and a lack of equilibrium with the environment, and even the opposite, viz., dysfunction. Thus, as shown by Bykov, more oxygen is consumed in performing a given task when the performance is preceded by a conditional stimulus, i.e., the oxygen consumed by the conditional reflex plus the amount consumed by the unconditional reflex alone not preceded by the conditional stimulus. We have shown a similar instance with the salivary secretion; more saliva is required for the same amount of food when the eating of the food is preceded by the conditional stimulus. The organism must pay in efficiency, i.e., in the amount of energy required, for its function of being ready for emergencies.

The fact that conditional reflexes are so often difficult to eradicate once formed makes the individual a museum of antiquities as he grows older, as I have pointed out previously. He is encumbered with many reactions no longer useful and even with some detrimental to life. This is especially true for the cardiovascular function, and it is these conditional reflexes that are the most enduring. A person may be reacting with his cardiovascular system to some old injury or situation which no longer exists, and he is usually unconscious of what it is that is causing an increase in heart rate or blood pressure. The result may be chronic hypertension. This may be the explanation of many cardiac deaths.

The persistence of the cardiac conditional reflex and of other general components in the absence of the more specific parts, e.g., the salivation and the movement, should lead to a revision of the idea of *inhibition*. Formerly we considered that the dog was in a state of complete inhibition in regard to a specific stimulus when he no longer gave the salivary secretion and the motor component, but now we see that inhibition can be and probably is, partial, incomplete, fractional. The animal may be quiet externally but violently agitated internally. This seems to me a usual and therefore normal occurrence instead of an exceptional and abnormal one.

Autokineses

By means of the chronic experiment, studying the subjective for a long period of its life, we can see important changes within the organism, changes which indicate interactions among foci of excitations stored in the central nervous system. To this function we give the name of autokinesis.

A familiar example is acquired immunity to disease. Having once had certain diseases—measles, mumps, chicken pox, whooping cough, typhoid fever—the person does not contract them a second time. But what remains? Certainly not the antigen, certainly not the same antibodies. It is the pattern of activity that is present, the ability to react when the stimulus has long since passed. There is some trace left in the living tissue somewhere. There are many other examples, occurring in biology or as a result of individual experience. One is the spontaneous restoration of the conditional reflex. Pavlov, as well as I and others, showed that generally a conditional reflex could be extinguished in one day but that it would reappear the next day, and that sometimes many separate days of repetitions were necessary for complete extinction. As he did not measure all components, this view would have to be modified somewhat at present in the light of the cardiac responses, but essentially the fact of spontaneous restoration remains.

I have noted that sometimes *one* injection of a drug will permanently, or at least for a long time, change the level of reactivity of the dog, the size of his conditional reflexes, though the drug is not repeated. Wiener, recognizing the development of pathologic reactions to formerly innocuous stimuli, explained it by saying that the *level* of feedback had been altered.

Every physician knows that a patient may steadily improve after one visit and consultation, and we all know how one experience in life may change our whole future. I call the development in the direction of making better adaptations positive autokinesis; when the direction is downward, negative autokinesis.

There is growing anatomical evidence that new connections can be made in the nervous system through emerging nervous processes or perhaps even through the origin of new nerve cells. Thus Jerzy Rose has shown that if one of the cortical layers are destroyed by radiation, the axons of the two layers adjacent, on either side of the destroyed layer will grow through the degenerate layer to make new connections with each other. At the XXIII Physiological Congress in Tokyo in 1965, Drs. M. Adal, D. Barker, and M.C. Ip, University of Durham, England, reported the growth of entirely new motor endings of nerves to muscles.

Organ System Responsibility

For the last few years we have been concerned with the comparative study of the renal and cardiac functions in the dog. It had been previously reported that the kidney was susceptible to conditioning to the same extent that the gastrointestinal functions were. However, after a number of years of trying to form renal CRs in the dog we have not found it possible.

When we begin to analyze renal function we come to an explanation of why there is this difficulty in forming a diuretic CR. The usual way of considering conditioning was a stereotyped one: you select an inborn type of reactivity, an unconditional reflex, you give the adequate stimulus to produce this UR, and then you precede this stimulation with any signal, the conditional stimulus, and *ipso facto* you get a CR. This has been the usual method for obtaining all CRs. There has been little question that the application of this stereotyped method will produce a stereotyped result, viz., the CR.

Recently I have looked for an explanation of why the kidney did not respond the way the salivary and the gastric secretions do, and the way the motor system does. The function of the motor system is to adjust in a useful way to the coming events in the external environment; the cardiovascular and respiratory systems prepare the organism for this action. In a like manner the salivary secretion, the gastric secretions prepare for the ingestion of food. When the signal, for one reason or another, does not activate the CR as it once did, no great loss occurs except that of a slight drop in physical energy. This is because the secretions, salivary and gastric, etc., are poured into the gastrointestinal canal and promptly reabsorbed; there is no loss of either fluids or solutes. Several gallons of saliva, gastric, pancreatic and intestinal secretions and bile are poured into the gut, reabsorbed and reused. It is as if a city continually reused all its sewage, for this happens with the aqueous solutions of the body, except those lost through the skin, lungs and kidney, and a small portion through the feces.

However, if the kidney were to function according to the same stereotyped paradigm, there would occur in the conditioning process a discharge of water and electrolytes which are unrecoverable. This would mean that a thirsty animal responding to the signals for water and also for foods could be depleting itself of these very essential items, leading to the death of the individual. For what the kidney discharges into its pelvis and into the bladder cannot be reabsorbed into the body system and it is therefore lost irrevocably.

The principle of organ responsibility means that the formation of a conditional reflex in greater or lesser degree is in relation to the physiologic function of the system upon which it is operating; a conditional reflex appears impossible to form if it would violate radically the function performed by this system in the body economy, thus opposing the principle of homeostasis.

Organ-system responsibility and the principle of teleology do not mean that we can always make a prediction according to logic, according to teleology; we do not know precisely the teleology of the organ or of the individual. We only know a little about it. So we cannot, as the great physicists Einstein and Planck have done, sit down with a few figures and, without performing an experiment, make predictions and come out with great laws. You cannot do that with a biological organism because of the tremendous number of factors which are at work. So you have to go to the dog and do the experiment to find out what happens; you cannot bypass the experiment simply by the principle of organ-system responsibility. This leads me to the conclusion, however, that I, as well as other people, would be quite mistaken were we to adhere to a stereotyped paradigm without looking at the underlying function of the physiology of that system with which we were working. And although it seems very popular and very alluring to say that everything can become conditioned, that you can cure heart disease, and that you can regulate every autonomic function of the body by the simple bell-and-food paradigm, I think that we have to exercise wisdom, look more at the physiology, and understand what are the organs doing—what are they for—and, thus, rid ourselves of stereotyped thinking.

Pragmatism, the product of Charles Peirce, was developed and applied by William James and John Dewey. In pragmatism, it is not the whole of reality with which we are concerned, but with only the parts accessible to us with which we can interact.

The laws of the external universe result in pragmatic control. We assume that the external sense organs record accurately the phenomena of the external world, and we work pragmatically with these laws.

Nerves from the internal universe give us a vague sense of the degree of well-being. Furthermore, we know when we are conscious, but these states are not recognizable in any scientific quantitative measurements. For the whole internal universe, we are unaware what goes on, except under pathological conditions.

The significance of the part of the information brought by the nerves of pain is subjective. The electrical impulses conducted over the nerves are of no significance to us, unless they are represented by the subjective feelings of pain.

The *content* of the states of consciousness cannot be communicated—first, these states are not quantitatively *recordable*, in the terms of which they are significant. Second, they are not communicable in their essence. There are objective correlates —e.g., heart rate, motor movements, etc.

With regard to communication, who knows what a baby is thinking when he looks at red? Therefore, the science that we have and use for the internal universe is a foreign science built on external data. We are lacking a science for what goes on inside. In all of this, an important, if not the central role is played by the information brought to the brain by the external sense organs, viz., the visual, auditory, olfactory, gustatory, tactile, and temperature functions. All these organs turn outward. They register what goes on in the external universe. Normally they cannot sense even their own existence—the eye does not see itself, the ear hear itself, the tongue taste itself, the olfactory organ smell itself, the skin feel itself. We are concerned here with the *conscious* experiences, not what may be conveyed to the subconscious, nor with the electrical potentials or chemical perceptions since it is the conscious perceptions that are the basis of our science. What the external sense organs bring into consciousness, as far as is obvious and demonstrable, is the *sine qua non* of the science that we know.

Thus our science is constructed from the building blocks of the external sense organs, arranged and cemented into place by the inner master architect, the brain.

Furthermore, science is a human product and practically all of this science depends on (involves?) the function of vision. The eye is not only the sense organ at the basis of our human science, but is the most sensitive instrument that we know, either in nature or man-made. This is true both with regard to the amount of energy it can detect—viz., several quanta, nearly at the theoretical physical limit of energy—and also the simplicity of its construction to perform its function. And as Sherrington points out, it is constructed mainly from water plus a little of the substance of egg white, entirely in darkness.

Although we do not know of a science devoid of the facts and involvement of vision, it is conceivable that, given our human brain, we could build a rudimentary science from other external sense organ data. Thus Helen Keller without the sense of vision could understand visual science, because the facts were supplied by other eyes which could see for her. If we had the auditory and tactile sense organs of a bat, or the olfactory sense organs of a dog, or of some worms, we could construct a certain kind of science, but it would include only things which could be heard or smelled and very circumscribed as to distance. Space would have to be estimated, as with a bat, by resonance of reflected sound waves emitted from the vibration of its own voice, or by the muscular sense of spanning the distance with arms or legs. We would know of the existence of the sun but not of the moon or stars, nor anything of its distance.

Some animals are guided by delicate sense perceptors, e.g., insects to their goals perhaps by heat radiations, salmon, eels, seals, etc., into streams by a chemical or pressure sense. Nevertheless, this is a long way from a science.

So far we have discussed the science that has been erected on the sense organ data of the external universe. But there is an internal universe bounded by our skin plus a few small areas of sensitive mucous membrane and modified visual epithelium, the boundary that prevents any unscheduled interchange of substance between the two universes. This internal universe of which we are a part is immeasurably more complex, and infinitely less comprehensible than the external universe of which we are not a part. By the standards of external science it is mainly an unstable aqueous solution comprising at any one instant vitriolic and toxic substances, perhaps many thousands of compounds of exact proportions, immersed together in a common medium, often strictly limited to one small area (e.g., HCl) or everywhere abundant (hemoglobin), confined rigidly to certain places, but under great pressure, by a watery membrane not visible to the naked eye and thinner than the finest tissue paper, yet strong enough to withstand a constant fluid pressure greater than that of the most powerful suction pump (the epithelial cells of the renal tubules). Without any known centrally and uniquely controlled mechanism, this living organism of thousands of simultaneous reactions, compositions, functions, structures, all infinitely varied and separate, yet with a common goal, maintains itself and contributes its prescribed allotment for the survival of the whole.

But what of the science for this complex internal universe? How does it compare with the science of the infinite external universe, relatively speaking? Have we evolved such an adequate science?

Let us compare the science of the external universe and that of the internal universe. As pointed out, the science of the external universe has been constructed on the data brought to the integrating organism, the brain, by the external sense organs. It has been a science which, though it may reveal only a very minute part of the external universe, of reality, provides us with a pragmatic basis for working with that part of the external universe to which the external sense organs are sensitive.

Now if the science of the external universe is dependent upon what the sense organs tell us of the external universe, how can we escape the conclusion that an adequate science of the internal universe must depend upon sense organ data from that internal universe?

But what are the sense organs for this internal universe? Sense organ data for the basis of science must bring information from the universe with which it deals, even though we admit the data is of a relatively small part of the whole. For example, the ear records only vibrations within the range of 16 to perhaps 30,000, the eye between the wave lengths of red and blue, or one octave.

The sense organ data from the internal universe that reach consciousness, and these are the only ones that science so far can deal with, are nil under normal conditions. All these myriad interactions work silently and, to our sight, blindly. None of us are conscious of the function of the liver, kidney, spleen, adrenals, stomach, or vestibular apparatus. We have a proprioceptive sense, but it is doubtful to what degree it normally enters consciousness.

It is true that under conditions of malfunctioning, or pathology, we sometimes feel discomfort or pain, but even this sense is not always present. Thus one can be dying of cancer, silent tumors, while being unconscious of their presence or location. The surgeon Blalock was not conscious of the cancer of the liver from which he died until it had spread throughout his body. Such facts are too commonplace in medicine to require elaboration.

Even when one has information from the internal universe it is usually vague and imprecise, comparable to what it would be to view an object through a ground glass window, a heavily smoked glass, or to listen for a specific sound in the roar of Niagara. We do often have a sense of well-being or the opposite, but it would be very difficult to measure or to record euphoria objectively.

On the same basis as we assess the science of the external universe, we have no adequate science for the internal universe. As we well know, the science that we have evoked for the external universe has produced remarkable results in biology. We have the cure for many diseases, e.g., diabetes, pellagra, scurvy, to say nothing of the drugs for combatting infections, the analgesics, anesthetics, stimulants, etc. Nevertheless, this science of the external universe applied to the internal universe, though it is useful and often alters profoundly biological processes, is still inadequate to explain life. The science that we have is foreign to life, borrowed from the science of the dead universe.

Even our language, when applied to the subjective, the most conscious part of the internal universe, is descriptive of spatial, auditory, visual relations. The terms for this idea, as well as the idea itself come from conversation with my friend John Lamb, who said:

> Our language is replete with words brought from objective descriptions of the external universe. For example: we turn now to the *sub*conscious from which ideas come to the *surface* in the form of mental *images* during a *flash* of insight. The *rate* at which this happens is taken to be a *function* of a person's psychic *energy*. *Deeply* felt emotions, though, are likely to *color* our ideas and *becloud* our thinking. Those who are deemed the *sharpest* thinkers seem to be most *adept* at *circumventing* these distractions in order to *penetrate* to the *core* of a *tangled mass* of abstractions.

Perhaps because of this inadequate science of the internal universe corresponding to our science of the external universe, we have practically no science of the most important part of the life as we estimate it for ourselves, viz., our subjective life. This we cannot even record scientifically, as we do the elements of the external universe. When we record the change in heart rate, blood pressure, respiration, muscular contraction in pain, we have an objective correlate, but a correlate of a zero function except when we experience it in ourselves. What we record is something of another category, the existence of which is known to ourselves but only inferred in others, animal or human. The science of the external universe does not touch this subjective experience.

Furthermore some subjective processes—thinking, feeling, perception, etc.—may be below quantum level and therefore theoretically never recordable by any instrument other than mind. This view is especially reinforced by the purest scientists, the modern physicists, Planck and Schroedinger, but also by the philosopher-physiologist Sherrington. Planck states that science cannot deal with our subjective life.

"Science thus fixes for itself its own inviolable boundaries. But man, with his unlimited impulses, cannot be satisfied with this limitation. He must overstep it, since he needs an answer to the most important, and constantly-repeated question of his life: What am I to do?—And a complete answer to this question is not furnished by determinism, not by causality, especially not by pure science, but only by his moral sense, by his character, by his outlook on the world."

And Schroedinger says that our psychical life does not involve energy.

"One can say in a few words why our perceiving and thinking self is nowhere to be found within the world picture, because it itself is this world picture."

And Sherrington:

"Mind, for anything perception can compass . . . remains without sensual confirmation, and remains without it forever."

The failure by Kety to measure any increased blood supply to the brain during consciousness or thinking, though still not conclusive, may be relevant.

Is it because of the lack of a specific science for the internal universe and the probable inadequacy of the science of the external universe when applied to the internal universe, that there is so much unknown about biology and life? Here the imponderables remain as stubbornly incomprehensible as they were in the dawn of recorded human history. Most of the eminent scientists sense that the existence of mind, love, individual free will, a world with a beginning or a world without a beginning, limited or unlimited space, time, and God, are equally difficult to comprehend. Even with our advanced and advancing science of the external universe, for each one of us what we value most highly are the emotions and the subjective. The objective science of the external universe has no meaning of its own—only as it can affect our subjective experience. This becomes apparent when we look at how the human values the idea of an after-life; it is not the body that he aspires to preserve, but the spirit, i.e., the subjective part. When there is the lack of interest in an after-life it is not because of the uncertainty of the objective body, but because of the doubt of such a subjective persistence. Thus:

Why if the soul can fling the dust aside,
And naked on the air in Heaven ride,
Were it not a shame, were it not a shame
In this clay house imprisoned to abide.

We could erect a similar though very limited science to the one we have now by using auditory sense data or a system of radar as used by bats. Thus we could form a science of music—pitch and the length of strings—but such a science would be limited only to what could be transmitted through actual matter, or perhaps through the thermal sense and heat rays.

But let us reverse the process of applying the science of the external sense organs to the internal universe, viz., using the internal sense organ data applied to the science of the external universe. The most definite and continually acting internal sense organs are proprioceptive, vestibular, which are mainly below consciousness and therefore, because they are below consciousness, inadequate by the criteria (sense organ data reaching consciousness) for our science of the external universe. The sense organ which preeminently brings us data from within and enters consciousness is the pain sense.

To reverse the process, to found a science of the external universe on the sense organ data from the internal universe: we would find the science, the relationships developed from the

117

perception of pain applied to the scientific understanding of the external universe. This would be a poet's world of images rather than a scientific world; the external universe would be explained by subjective terms such as groaning, suffering, etc. Such an idea is evidently preposterous, but I raise the question of whether it is not equally absurd to look for an adequate science of the subjective world and of the whole internal universe from the sense organs which bring data from the external universe.

Without doubt it is true that we can produce certain results by studying the living organism as if it were a part of the dead external universe.

When we measure the effect of meditation and other mental states in objective physiological terms—heart rate, blood pressure, oxygen metabolism, etc.—we are doing no more than Pavlov did seventy-five years ago when he converted the state of hunger to a quantitative record, drops of saliva.

What is to be done?

Given the structure of the nervous system and the lack of a basis for a science of the internal universe comparable to the science of the external universe, it is hardly likely that we can ever develop such a science. We then must make what pragmatic use we can of the science that we have.

But if one chief goal of science is to comprehend the nature of the biology of our subjective life we should understand the differences in the study of the external universe compared with the internal universe. Such a point of view will not blind us to the pragmatic value of science, of the wonders revealed by science, of the adventures ahead into the Unknown, or what is knowable and what is unknowable.

In conclusion, we must assess the inadequacy of our present science of the external universe for the complete study of the internal universe, of consciousness and our various subjective states. And despite our misgivings, we should face all the universe, the external and the internal, with an open mind and in the spirit not of despair but of adventure.

Discussion

Sir John Eccles: I am, of course, in general agreement with Dr. Gantt on his external and internal universes, but I would like to point out that I have some differences also. We do have far more sense organs within the skin, shall we say, than pain. And some of these have recently been investigated quantitatively and shown to be very important. Of course, we have known for a long time about proprioception and, for example, the position of a limb is known accurately from joint sensing and from muscle and tension sensing in fascia. But more than the muscle contraction can actually be now sensed and Gantt has shown that this sensing gives rise to many kinds of illusion. We have knowledge of more and more sensing that comes from within the body and which is quantifiable. It has not been recognized until recently because it isn't so overt as other sensing. It is rather like the sense from your vestibular system. You don't normally notice it, but if you are put on a turntable, you get vertigo. Vertigo is a sense derived from your vestibular mechanism. There are many internal senses which can be quantified. That is the first point I want to make.

Secondly, about the subjective states. There is a science of subjective states; in fact it is a very extensive science. One part is called psychophysics, where all kinds of measurements of stimulations are made and compared to the resulting subjective experiences, for example in vision and in hearing with matching a sense with the signals. In fact, Stevens has erected a power law according to which the experienced sense intensity is proportional to the stimulus intensity raised to some specific power. The exponential of this power law has been found for many senses, but has very different values for the kinds of sensing—vision, pressure, vibration and sound. So what I am trying to say is that we do have, in fact, a way of evaluating our internal senses, not perhaps as accurately as the external. Even our scientific observations in the way of measuring and assessing necessitate an internal evaluation of what comes through our senses. We would all agree that we build up the whole of science on sensory impressions. There is no other way, but many of these senses come from the inside and are strictly speaking internal.

Gantt: I would just make the comment that although this does throw light on whether we have nerves for internal states, the other part of what I am saying is that the subjective remains forever beyond measurement, in any degree and with any measurement that is essential to itself. You can get measurements of correlates, but they are not the essence of the subjective, and I am sure Sir John would agree with me in that. It is said many times in Sherrington's book; here is just one sentence: "Mind, for anything perception can compass . . . remains without sensual confirmation, and remains without it forever."[1] Now, of course, you can always say that new things will be discovered, but this statement throws light on some possibilities of nerves that come from inside. If you compare these with the precision of the external sense organs, there is no comparison if you talk about what comes into consciousness. These things are probably acting all the time in some subconscious way.

Eccles: Yes, I agree with that, but lest Sherrington be misunderstood in your little quotation, I would like to read your other quotation from Schroedinger here if I may. It reads, "One can say in a few words why our perceiving and thinking self is nowhere to be found within the world picture, because it itself is this world picture." That, I would agree with completely. I think it is a very good quotation.

Editor's Note: The author of this chapter is deceased. Therefore, the footnotes are incomplete.

Notes

1. C.S. Sherrington, *Man on his Nature* (The Gifford Lectures, Edinburgh 1937-38, New York: Macmillan and Cambridge University Press, (1941).

10.

Adaptability of the Nervous System and Its Relation to Chance, Purposiveness, and Causality

Ragnar A. Granit

To the biologists themselves biology nowadays is either organismic, physico-chemical or molecular but if you ask a layman what biology might be however, he or she would almost certainly think of the evolution of animals, genetics, chromosomes, hybridization, new species of plants, or the breeding of horses or dogs. Behind this is, I suspect, a flood of popular conceptualization based on slogans such as the *survival of the fittest, the struggle for life, our origin from apes* and perhaps also the tough resistance of anti-Darwinism in some well-known trials in a certain state within the United States. To many of these topics people feel an irresistible urge to add their own contribution.

In the science of neurophysiology experimenters are cautious, unwilling to popularize and hesitant to discuss general principles for fear of exposing themselves to disparaging remarks from their colleagues. As a consequence their science stands isolated from contact with the rest of the biological sciences in which a running discussion of first principles is being maintained. In formulating the following remarks, I hope to show how our science can add a note of our own to the concert of voices explaining concepts such as purposiveness, adaptation, causality and chance. How do we look upon them in our field?

121

I shall use as a background evolutionary theory where purposiveness is given a definite role in the disguise of "directiveness." While physiologists may speak about teleological explanations, the evolutionary biologist speaks about "teleonomic directivess" of "teleonomic purposivess."[1] Pantin maintains that it is impossible to use "purposiveness" because purpose implies "striving after a future goal retained as some kind of image or idea."[2] The neurophysiologist can immediately mention any number of highly purposive reactions that are wholly automatic, be they inherited or acquired. Thus he has no reason to discard the classical term: teleological explanations—without or with an image of the goal. When in evolutionary theory "purposiveness" has to be toned down by the attribute "teleonomic," the reason for this is that the consensus of opinion in this field holds "purpose" to be apparent only and the direction of evolution to be fundamentally explainable on the basis of mutations and recombinations. Their viability is tested by natural selection. The testing itself takes place in the phenotype and the whole operation in a population. It is thus statistical.

If one asks how the effect of the testing ultimately leads to fixation of the mutant in a population, the answer may be illustrated in the following experiment by Waddington:[3] a strain of *Drosophila melanogaster* produced flies with a break in the posterior crossvein of the wing only when pupae aged 21-23 hours were subjected to 40° for four hours. They did not do so at 25°. After 14 generations of selection with the heat treatment some flies were found to show the effect without being exposed to the heat shock. Thus this typical acquired character had entered the genetic make-up by selection which so increased the frequency of the salient gene that it became stabilized for some generations. The evolutionary progress is postulated to have taken place by small changes over millions of years of exposure to natural selection. These have ultimately been fixed in the coded genome.

Mayr points out that evolutionary biology deals with two questions, "how come," and "what for."[4] I take it that the synthetic theory of evolution, as briefly outlined above, deals with both of them simultaneously in their explanations. This field is distinguished from "functional biology"—says Mayr—which deals with questions of "how" in a manner inseparable in principle from that of physics and chemistry. I shall come in a moment to the fact that no one can think of understanding the central nervous system without encountering any number of "why"questions.

In the meantime let us realize that the coded instructions of evolutionary theory cannot be easily translated into characters paired with genes. Characters are polygenetic and an additional complication is polymorphism, an important variability reflected in the process of natural selection. The programmed codes, for these and many other reasons, cannot be rigid. The genetic instructions are, within limits, open. An outsider would like to understand why this sometimes is obviously true, while at other times it is equally obvious that great rigidity has prevailed, for instance, in species which have been constant for 500 million years.

Perhaps I should also add an instance of open instructions. We can take it from Lucretius, *De rerum natura*, Chapter IV, where he pointed out that the tongue existed before speech became possible. Everybody knows that the dog also uses the tongue for heat regulation. This is what one might call the serendipitous trait in evolution. Something is begun somewhere in the phylum and after millions of years is found to be useful for something else. Because the coded instructions are open and tested by the environment in the phenotype, such strokes of inspired magic are possible.

The leading workers in evolutionary biology realize that the explanation of evolution by the synthetic theory is a postulate, and also that it is non-predictive. Nevertheless it is the best explanation we have. It embodies deep insight, a great deal of real creative knowledge, and it will live with us into the future.

Approaching this theory from the point of view of the neurosciences, I believe that a significant contribution might be a discussion of the act of testing of the phenotype, as it is seen from the physiological end. It seems to me essential that if we can understand the role of "purpose" in neurophysiology and thereby its role in the elaboration of the phenotype, we have in a way given teleological purposiveness a place also in evolution."

It is of course not difficult to show that teleological explanations play a decisive role in practical neurobiology. We ask *why* an observed event takes place and by this means arrive at an essential element of understanding. A very good example is the work of Karl von Frisch on the communication and orientation of the bee.[5] The two questions of "how" and "why" are clearly outlined. *How* is it that the bee can orientate itself over long distances of flight? The answer was, as is well known, that it differs from us in having retinal units with eight radially placed detectors of light polarized in different planes. Sunlight is naturally polarized as it is reflected from the blue sky and, thus, as long as part of the sky is visible, the bee has at its disposal a map by which to adjust its angle of flight.

Why is it that bees returning to the hive from distant sources of honey execute a curious dance on the glass wall of the observation hive? Von Frisch called it "Schwanzeltanz." To many scientists this would have been merely an oddity, a curio to be placed on the roomy shelf of other innumerable curios in the biological world. The phenomenon could in fact be understood simply by asking for its purpose. Von Frisch proved that its purpose was communicative. The bee danced in a circle divided into two semicircles by a diagonal which showed the direction of the flight, while the number of tours in the dance indicated the distance from the hive. In the observation hive the bee danced on a vertical plane so that its companions in addition had to project it on a horizontal plane—rather an intricate piece of geodetic geometry on the part of such a relatively small mass of neurons.

So far my questioning has only been concerned with the practical use of "why" questions. These questions make it possible to detect biological adaptions and the evolutionary biologist would agree and maintain—as to the bee—that this is a typical instance of *telenomic* purposiveness laid down in the genetic instructions.

True *teleological* purposiveness, however, is what evolution has produced in developing our brain. Let me quote Sherrington: "The dog not only walks but it walks to greet its master. In a word the component from the roof brain alters the character of the motor act from one of generality of purpose to one of narrowed and specific purpose fitting a special occasion. The change is just as if the motor act had suddenly become correlated with the finite mind of the moment."[6] This is meant to emphasize that the conscious purposive brain represents the final hierarchic stage in the development of our capacity to adjust ourselves to the environment. An adaptation—the dog walks—has become *adaptable* by being subjected to cerebral control—it walks to greet its master. In the neurosciences the great and fascinating problem is what to do with *adaptability*. From the genetic point of view evolution has led to diverse adaptations. Animals are adapted to swim, to fly, to feed on grass, etc. But purposive adaptability deals with the range and pliability of such genetically fixed adaptations.

To begin analyzing such problems with "the dog walking to greet its master," is to begin from the end, the top level of dog performance. Pavlov did this when he trained dogs to salivate to a tone by the simple expedient of letting a reward of food in repeated trials succeed the tone. In order to appreciate the role of purposiveness in creating such "conditioned reflexes" one need but imagine the "reward" (today called "reinforcement") to be given *before* sounding the tone instead of *afterwards*. Purpose, meaning motivation, is a term that in different ways show what made sense of this undertaking.

We have to begin with simpler questions. The one I propose is as follows: can we change a normal response of a single cortical cell or a number of them by impressing upon them properties which are at cross purposes with an ingrained purposive adaptation? This question is particularly interesting from the evolutionary and developmental points of view.

My first example is Sperry's experiment[7] in which the optic nerve of a frog was cut, the eye bulb turned round in its socket by 180° and regeneration allowed to take place. It was found that by some kind of chemically determined specificity the nerve fibers grew into their original sites in the optic tectum. The frog never adapted itself to this reversal of the optical image. A fly in the upper field of vision excited the animal to catch it in the lower field. Once established the ingrained adaptation was too resistant to allow any adaptability.

In his experiment inherently open genetic instructions have been closed, but it can be shown that originally they had been open at an early stage of amphibian ontogenetic development if at the time rotation took place normal purposive (fly-catching) reflexes developed. Jacobson and Hunt's analysis showed that the critical period for the operative rotation in *Xenopus*, another amphibian, was between 32 and 40 hours of amphibian life. Its retinal ganglion cells were born approximately 34 hours and their nerve fibres reached the optic tectum 15 hours later. The empirically established new correlations between the retinal and the cortical maps closed the genetic instructions, possibly aided by functional saction of synaptic chemical "markers."

It is easy enought to enumerate cases of developmental plasticity which are lost later in life, even in man. The language areas in the brain are well known to be in the parietal and temporal lobes of the left hemisphere. Destruction of them leads to permanent aphasia. But, if this region is lost before the age of about twelve, the right hemisphere takes over and develops new language areas.

On the other hand, there are also functions of the roof-brain or cortex in which re-purposing against an ingrained purpose succeeds. In this respect man is supreme. Long ago it was shown by Sperry that operative exchange of flexors and extensors even in the monkey was not perfectly compensated.[9] But if one looks up "Bennell's Surgery of the Hand" one finds it stated explicitly that in the hand and the forearm any muscle and tendon, when transferred to a new site, can carry out any desired motion. "A wrist extensor can act as a digital extensor, a digital flexor, a wrist flexor or a motor for opposition and adduction of the thumb" (p. 444).[10] These movements have then been reprogrammed in the brain under the guidance of feedback from the eye, the muscles, and, oddly enough, from the skin, which has been found to be very important for programming a prosthesis (Moberg). In Sperry's experiments training for example one flexor movement was not transferable to flexion in another situation: the measure of re-adaption achieved required months, even two years.

However, I would like to return to vision and make some comparisons between cat and man with respect to adaptability tested by "repurposing" an afferent response of the brain. This concerns the perception of orientation of lines appearing in the receptive field of a cortical cell in the primary visual projection area 17. It presupposes knowledge of the discovery of Hubel and Wiesel that the cells of the type called "simple" are sensitive to the orientation of oblongs or lines and yield optimal responses for correct orientations.[11] In the visual cortex of the cat an assembly of such cells represents all orientations of visual stimuli in a non-preferential manner. But if young kittens are reared in a vertically or horizontally striped environment the cortical cells begin to respond preferentially to these directions. Blakemore[12] who did this work, following Hirsch and Spinelli,[13] found that no more than an hour's exposure to such visual experiences sufficed to modify the preferred orientation of most units, provided that this experiment was followed by a minimum of two weeks in the dark. But if the kittens had more than 5 hours of such abnormal experience the effect became virtually ineradicable by other visual stimuli. Nothing else distinguished these cortical units from normal ones.

What about ourselves? There is now a large number of experiments in which people have been wearing inversion lenses or prismatic goggles or even colored filters to create a visual world at cross-purposes with ingrained experience. The first ones, by Stratton in 1897, showed that on the fifth day of wearing a monocular inversion lens with the other eye covered, Stratton had adapted so well to the originally inverted world that "there was no anticipatory drawing in of the chin and chest when a solid object passed through the visual field in the direction which in normal vision would have meant a blow."[14] Both the perceived world and the reflexes were adapted to the new experience.

From work on monkeys we are entitled to conclude that directionally sensitive cells also exist in our visual cortex. An average response of such cells can actually be studied objectively by measuring on the scalp the amplitude of electrical potentials evoked in response to visual stimuli of variable orientation. It is known that vertical and horizontal targets are better resolved by human observers than oblique patterns, also that evoked potentials by their amplitude indicate these preferential sensitivities.

In Pisa, Fiorentini, Ghez and Maffei proceeded to investigate what happens when seven adult subjects wore tilting prisms continually for seven days.[15] The prisms produced a tilt of the target of 30° or 40° from the vertical, and the angle between the apparent vertical and the real vertical was measured and compared with the amplitudes of their evoked potentials. These served to indicate the degree of perceptual compensation. In all subjects perceptual "re-purposing" to the tilt occurred in the first hours, and compensation was virtually complete on the second day. The adaptive effects were accompanied by a decrease of the mean difference between the amplitudes of evoked potentials for the vertical and oblique patterns. And this is now the final experiment that I shall mention in support of the fact that man has carried a high degree of plastic adaptability with him into maturity. I would now like to discuss the facts rather than multiply them.

There are many things we would like to understand in these

127

observations, such as (i) the mechanism of compensation, (ii) why man is superior to cat and (iii) their general significance in relation to purposiveness, chance and causality.

(i) Verticality, like most percepts, is a complex affair. If we tilt our head, a vertical oblong remains vertical in spite of the tilted retinal image and the new receptors concerned. Verticality has a kind of relative constancy, like size, velocity of movements, and object color. The size of our hands alters continually, regarded as a retinal image, but is constant as a percept. There are clearly definite frameworks of reference, some external, but probably most of them internal. The percept of verticality has important components other than visual ones. There is first and foremost an internal world of reference based on feedback from the balance organs in the head, on sense organs in the neck muscles, along the spine, in muscles of the leg, and skin sensations from the soles. The perennial necessity of compensating for gravity sees to it that the experience of verticality is solidly anchored by those feedback impulses in a cellular organization capable of error detection. This is based on the information returning to it.

A permanent distortion of the visual input by prismatic goggles is a non-plausible illusion which goes against the grain of all the other sources of information, in particular against those most directly concerned with the position of the head in relation to gravity. Error detection leads by feedback to error correction in this highly purposeful, or let us say, sensible brain of ours. These events produce alterations in the wiring diagram which is wired up with a redundancy, very likely exceeding that of all other mammals. We do not know which particular processes are responsible for the error correction but there is no lack of possible alternatives, judged by experimental results from adjacent neurophysiological fields. The axoplasmic flow of chemical material in nerve fibres is well known and intensely studied today. It may serve to cement new connections, the old ones may withdraw in a mechanical sense because of disuse while new ones may expand by use. A synaptic cleft, after all, is no more than a few hundred Angstrom (2 nm), or there may be active inhibition involved in the error correction. Even if we do not know what the explanation is it is one that does not seem to be wholly beyond reach by experimentation. From Cragg's work we are also quite familiar with electronmicroscopically recordable synaptic alterations by use and disuse.[16] Error correction by feedback is well known from the experiments on maintaining constant length and tension of a muscle in the face of load variations. We have the wiring diagram of this circuit and the whole process is essentially spinal though the sensitivitiy of the error detectors (muscular sense organs) is adjustable from the brain. The new element introduced by the experiments on perceived verticality reviewed here is the durable effect of error detection, the permanent nature of the compensation. This may be maintained by use.

(ii) In considering a likely explanation of why man is superior to the cat, the enormous expansion of our cortex and the high degree of encephalization, that is, of the shift of final control to this cortex, suggest themselves as the basic elements in any workable hypothesis.

Beginning with the question of why in early development the genetic instructions are open, later on to become closed, I feel much attracted by the hypothesis of Jacobson, which is well-founded and capable of an experimental expansion. Jacobson, a developmental physiologist, uses the term "specification" and speaks of non-specified cells: "Some neurons are highly specified and all their connections are fully determined, but there are also some incompletely specified neurons with indeterminate connections. During ontogeny there is a tendency for neuronal specificity to increase and for connections to become more highly determined, but the developmental stage at which these changes occur, as well as their extent and duration, varies for different neurons . . . Neurons of class I are those that originate early in embryonic development. They are mainly macroneurons, that is, large neurons with long axons. They form the primary afferent and efferent neurons of the central nervous system of vertebrates, and their central connections usually have a topographical arrangement. Their connections are specified during early embryonic development, and are invariant and unmodifiable thereafter. Sensory stimulation is not required for their development and there are few, if any, lasting changes following electrical activity of class I neurons. By contrast, class I neurons are interneurons of various kinds, especially the small neurons with short axons, the Golgi II type. They originate later than class I neurons in any particular part of the nervous system, and the production of class II neurons continues into postnatal life in some parts of the brain. The connectivity of these neurons is more variable than that of class I neurons. Specific kinds of sensory stimulation are required for the full development and maintenance of class II neurons or of their connections. Electrical activity in these neurons may result in changes on long duration. Specification of class II neurons occurs slowly and is contingent on specific kinds of sensory stimulation."[17]

The talent for re-purposing against an ingrained purpose is thus not a universal property of all brain cells. It is based on the variable connectivity of the interneurons of the Golgi II type of cell, which are the large majority of all cells in the cortex. According to Ramon y Cajal their number increases upwards in the phylum.[18] One of the directive purposes of evolution in creating such an organ for encephalization of control may well be to give the new instrument the adaptability of which I have spoken. The ultimate controls are drawn into the sphere of action of the small internuncial cells at a site where their number is great enough to be decisive in responding purposively to experience beyond the stage of ontogenetic development.

From this point of view it seems to follow that man should be the most adaptable adult organism in existence. His brain is the relatively largest one. Relative to what? With its average of 1350 cc, it is smaller than, for instance, that of the blue whale which is 2800 cc. But phylogenetically brain volumes are related to body surface, the formula relating brain size to weight being the same as the one relating weight to surface. We are apparently more significantly related to the environment by our surface than by our weight. But in the formula there is also a constant that determines the degree of encephalization and this is wherein man excels.

(iii) I wish I could do better on degrees of connectivity in this cellular organization that is our cortex. Such figures are very difficult to come by, because there is no good technique for measuring what Cragg's average figure of 30,000 synapses per cell or 60,000 synapses for the large cells really means. Is it an enormous branching of a few fibres of contact or does it represent a very large number of projecting axons and thus a high degree of connectivity? Following Cragg there would, at a conservative estimate, be 56 neurons interconnected with each neuron in the monkey visual cortex, 600 in its motor cortex where the neurons are larger. In another paper dealing with the rat visual cortex his estimate is 300 for each neuron. Man tends to have more large neurons than other animals of the same size. For the cat Sholl found each stellate neuron to branch around 4000 other neurons.[19] For man Cragg gives the average figure of 50 million cells per cc in the visual area. Others give values of 78 and 97 millions, as collected and tabulated by Cragg. But then, of course, the absolute number of neurons also would be relevant and there the estimates for the whole cortex of man range from 2.6×10^9 to 14×10^9.

Despite all these variations I think we move on certain ground when we state that no man-made computer has a connectivity anywhere near this order of magnitude. It simply is fabulous and adds an element of futility to the hope of ever solving the riddle of brain function merely by wiring diagrams.

What it does show, however, is that the numerous small cells of Group II with their adaptability or plasticity relative to environmental changes are numerous enough to give chance a chance. At this stage we have to turn to biological analogies to realize that we are up against a trick that Nature has used elsewhere. There are plants producing an enormous number of seeds, and in one ejaculation of the rabbit there is said to be an average of 700,000,000 sperms. Behind all this is, of course, a basic stability of the genetic code, just as in the brain there are fixed connections by cells of Type I and variable one by cells of Type II, capable of being influenced by environmental challenges.

Brain function can be compared to the immuno-system.[20] The small B-lymphocytes, rather than specializing in certain common diseases, generate an extraordinary number of antibodies. Specialization would have led to a fixed rather than to an adaptable adaptation. Adaptability is achieved by the existence of random chemical specificities for pattern recognition, their number being large enough for matching antibodies to most of the inimical epitopes that are likely to occur. These fits are remembered by the system and we know them as immunities for the agents that provoked them, at least when the immunity refers to a diagnosed disease with a name fixed to it. In this manner the immuno-system responds adequately to an enormous variety of signals; it learns from experience and remembers the lessons it has been taught by foreign agents. The chemical markers concerned in this activity are the immunoglobulins.

The analogy implies that in both cases there are systems making use of chemical specificities and that these systems rely on chance for adaptability to environmental challenges. Chance enters in as a multiplication of alternatives. Both systems have other cells for fixed tasks. In brain physiology and anatomy the fixed organizations and the various adaptations that they represent have obviously been in the center of neurophysiological research. To quote Brodal: "We may consider the brain as consisting of a multitude of small units, each with its particular morphological (and presumably functional) features. These units collaborate by way of an immensely rich, complicated and different network of connections, which are very precisely and specifically organized. The anatomical possibilities for (more or less direct) cooperations between various parts of the brain must be almost umlimited."[21]

Finally, having seen now how purposiveness and adaptability are, so to speak, partners in an indissoluble marriage between the organism and its enviornment, what about causality? It is perfectly clear that teleological explanations do not imply that we are casting adrift from causality. The aim of a purposive response is predictive; it assumes that the environment behaves in a predictable manner, and adjusts itself to correct for deviations from the predictable. Thus, inasmuch as the external world is concerned, purposiveness relates to definite causes. The experimenter can relate different purposes to the responses he is engaged in studying. We can never escape from the purposive causal relation to the environmental challenge. The teleological explanation may be put aside while we try to study the mechanisms by which it is realized in the organism, but it is nevertheless there clamoring for an answer.

The limitations we encounter in discussing casual teleology are on the inside of the organism. We don't know the inside causes residing in memory, motivation and in as yet unknown properties of the nervous system. To these unknown quantities we can add mind or consciousness which, of course, is the supreme instrument for dealing with purposiveness in all its aspects. I have left consciousness outside of this address because I have been interested in seeing to what an extent it is possible to get at the "hardware" of purposive responses in relation to definite environmental factors. In other words, I have wanted to find out how far we can go with things accessible to physiological and anatomical approaches. There is no denying that it would have been an easy choice to go for experiments that emphasize the complexity of internal causes, as, for instance, those referring to numerous illusions.

If I may return for a brief moment to evolutionary theory on the notion that lectures should end where they begin, I would like to point out that my reasoning amounts to a study of the act of testing of the phenotype and that this process is an essential component of the synthetic theory. I think my analysis has shown that adaptability is a teleological concept, with or without awareness of goal. I would not hesitate one moment to speak of an *immanent teleology*. People are afraid of this because they think it implies accepting a vitalism, which in my opinion has been dead for half a century. I would just as happily speak about immanent gravity or immanent magnetism. In all three cases no knowledge about ultimate causes is assumed. On the contrary, the term "immanent" means that we have no idea about the nature of the gravitational force and therefore have to accept it as a fact, inherent in our world of observations and for this reason as an essential element in our scientific superstructure. Similarly immanent teleology belongs to the scientific structure dealing with the living organism in its relation to the environment and we should try to make sense of it. My view has been that attempting to understand adaptability, in the present phase of physiological work, is a step in the right direction.

Notes

1. E. Mayr. 1963. "Cause and effect in biology," *Science 134*, 1501-06.

2. C.F.A. Pantin, *The Relations between the Sciences* (Cambridge University Press, 1968).

3. C.H. Waddington. 1953. "Genetic assimilation of an acquired character," *Evolution 7*, pp. 118-26.

4. E. Mayr, "Cause and effect in biology."

5. K. von Frisch, *Aus dem Leben der Bienen* (Gottingen and Heidelberg: Springer-Verlag, 1953).

6. C.S. Sherrington, *Man on his Nature*. The Gifford Lectures, Edinburgh 1937-38 (New York: Macmillan and Cambridge University Press, 1941).

7. R. W. Sperry, "Mechanisms of neural maturation," in *Handbook of Experimental Psychology*, S. S. Steven, ed. (New York: John Wiley & Sons, 1951), pp. 236-80.

8. M. Jacobson and R.K. Hunt. 1973. "The origins of nerve-cell specificity," *Scientific American, 228*, pp. 26-35.

9. R.W. Sperry, "Effect of crossing nerves to antagonistic limb muscles in the monkey." 1947. *Archives of Neurological Psychiatry 58*, pp. 452-73.

10. J.H. Boyes, ed. *Bunnell's Surgery of the Hand*, 4th ed. (Philadelphia: J. B. Lippincott, 1964).

11. D.H. Hubel and T.N. Wiesel, "Receptive fields of single neurons in the cat's striate cortex," *Journal of Physiology 148*, pp. 574-91.

12. C. Blackmore and G.F. Cooper. 1970. "Development of the brain depends on the visual environment," *Nature 228*, pp. 447-78. C. Blackmore and D.E. Mitchell. 1973. "Environmental modification of the visual cortex and the neural basis of learning and memory," *Nature 241*, pp. 467-68.

13. H.V.B. Hirsch and D.N. Spinelli, "Visual experience modifies distribution of horizontally and vertically oriented receptive fields in the cat," *Science 168 (1970)*, 869-71.

14. G.M. Stratton. 1897. "Vision without inversion of the retinal image." *Psychological Review 4*, pp. 341-60; 463-81.

15. A. Fiorentini, C. Ghez, and L. Maffei. 1972. "Physiological correlates of adaptions to a rotated visual field." *Journal of Physiology 227*, pp. 313-22.

16. B.G. Cragg. 1967. "The density of synapses and neurons in the motor and visual areas of the cerebral cortex." *Journal of Anatomy 101*, pp. 639-54.

17. M. Jacobson, *Developmental Neurobiology* (New York: Holt, Rinehart & Winston, 1970).

18. S. Ramon y Cajal, *Histologie du Systeme Nerveux de Phomme at des Vertebres* (Madrid: Instituto Ramon y Cajal, 1952).

19. D.A. Sholl, *The Organization of the Cerebral Cortex* (London: Methuen, 1956).

20. N.K. Jerne. 1973. "The immune system," *Scientific American 229*, pp. 52-60.

21. A. Brodal, M.I.T. Conference (1974), to be published.

Discussion

Stephen Prickett: I was fascinated by the Kantian possibilities that seem to be illustrated in Professor Granit's address, where it became clear that so many of the attributes we push into the external world can in fact be seen as qualities within the mind. Could Professor Granit comment further?

Granit: As a matter of fact, there is a secret undercurrent in all this work, and that is that we are trying to discover clues for the mind. The physiology of the special senses is in many cases a physiology designed to discover the clues for any kind of mental processes. We have gone rather far now in this direction in present day physiology. We are now at single cells in the cortex of animals and I think even sometimes in man—they can be obtained in surgical operations on man since the brain doesn't feel any pain and so people allow such experiments to be done. Some clues are very direct, like that of horizontality and verticality. There are many other clues that are not so directly translatable now. For example, we can locate distances acoustically—it is the difference in time between the two ears that is decisive, but it doesn't give any indication of the location of the source; whereas these experiments on horizontality and verticality have a more precise connection with the mind, if I may say so.

Erick Jantsch: I wonder whether the concept of immanent teleology is not convergent with the aims and the concepts of general systems theory?

Granit: Well many people do like to think of cybernetics as a teleological science, but I am a little hesitant on that. I think that if you have say a Kreb's cycle and push a good reaction into a Kreb's cycle you have done something important—you have put a new reaction into an old structural process. In the same way we have these cybernetical restrictions and many things can be put into this concept, but personally, I think it isn't so very different from pushing a reaction into the Kreb's cycle, or pushing a reaction process into the cybernetic machinery or constraints which can be of course handled mathematically.

Nand Keswani: You spoke of the adaptability of the nervous system to the needs of the human body. How about the relationship of the brain to the adaptabiliy of the human being to a community and to the society? We know that the brain, in experimental animals as well as in man, has centers controlling feeding and also the sex urge. The herding mentality is also closely associated with these urges. Some chromosome aberrations have also been blamed for criminal tendencies and antisocial behavior in these individuals. What is your comment?

Granit: Well, you are asking me to go far beyond my limits of competence. I am a neurophysiologist and I therefore have thought very little about the application of these ideas into society. I think that I shall leave it to you.

R.V. Jones: Could you tell us anything about the "moon illusion" and how it arises. You have explained about the vertical perception.

Granit: When I was a child I was riding on a horse and saw the moon jumping along the treetops at the speed at which the horse moved. The explanation is that the image on the retina is a constant, but as you are moving, the trees are being left behind you, and then you have an illusion—a sensible movement —because something which goes ahead with the trees must be moving in order to remain in the background. These fall into internal frameworks of reference for which we have very little physiological knowledge but we have to accept them, since we have created such frameworks.

Tor Ragnar Gerholm: In the 18th century a physicist named Mobertius advanced the theory that every action for every natural phenomenon occurs according to a principle of least action. This was clearly a teleological idea which was very much detested by the Newtonian physicists. The Principle of Least Action has been formulated into a mathematical language, finally arriving in a pure logical mathematical way at a formula, which is exactly the same one as one obtained by Newtonian Mechanics. It followed that the distinction between the teleological explanation and a causal one is actually a matter of how you speak about it, rather than accounting for a difference in principle in nature. I don't know if this has any relation to what Professor Granit was speaking about today. It seems to me that there is really no difference in principle between teleological explanations and causal explanations, but that depends on a particular situation which you are dealing with as to which one of the two modes make more sense. Certainly in physiology, it makes more sense to have a teleological explanation. Would Professor Granit please comment?

Granit: This is very much in line with what I wanted to say. I agree that causal explanations are teleological explanations, but the only difficulty is, within us, internal forces have become master. With respect to the environment we can very often do very well with teleological explanations because they are causal and essentially the same. We can't help doing it, but when dealing with organisms that have to eat, have to reproduce, have to defend themselves, so they are related to the environment in a causal way and that's what I wanted to do, merely to show you how far we can go experimentally in this field these days.

Earl of Halsbury: When I refer to the blackboard, I take a piece of chalk and draw a curved line across and I record the results as a graphical fact. Now, given that graphical fact, I can invent various alternative analytic descriptions. One can set up a coordinate system and express it as an equation between the dependent and independent variables. Alternatively I can set up a differential equation and provided I know one point on this curve and the tangent at that point as a first order differential equation, I can describe it exactly in the same way, but by an alternative means. Now, if instead I choose to take a point at the beginning of the curve and a point at the end of the curve, and say that the curve goes through those two points subject to an external condition such that there is some constraint on the action, there is a third

137

analytic desciption of a graphical fact. Now it is only when we introduce an anthropomorphic rejection into these alternate descriptions of graphical facts that we begin to talk of:

Description for the first;
Natural Law for the second;
Teleology for the third.

We imagine that we human beings are the tip of that piece of chalk. That, in the first sense we are doing what we are doing. In the second sense we are obedient to a law, and in the third sense that we are trying to accomplish something.

Now, goal-seeking mechanisms were rather mysterious creatures to the biologists of the last century who drew from Aristotle the concept of teleology as a means of explaining the rather unfamiliar properties of living organisms. But even then, Clark Maxwell, at about the time that he was inventing the electromagnetic theory of light gave the first analytic description of the centrifugal governor of the steam engine which we would now call a linear control device. Goal-seeking mechanisms are now the commonplace of the control engineer's laboratory. You can have mechanisms like those that are at Edinburgh University where they take a child's toy in pieces and by trial and error find out how to put it together. Then when they feel a little tired, they plug themselves into a source of electricity in order to have a meal and be able to carry on. These are really almost the trivia of control engineering and the great question is: Have the teleological descriptions of anthropomorphic character which we project into them really got anything in common with human purpose, which is self-conceived. Because the one thing that no computer I can imagine can do for itself is to decide the next problem which to work on. This has got to be done by human beings and so long as that is true, all mechanical analogies of human purposes will, I believe, fail.

Granit: I agree completely with you, and have nothing against your point of view. We can't go too far with such things as cybernetics and so on, but I think there are some concepts in Information Theory which are very useful for us. After all, the engineer cannot design any machines that his brain cannot design for him. Nevertheless there are some things different in the whole machinery that we don't understand.

I have been thinking throughout in hierarchic terms. You can't explain by the potential of the individual cell, you can't explain the whole operation that is performing. But, when you come to a higher level of hierarchy you cannot explain it by going down and down. There is a limit to that.

11.
The Brain, Learning and Values

Holger Hyden

Thoughts on the Problem

The problem of higher brain functions is very much involved in the question of the unity of sciences, if the ultimate aim is that brain should understand brain. All statements about learning and memory should attach quantitative values to definite positions in a space-time of coordinates, provided the different systems within the brain could be defined by qualitative criteria.

There is a big gap between the psychological experience of a "memory," its expression as complex behavior of an animal or homo and the knowledge of the structure, biochemistry and physiology of brain. An understanding of e.g., insight learning should imply that physical laws suffice to explain biological phenomena. Given mathematical methods to solve nonlinear, partial differential equations, a general systems theory such as proposed by von Bertalanffy could in time express such higher brain functions by isomorphic concepts, at both biological and physical levels for the different hierarchies of the brain.[1] When this is realized then also the unity of sciences will be granted.

When we revisit a summer place from our childhood and take in the smell of wet grass and jasmine, look out on the familiar sight of the sea and feel the rough surface of the old fir tree, we experience these sensory modalities as a whole; the brain is a whole with interacting hierarchies. We look at one instant at a butterfly on a flower—and we discover a moment later that the butterfly is gone. We do not consciously scan the area and subtract the picture minus the butterfly from the picture in our memory in order to make the discovery of the missing butterfly. We take in the sight as a whole.

If we reduce the brain unit to subunits, a simple account of the combinatorial explosion says that one nerve impulse travels to the synapses and triggers the activity in let us say 10 cells by means of synaptic chemical mechanisms. Each of the 10 cells triggers 10 more interactions. The combinations increase from 100 to 10,000. Since each of 10 billion nerve cells may have 100 to 10,000 connections there will be an enormous input from the activated cells. The activation of neurons is very selective!

The activities through the brain are channelled in certain systems, deviated to millions of certain neurons which may be dispersed in several areas. Electrical and chemical activities take their course determined by phylogenetically developed systems and hierarchies in the brain. The detailed processing will, however, be determined by the way in which most of the brain cells have been modified or labeled by experience. We assume that this process goes on for most of the life cycle. This paper will discuss mechanisms by which a protein differentiation of nerve cells can serve all brain systems in establishing long-term memories.

Leaving psychological approaches and applying the approach of molecular biology, a direct question is: does the learning process imply that brain cells—their structure, molecules and metabolism—undergo remaining changes?

On the basis of present experimental knowledge I would like to present a theory *in principle* of learning and memory which implies that both short-lasting, (reversible) and long-lasting, remaining, cell protein changes are biochemical correlates. When an animal begins to learn a suitable and sufficiently difficult task of an "image-driven" type, a short-lasting production of protein starts within minutes. The increased synthesis involves at least two proteins which are specific for the brain—one is called the S100 protein. This production starts in the hippocampus, a phylogenetically old part of the brain. Non-learning controls do not show this activity. The same type of brain cell production follows in brain cortical areas after a certain delay. During learning at least two other protein fractions are synthesized in the membranes of synapses, the contacts between neurons. This short-lasting protein production (around 24 hours) is redundant and increases the statistical probability for the remaining nerve cell changes to be made.

The long-lasting nerve cell changes involve protein molecular changes which become inscribed in a certain pattern into the membrane of millions of neurons. This brain specific protein interacts with another, contractile protein by mediation of calcium. On the same stimulus, all neurons with the same membrane protein pattern and synapse differentiation are assumed to become activated. The renewed, same stimulus makes all those neurons active that share most of the same molecular membrane pattern. This is experienced as a memory.

Between the short-lasting protein synthesis in nerve cells during learning and the long-lasting, membrane changes occurs an increased production in the whole brain of a certain protein with a molecular weight around 60,000. We assume that this protein mediates the consolidation of the long-term memory.

When learning starts, there occurs (only in learning animals, not in controls) a new synthesis of messenger RNA (8S and 16S hn RNA and 25S polyadenylate-associated RNA) in nerve cells which will induce the production of certain proteins and molecular patterns as described above. Calcium is the element which helps to translate electrical field changes during learning into long-lasting molecular changes in brain cell membranes. The stimulus to learn can thus penetrate to the genome of brain cells and the learning mechanism has its root in the same molecular mechanism as has "instinct behavior," although experiential learning operates only for a life cycle.

Brain and the Critical Period

The present paper will mostly discuss the S100 protein inside and outside the cell membrane, and also a contractile network of protein filaments close to the inside of the nerve cell membrane and attached to the knob-like synapses on the membrane, the contacts between neurons bridged by the thin nerve cell processes. Both S100 and the contractile network interact with calcium. By this reaction we have reason to believe that they interact also with each other. In doing so, the synapse function is affected within that area of the nerve cell surface which has incorporated S100. The effect is in the nature of inhibition.

Observations on man and animals show that the visional, auditory and sensory-somatic modalities converge to a part of the temporal cortex, called the entorhinal cortex, and from there to the hippocampus. An intact and correctly functioning hippocampus is a prerequisite for formation of the long-term memory (if the task is sufficiently difficult and not only a conditioning reflex). From the hippocampus the activities spread out over cortical areas via subcortical centers and one part goes back to the hippocampus.

The hippocampus and surrounding areas belong to the so-called limbic system, deeply hidden by the hem of the temporal lobe, and are parts of the evolutionary old brain.

Around 10 million different pathways are built up in the brain during the embryonic period in the form of systems between collections of nerve cells surrounded by the other type of brain cells, the glial cells. This occurs by a genetical and chemical labelling method. When the outer shape of the brain is sculptured by firm rules, the visual, auditory and sensory-somatic pathways are laid down together with association paths and the still mysterious small and short neurons intermixed with glia in the outer part of the brain cortex. All activity is specific for the pathway proper. The nerve cells are highly differentiated cells. Like all other somatic cells each nerve cell has in its nucleus all genes necessary to produce a complete individual. The genes direct the synthesis of the cell's special products for the daily activity via different types of RNA molecules and proteins in the form of enzymes. The differentiation into specialized cells means that only a certain number and combination of the genes are active. The rest is inactive or blocked but some can be activated by proper stimulation. For neurons in general and for the whole brain there exists a critical period in the beginning of the life cycle during which the proper stimuli seem most important for the development of brain functions, structures and biochemistry in the whole brain. One such period for man is the first two years. When the critical period is over—and there are different periods correlated with different abilities—the possibility of undergoing further plastic changes seems to be blocked.

Several types of behavior are present at birth through the bank of information in the genes of the brain cells. More than 99% of all nerve cells are present in the brain at birth. During the first year in homo, the branching processes of the nerve cell body, called dendrites, grow extensively in number and length. The points of contact between neurons, the synapses, will be structured and grow. A number of already formed synapses disappear. Intricate relationships are set up between neurons via neighboring small neurons. During this first postnatal period genetically pro-grammed activities are started by triggering stimuli. Learning by experience begins. For all species the first part of the life cycle is the concentrated period of learning in all its aspects. Expressed in another way, a whole spectrum of stimuli is necessary to realize the genetical potentialities of the brain in an individual. In man, a warm contact between the small child before the age of 2 and an adult is necessary for the development of its emotional life and higher brain functions. This has been amply shown by Skeels and Goldfarb. In animals, brain analyses have been performed during the corresponding critical period. Young rats or mice living in a normal hierarchical group and with a detailed environment to investigate get a thicker brain cortex with a more intensive chemical metabolism and bigger synapses than animals living isolated in a single cage during this critical period. The animals in the "enriched" environment also do better in behavioral tests. What has been lost by lack of proper stimuli during the critical period cannot be regained later on. Results from animal experi-ments cannot, however, be directly translated to the conditions of man.

It has been convincingly shown that skills learned during one generation cannot be inherited by the next. There is no Lamarcki-an mechanism in learning.

A pertinent question is whether learning and memory by experience utilize the same mechanism which operates during embryonic life to build up instinct behavior. Certain results indicate that this is the case, and I would like to return to this problem later on.

The Behavioral Test

How shall an animal learning experiment best be arranged to elicit the same response of the brain as a similar learning demand produces in the animal's natural environment and living condi-tions? This question has been vastly ignored by many neurobiologists working on behavior. Mostly rats have been used. The rat is a highly intelligent animal, inquisitive and ecologically and socially successful. Briefly put, the rat learning test should be of image-driven behavior type, rather difficult to solve and modeled on behavior in the natural environment. Conditioning tests, such as jumping onto a shelf to escape electric shock, or, pressing a lever to get a food pill, are poor choices. Why is this so? One answer is the following: That part of the old areas of the brain called the hippocampus must function correctly if learning shall occur and memories be formed. This has been found for man, monkeys and also for the rat. The hippocampus is a paired structure, deeply hidden by the overlaying brain cortex. If the hippocampus is damaged in the rat, it cannot learn to solve a task of medium difficulty, within the capacity of the species. But—and this is significant—the rat without correctly functioning hippocampus will learn conditioning tasks even better than normal rats! The hippocampus has also another function in the rat. It informs the rat about space-time relations and helps the animal to make three-dimensional maps. In our rat learning experiments we have for twelve years used a "transfer of handedness" task in retrieving food pills one by one by grasping it by inserting the paw in a narrow glass tube. The control to the learning animal is a rat uses the preferred paw to get the same number of pills in the same arrangement. The control who works under the same conditions as the learning rat. The control can improve its performance but does not learn anything new.

Remaining Protein Changes During a Learning Period

As was mentioned above, during the first part of the postnatal period the neurons develop their intricate processes, and the synapses grow and become structured. Contacts are being established with other neurons. The insulating material around the main nerve cell process becomes finished. Genetically programmed activities become activated according to their built-in time schedules. For all species it is a concentrated period of learning. To mention a striking example, between 2 and 4 years a child learns to speak its language, including meaning, grammar, and syntax!

To go back to the molecular and structural studies: parts of the neuronal membrane from adult mammals contain the brain specific S100 protein, firmly bound. The S100 protein is incorporated into the nerve cell outer membrane during the first part of life. The membrane S100 constitutes around 10% of the total S100 which in turn is 0.1% of the total brain cell proteins. The S100 is an acidic protein with a molecular weight of 21,000. It is produced by glial cells but is localized also to the nerve cell outer membrane and nuclear membrane. Characteristically, S100 binds calcium and undergoes with this process "conformational" changes. The molecule partly opens up and certain groups are exposed. This enables the protein to react with membranes which then acquire the ability to regulate the in- and outflux of ions.

Species differences with respect to the formation of membrane-bound S100 are striking and interesting. As examples, the rat and the rabbit are poorly developed at birth; they are like embryos. At two weeks after birth they first get the young animal's metabolism and then begin to show the alert behavior of the young. Rats and rabbits lack membrane S100 in their nerve cells. At the end of the first fortnight, S100 begins to be incorporated into the nerve cell membrane. It becomes redistributed in a dramatic way during that period of intensive learning. S100 changes its main localization from the top of the cell to the basal part of the cell body from which the impulse carrying process emerges. During the first month in rats the membrane S100 widens into a pattern of the cell surface. Eventually it will take up 30-50% of the surface including the receiving part of the synapses within that area. As you know, the newborn guinea pig is well developed, alert and lively at birth and begins almost at once to explore the environment. It is interesting that already at birth membrane S100 is present in the nerve cells of the guinea pig. This differentiation of the nerve cell surface, including the synapses into one area which is rich in S100 and another area which lacks S100, may be of great importance for learning. The reason is the following. Close to the inner side of the nerve cell membrane and attached to the synapses lies a continuous network consisting of two intercoiled protein filaments. These filaments contain the contractile protein actin. Both the coiled filaments of the network and the membrane S100 bind calcium, S100 most avidly. When the network binds calcium the filaments uncoil. From a physicochemical point of view, this is a cooperative process. S100 has at least 8 different binding sites for calcium and undergoes a conformational change at binding; the molecule partly unfolds. If one looks at the arrangement of the two proteins in question on the nerve cell, a mechanism reveals itself which seems to affect both synapses and membrane.

An important observation has been that during learning calcium increases in the hippocampus. This is a specific reaction since sodium, potassium and water do not change, so it cannot be increased circulation which is the cause of calcium increase. When calcium is taken up by the S100 that molecule undergoes conformational changes. Inside the cell the concentration of calcium is low, 10^{-7}M, and the network remains coiled and exerts a tension on the synapses and that part of the membrane which contains S100. Outside that area there is no competition by S100 for calcium. Therefore, the filaments can bind calcium and uncoil, which may result in a relaxation of synapses and membrane in areas lacking S100. Thus, there exists *a functional linkage between the membrane S100 and the network of contractile protein, and the relation between the cooperative processes is regulated by calcium.*

What may be the function of such an arrangement of two proteins in the nerve cell membrane? The working hypothesis is that the protein differentiation, caused by experience and learning, will secure the concomitant activation of all neurons which have undergone a similar differentiation and on the same stimulus. It does not matter where in the brain the neurons are located.

Shortlasting Synthesis of Brain Cell Protein as an Inducing Phase at Learning

The observations on the nerve cell membrane and theory discussed in previous paragraphs depict a mechanism which introduces cooperative phenomena and functional linkage between brain cell proteins. It could add a further combinatorial level to the already known mechanism of the nerve cell membrane.

The short-lasting, reversible protein production starts within minutes after the training to learn has begun. In general terms it can be stated that at learning neurons become highly active. I would like to contrast *active* against *re-active*. The data available indicate that the learning mechanism of the brain in the first hand is *active*, not *re-active* like a reflex in a conditioning system.

The amount of S100 in the hippocampus increases by 15-20%

and the incorporation of radioactive amino acids into cell protein by 300%. A similar increase is shown by another brain specific protein which is localized to the neurons and called 14-3-2. There thus occurs an increased synthesis of defined proteins in the hippocampus when the animals learn a new complicated pattern of behavior. The calcium increase in the hippocampus during learning causes part of S100 to undergo conformational changes. As a sign of the stability of this molecular change S100 has a higher mobility on electrophoresis. The active controls do not display such a response. An increased synthesis of brain specific proteins is observed in cortical areas with a time delay in comparison to that in hippocampus. This series of observation demonstrates that a wave of protein synthesis pervades the brain at learning and starts in the hippocampus. In other words, *system changes occur in brain cell protein during learning.* The leading role of the hippocampus during learning does not seem to be dependent upon the type of learning task. It occurs during the change of handedness in a complicated sensory-motor task as well as during maze learning.

Is the observed synthesis and alterations in brain proteins specific for learning *per se* or is the phenomenon only a sign of increased activity? The specificity of the response has been demonstrated by injecting a monospecific antiserum against the S100 during the training into the lateral ventricles of the brain. By the technique used, it was shown that the antiserum reaches and precipates on the S100 of brain cells in the hippocampal and related regions which are situated closely to the ventricles.

The effect of the antiserum to S100 is seen in the deviation of the learning curve towards zero on further training. Careful controls with antiserum from which antibodies against S100 had been removed did not show any impairing effect. Nor did the injection of other gamma globulins.

In 1976, Rapport and collaborators observed that besides antiserum against S100 also antiserum directed against synaptic protein had such an impairing effect on learning. No other motor or sensory symptoms were observed in the animals treated with antisera.

If one considers the dominating role of the hippocampus in the protein response during learning, it is not surprising that if the membrane mechanism involving S100 is blocked by antiserum, functional disturbances will ensue. The blocking of further learning is clearly observed. It is interesting that the reaction between a membrane antigen of nerve cells and the corresponding antiserum gives rise to an increase of the antigen, the S100 protein. Within half an hour the production of soluble S100 increases significantly in the hippocampus, from 350 g/g net weight to 450.

A conclusion from these experiments on S100 and behavior is that S100 has an inhibiting effect on neurons.

Several hours after training, when the animals are back in their cages, a protein fraction with a molecular weight of 60,000 is synthesized in the cortex and other parts of the brain. It may emerge at 8 hours after finished training and reaches a considerable peak after 24 hours. The response has disappeared after 48 hours. As a working hypothesis, this protein fraction may consolidate the long-term memory.

The S100 was localized to the outer cell membrane. The synaptic membrane protein is likewise an object of great interest since synapses are the functional contacts between neurons.[2] We have therefore analyzed membrane bound protein in synapses in the hippocampus and cortical areas during learning in rats. The training was followed by an increase of protein around 30,000 and 80,000 molecular weights, beginning in the hippocampus. Later on similar proteins increase in cortical areas. Thus, the distinctive activity of the hippocampus at learning is also observable in the synaptic membrane protein and the synthesis in the cortex follows with a delay.

Shashoua[3] has found an increased synthesis of three different protein fractions from nerve cells in goldfish trained to acquire a new behavior.

Gene Activation During Learning

It is indeed a puzzling observation that an animal engaged in learning for which it is motivated starts a synthesis of specific brain proteins in its nerve cells which cannot be observed in the corresponding nerve cells of the active control. The latter performs all the movements, is in the same environment and gets the same amount of food as the learning animal. But the control does not learn. Stress has been excluded as a possible cause of such protein changes although it is recognized that a certain amount of stress is always involved in all learning experiments. Several years ago we took up the question of whether the stimulus involved in the acquisition of a new behavior can penetrate to the nucleus of brain cells and activate part of the genome. A positive answer would demand that learning experiments could be shown to lead to a production of messenger RNA (mRNA). Attempts in various laboratories including our own could, to begin with, only show indirect evidence for mRNA production in brain cells in learning animals. Recently, we have, however, succeeded in demonstrating that hippocampal nerve cells in a learning rat show in increased synthesis compared to active controls of 8S and 16-18S heterogeneous RNA and a synthesis of polyadenylic-associated mRNA of 25S. Both these species of RNA belong to mRNA[4]. This means that cognitive stimuli can penetrate to the nucleus of nerve cells and activate genes which results in specific protein synthesis. This phenomenon does not exclude that mRNA, which is already present in the cell body, can be utilized for protein synthesis before the new mRNA has been assembled, transported to the cytoplasm and organized for protein synthesis. Learning and formation of long-term memories seem therefore to have their roots in the same molecular mechanism as genetically programmed activities.

A Hypothesis

A hypothesis *in principle* of learning and formation of long-term memory can be based on available data, with certain assumptions. Perception may take less than a second; formation of a short-term memory seconds to minutes. Processing and consolidation of a long-term memory may take seconds to many hours, depending on the characteristics of the new information and the level of emotion.

An unknown factor is the stimulus to learning and its nature. It initiates, via messenger RNAs, a specific protein synthesis in learning animals. This synthesis is absent in control animals subjected to the same experimental procedure but without learning.

When learning begins, we assume that outer and inner stimuli cause electrical field changes, which induce the shortlasting synthesis of at least two brain specific proteins. Calcium effects and calcium binding proteins have amply shown the important role of that divalent ion for cell processes. Calcium increases with learning and acts as a translator of electrical phenomena to remaining molecular changes. Calcium causes the membrane S100 to undergo conformational changes whereby hydrophobic groups are exposed. This enables S100 to interact with the membrane and to change its behavior towards ions. It is assumed that during acquisition of a new behavior the pattern of the membrane S100 on neurons enlarges successively with more learning. The short-lasting synthesis of S100, which begins in the hippocampus and spreads to cortical areas is a redundancy phenomenon securing that the nerve cells to achieve a metabolic state which favours the process of membrane differentiation.

Eight to twenty-four hours after finished training to learn, a soluble protein, molecular weight around 60,000, is synthesized in several brain areas. This protein disappears in some hours. We assume that this protein helps to consolidate the new information into a long-term memory.

The shortlasting protein production which is observed in the hippocampus and cortical areas with a time phase shift suggests that small molecules, like peptides, may act as triggering substances. The increased synthesis remains for hours and a steering of the activity by electrical impulses seems unlikely. A diffusion of smaller molecules from area to area is a more likely proposition.

Perception from the outer environment or stimuli from the inner environment activate during learning many millions of neurons belonging to different modalities. Each activation seems at the beginning to be kept within its own system but will soon spread by association mechanisms to other parts. The further paths of the activities lead to the entorhinal and related areas in the cortex and pass on to the hippocampus. The new information processed does not seem to be stored in the hippocampus. Instead, the hippocampus activates its cellular mechanisms, electrical and molecular. The biochemical activity inducing protein differentiation of nerve cell membranes and synapses via subcortical areas to different parts of the cortex. According to this view, learning means protein differentiation of brain cells governed by the genetic mechanism. The experiential learning is superimposed upon the structures and mechanisms for genetically programmed activities but belong to the same categories. At retrieval, it is supposed that the same stimuli which induced a growth of brain cell differentiation can activate all brain cells wherever they are located provided only that they share the same pattern of protein differentiation. These brain cells have the same qualitative and quantitative values in the space-time of coordinates. The sum of differentiated activation in the three-dimensional brain is experienced as "memory." Viewed in this way the engram is a process.

Notes

1. L.V. Bertalanffy, *General System Theory* (New York: George Braziller, 1968).

2. H. Hyden, P.W. Lange, L. Mihailovic, and B. Petrovic-Minic. 1974. "Changes of RNA base composition in nerve cells of monkeys subjected to visual discrimination and delayed alternation performance." *Brain Research* 65, p. 215.

   H. Hyden, P.W. Lange, and C. Seyfried. 1973. "Biochemical brain protein changes produced by selective breeding for learning in rats." *Brain Research* 61, p. 446.

   S.E. Karpiek, M. Serokoz, and M.M. Rapport. 1976. "Effect of antisera to S100 and to synaptic membrane fraction to maze performance and EEG." *Brain Research* 102, p. 313.

   V.M. Pickel, D.J. Reis, P.J. Marangos, and C. Zomzely-Neurath. 1976. "Immunocytochemical localization of nervous system specific protein in rat brain." *Brain Research* 105, p. 184.

3. V.E. Shashoua. 1976. "Brain metabolism and the acquisition of new behaviors. I evidence for specific changes in pattern of protein synthesis." *Brain Research* 111, p. 347.

   F. Zilliken and K. Abdallah, *Molekulargiolohishe Grundlagen des Kurzund Langzeitgedachtnisses* (Stuttgart: F.K. Schattauer, 1973).

   C. Zomzely-Neurath, P.J. Marangos, N. Hymowitz, W. Parl, A. Ritter, V. Zayas, W. Cua, and C. York, "The effect of behavioral task on neuronal and glial specific proteins." In press.

4. A Cupello and H. Hyden. 1976. "Alterations of the pattern of hippocampal nerve cell RNA labeling during training in rats." *Brain Research* 114, p. 453.

   K. Haglid, A. Hamberger, H.A. Hansson, H. Hyden, P. Persson, and L. Ronnback. 1974. "S-100 protein in synapses of the central nervous system." *Nature*, 251, p. 532.

   H. Hyden, "Changes in brain protein during learning. Nerve cell and their glia: relationship and differences. RNA changes in brain cells during changes in behavior and function." In *Macromolecules and Behavior*, edited by G. Ansell and P.B. Bradley (London: Macmillan, 1973) p. 3.

   H. Hyden. 1974. "A calcium-dependent mechanism for synapses and nerve cell membrane modulation." *Proceedings of the Natural Academy of Science* 71, pp. 2965.

H. Hyden and A. Cupello, "A comparison of poly (A)⁻ associated RNA from synaptosomes and cytoplasmic subcellular fraction of rat brain." *Brain Research*, In press.

H. Hyden and P.W. Langem. 1972. "Protein synthesis in hippocampal nerve cells during re-reversal of handedness. *Brain Research* 45, p. 314.

H. Hyden and P.W. Lange, "Protein changes in different brain areas as a function of intermittent training. *Proceedings of the Natural Academy of Science* 69, p. 1980.

H. Hyden and P.W. Lange. 1975. "Brain proteins in undernourished rats during learning." *Neurobiology*, 1975, 5, p. 84.

Commentary

Robert J. White

Professor Hyden has reviewed for us his unique contributions to the neurochemical understanding of memory and learning necessarily heavily based on his extensive studies of the protein alterations of nerve cells and their membranes associated with the acquisition, storage, and expression of information in the rodent brain. Happily he has gone further, for in his efforts to unravel the intricate properties of the short and long-term memory traces and their intimate relationship to each other, he has provided us with a multidimensional general system theory incorporating genetic mechanism and ionic participation to explain learning memory. Without question, his approach is controversial and to some degree conjectural. It will certainly not satisfy the molecular or mathematically oriented neurophysiologist who characterizes such brain functions as memory and learning in terms of nerve nets, steady state ionic equilibrium and fluxes, computer analogies and high ordered mathematical formulations —to name only a few. Nor would many experimental psychologists be pleased with these conclusions and theories for they would question and emphasize the lack of exactness in anatomical localization, appropriateness of the testing design and interpretation, and finally relevance to these neurochemical findings to memory and learning in general. Be that as it may, Professor Hyden's exquisite analytical chemical techniques have repeatedly demonstrated statistical changes in the protein composition of the appropriate loci of the hippocampus and somato-sensory cortex of the rat during and following the learning of a specifically designed difficult task; however, his personal attempt to provide a total conceptualization of memory and learning transgressing both genetics and phylogeny and based on his own experimental work is, of course, open to serious challenge not only neurophysiologically and biophysically (as stated previously) but philosophically.

Before considering this aspect of the problem, let's briefly review several interesting experiments conducted in the subhuman primate which add new dimensions to the stability of the memory trace in this highly encephalized animal. Monkeys trained in the Wisconsin testing device on six separate cognitive tests were subjected to localized cooling of the brain (to 15°C or lower) employing a simplified extracorporal circuit; at these lower temperatures the brain was rendered totally ischemic for thirty minutes. Upon recovery the animals were retested, demonstrating no diminution of intellectual or memory performance: additionally, the Rhesus monkey's cephalon has recently been successfully transplanted for short periods of time to the isolated body of another Rhesus, and with the regaining of the conscious state, gives every evidence of preservation of behavior and intellectual performance (cf. Chapter 10). In addition, the subhuman primate brain has been completely isolated, removed from the cephalon and maintained in a high performance state utilizing a completely mechanical extracorporal perfusion circuit. Studies employing evolved potentials (visual and auditory) indicate preservation ("normalization") of the circuitry subservient to these high ordered functions. This is also true of the neuroelectrical recordings at both a cortical and subcortical level. Thus the memory and intellectual functioning of the subhuman brain demonstrates remarkable stability in spite of drastic physical (cooling and ischemia) and/or surgical (transplantation) dislocation. Perhaps this is a further subtle argument in favor of Professor Hyden's tenet regarding the memory trace representation in the protein permanency of the cell body and membrane.

Experiments on monkeys and rodents are fine, but in the final analysis can we extrapolate these findings to man? For it is man and his values that we are primarily concerned with at this conference.

The human brain is the most complex, most superbly designed biological system known. Before it all human achievements in science and engineering is humbled. Truly the elements and their relationships that compose the "inner space" of the brain-mind continuum are as awesome and challenging as the galaxies and their solar systems in "outer space." Yet it is the human mind utilizing the tissue substrate of the brain which must solve the mysteries not only of the universe, but of itself. As Professor Hyden has stated: "That the brain should understand brain." Surely one would hope as the intricacies of the central nervous system are unraveled, and human performance and action are explained, scientific unity will be born of the diversities and inconsistencies which presently characterize intellectual endeavor.

Thus the exciting and thought-provoking experiments and theories of Professor Hyden, dealing with memory and learning in the rodent require re-examination of the uniqueness of the mind-brain relationship, which must characterize all human relationships and acquisition of all knowledge. Wilder Penfield, in the volume entitled: *The Mystery of the Mind,* published just prior to his death, concluded: "That it is easier to rationalize man's being on the basis of two elements than on the basis of one." This famous brain surgeon, however, further adds: "But I believe one should not pretend to draw a final scientific conclusion, in man's study of man, until the nature of the energy responsible for mind-action is discovered as, in my own opinion, it will be."

Thus this world authority in his concluding literary effort is on one hand forced to accept "scientific dualism" as an explanation of the mind-brain continuum, yet even he, after years of work on the problem, was hopeful of eventually solving the relationship based on a unitary hypothesis. One wonders if neuroscience may eventually be reaching limits in this area—limits that will require the defining of a new "Heisenberg Indetermancy Principle" operant in expressing the intimate association between the mind and its tissue substrate. Sir John Eccles has likewise expressed himself on this vexing problem and has found it appropriate to employ the "three world" concept of Popper, stating: "But realizing their existence in the world of self-awareness (World 2) and so having in the religious concept, souls." He further recalls a conversation with the great neurophysiologist, Sherrington, who stated: "For me now the only reality is the human soul." Thus many of our most distinguished neuroscientists, after decades of investigation, acknowledge the impossibility of explaining the human mind in terms of computer science, neurochemistry, or neurophysiology. Acknowledging these weighty opinions as well as contemporary theology, the question remains to plague us as

157

to whether the mind-brain problem (including human learning and memory) will ever be completely understood regardless of the expected advances in experimental science. Nevertheless, one must hope and persevere that as the nature of brain, in its biochemical and neuroelectronic dimensions, is slowly unraveled, mankind will be enabled to better appreciate and understand human motivations and values, permitting a better design of life and living for all.

Notes

J.C. Eccles, *Facing Reality* (Heidelberg, Berlin and New York: Springer-Verlag, 1970).

W. Penfield, *The Mystery of the Mind* (London and Princeton: Princeton University Press, 1975).

K.R. Popper. 1968B. "On the Theory of the Objective Mind." *Akten des XIV, Internationalen Kongresses fur Philosophie*, vol. 1, pp. 152, 164, 169, 176.

R.J. White, L.C. Massopoust, Jr., L.R. Wolin, N. Taslitz, and D. Yashon. 1969. "Profound Selective Cooling and Ischemic of Primate brain without Pump or Oxygenator." *Surgery* 66: pp. 224-32.

R.J. White, "Experimental Transplantation of the Brain." Chapter 45 in *Human Transplantation*, F. T. Rapaport and J. Dausset eds., (New York: Grune & Stratton, Inc., 1968).

R.J. White, L.R. Wolin, L.C. Massopoust, Jr., N. Taslitz, and J. Vendura. 1971. "Cephalic Exchange Transplantation in the Monkey." *Surgery* 70, pp. 135-38.

R.J. White, M.S. Albin, J. Vendura, and G.E. Locke. 1967. "The Isolated Monkey Brain: I-Operative Preparation and Design of Support Systems." *Journal of Neurosurgery* 27, pp. 216-25.

L.R. Wolin, L.C. Massopoust, Jr., R.J. White. 1973. "Behavioral Effects of Autocerebral Perfusion, Hypothermia and Arrest of Cerebral Blood Flow in the Rhesus Monkey." *Experimental Neurology* 39, pp. 336-41.

12.
Cerebral Activity and the Freedom of the Will

Sir John Eccles

Introduction

In Chapter 20, I give an account of the philosophical position which will form the basis of my discussion. I refer to the trialist philosophy of Sir Karl Popper in which everything in existence or experience is subsumed in one of the three worlds: World 1, the world of physical objects and states; World 2, the world of states of consciousness and subjective knowledge of all kinds; World 3, the world of man-made culture, comprising the whole of objective knowledge.

Fig. 1 indicates the three levels of World 2, outer sense, inner sense and central to these, the self of pure ego which for each of us is the basis of our unity as an experiencing being throughout our lifetime.

The Ego and the Freedom of the Will

"An action to be free must be conscious, purposive, follow open alternative choices; and it by no means follows, as empiricist philosophers always maintain, that because it could be otherwise it need be arbitrary or because it is not mechanically caused, it is not caused at all."[1]

That we have free will is a fact of experience. Furthermore I state emphatically that to deny free will is neither a rational nor a logical act. This denial either presupposes free will for the

159

WORLD OF CONSCIOUSNESS

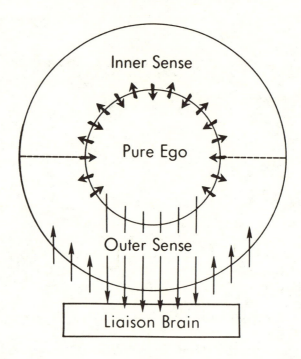

Outer Sense	Inner Sense	Pure Ego
Light	Thoughts	The self
Color	Feelings	The soul
Sound	Memories	
Smell	Dreams	
Taste	Imaginings	
Pain	Intentions	
Touch		

Figure 12-1: World of consciousness. The three postulated components in the world of consciousness together with a tabulated list of their components.

deliberately chosen response in making that denial, which is a contradiction, or else it is merely the automatic response of a nervous system built by genetic coding and moulded by conditioning. One does not conduct a rational argument with a being who makes the claim that all its responses are reflexes, no matter how complex and subtle the conditioning. For example, one should not argue with a Skinnerian, and moreover a Skinnerian should not engage in argument. Discourse becomes degraded into an exercise that is no more than conditioning and counterconditioning—what we may characterize as Skinnerian games! Nevertheless, despite these logical problems, it is widely held that free will must be rejected on logical grounds. The question can be raised: can free will be accommodated in a deterministic universe?

The diagram of Fig. 12-1 gives the basis for defining the postulated mode of operation of free will, which is represented symbolically by the arrows stemming from the pure ego or self. Polten states:

> *"The pure ego is the necessary ingredient which changes determi-
> nation to self-*determination or libertarianism. If we did not have
> such an 'unmoved mover' (and it must be the *core* of that which
> makes up the self!) then we could not master our environment with
> science and technology, as we undeniably do. Far less would it be
> possible to give ourselves autonomously the moral law, and act with
> freedom of choice and responsibility. Both technologist and practi-
> cal moralist can interfere with natural casual chains only because
> they themselves (i.e., their pure egos) are not pushed along these
> inexorable sequences; the pure ego rather impinges its own inten-
> tions upon the course of nature, and thus utilizes the laws of nature
> for its own ends. . . . Those who uphold free will need a pure ego,
> and the meaning and existence of free will has been so notoriously
> unclear and vexing largely because the meaning and existence of
> the pure ego has so far been so unclear. Thus human reflex actions,
> such as a knee jerk, are unfree because the pure ego is not involved;
> but conscious thoughts and purposive actions are free because the
> pure ego directs them."

When discussing casuality, Max Planck[2] made a statement that is relevant in this context.

> *"The question of free will is one for the individual consciousness
> to answer: it can be determined only by the ego. The notion of
> human free will can mean only that the individual feels himself*

to be free, and whether he does so in fact can be known only to himself."[3]

The Neurological Problems Arising from the Postulate of Free Will

My position is that I have the indubitable experience that by thinking and willing I can control my actions if I so wish, *although in normal waking life this prerogative is exercised but seldom.* I am not able to give a scientific account of how thought can lead to action, but this failure serves to emphasize the fact that our present physics and physiology are too primitive for this most challenging task of resolving the antimony between our experiences and the present primitive level of our understanding of brain function. When thought leads to action, I am constrained, as a neuroscientist, to postulate that in some way, completely beyond my understanding, my thinking changes the operative patterns of neuronal activities in my brain. Thinking thus comes to control the discharges of impulses from the pyramidal cells of my motor cortex and so eventually the contractions of my muscles and the behavioral patterns stemming therefrom. A fundamental neurological problem is: how can willing of a muscular movement set in train neural events that lead to the discharge of pyramidal cells of the motor cortex and so to activation of the neural pathway that lead to the muscle contradiction?

If we have not this ability to exercise a willed or voluntary control over our actions, if we are illuded in this belief, the logical consequences lead to a denial of all personal responsibility for actions no matter how clever the philosophical discussion. Praise or blame become but meaningless noises because all people would be trapped in an inexorable web of cause and effect. To claim freedom of will does not mean that actions are uncaused: It means that some are not caused or controlled solely by purely physical events in the neuronal machinery of the brain, but that the events in this neuronal machinery are to some extent modulated by the self or ego in the mental act of willing. It is postulated that there is a true interaction of the mental and the physical, and that mental events actually are casual agents in their modulating influence on the patterns of neuronal events that lead to the expression of willed movements.

I will not discuss the many philosophical theories (c.f. Chapter 18[4] [5]) that have been developed in order to evade the crucial and fundamental problems raised by the postulate of interaction —that mental events can effectively interact with brain events both in giving and receiving. The existence of mental states is not denied in these various philosophies, but it is regarded as being ineffective—a kind of spinoff from the neural events as in parallelism, epiphonomenalism and even in the more sophisticated version of the psyconeural identity hypothesis.[6] This philosophy is reducible to a materialist monism, but it accepts fully all varieties of conscious experience and explains them as being necessary components or aspects of brain states, there being strictly a psychoneural identity. It is postulated that every brain state has its counterpart in a conscious experience, the analogy being that the brain state can be recognized by external observation, and consciousness is the inner experience of that same state. Unfortunately the philosophical formulation is naive with respect to brain states.

I will not embark on a philosophical disputation, but recently there has been a most critical appraisal of the psycho-physical identity hypothesis by Polten[7] who has demonstrated that it leads to paradoxes and contradictions and so stands refuted. My attack on the hypothesis is based on a consideration of the brain events and of the manner in which the identity hypothesis relates them to consciousness.

We are now in a position to consider the experiments of Kornhuber and associates[8] [9] on the electrical potential generated in the cerebral cortex prior to the carrying out of a willed action. The problem is to have an elementally simple movement executed by the subject entirely on his own volition, and yet to have accurate timing in order to average the very small potentials recorded from the surface of the skull. This has been solved by Kornhuber and his associates who use the onset of the movement to trigger a reverse computation of the potentials up to 2 sec before the onset of the movement. The movement illustrated was a rapid flexion of the right index finger. The subject initiates these movements "at will" at irregular intervals of many seconds. In this way it was possible to average 250 records of the potentials evoked at various sites over the surface of the skull, as shown in Fig. 12-2 for the three upper traces. The slowly rising negative potential, called the *readiness potential*, was observed as a negative wave with unipolar recording over a wide area of the

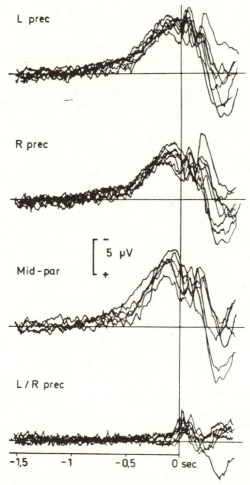

Figure 12-2: Cerebral potentials, recorded from the human scalp, preceding voluntary rapid flexion movements of the right index finger. The potentials are obtained by the method of reverse analysis (Kornhuber and Deecke). Eight experiments on different days with the same subject; about 1000 movements per experiment. Upper three rows: monopolar recording, with both ears as reference; the lowermost trace is a bipolar record, left versus right precentral hand area. The readiness potential starts about 0.8 sec prior to onset of movement; it is bilateral and widespread over precentral (L. prec, R. prec) and parietal (Mid-par) areas. The premotion positivity, bilteral and widespread too, starts about 90 msec before onset of movement. The motor potential appears only in the bipolar record (L/R prec), it is unilateral over the left precentral hand area, starting 50 msec prior to onset of movement in the electromyogram. (Experiment of W. Becker, L. Deecke, B. Grozinger, and H.H. Kornhuber, presented at the German Physiological Society Meeting 1969, Pflugers Arch. Physiol. 312:108).

164

cerebral surface, but there were small positive potentials of similar time course over the most anterior and basal regions of the cerebrum. Usually the readiness potential began almost as long as 800 ms (0.8 sec.) before the onset of the movement, and led on to sharper potentials, positive then negative, beginning about 90 ms before movement. Finally, as shown in the lowest trace, at 50 ms a sharp negativity developed over the area of the motor cortex concerned in the movement, the left precentral hand area in this case. We can assume that the readiness potential is generated by complex patterns of neuronal discharges that eventually project to the appropriate pyramidal cells of the motor cortex and synaptically excite them to discharge, so generating this localized negative wave just preceding the movement.

These experiments at least provide a partial answer to the question: What is happening in my brain at a time when a willed action is in process of being carried out? It can be presumed that during the readiness potential there is a developing specificity of the patterned impulse discharges in neurons so that eventually there are activated the correct motor cortical areas for bringing

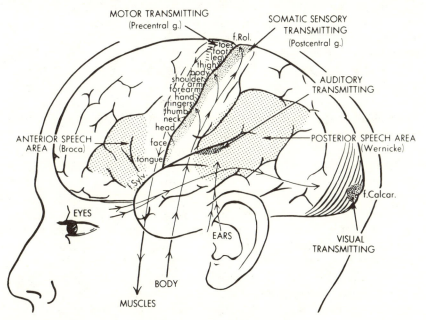

Figure 12-3: The motor and sensory transmitting areas of the cerebral cortex. The approximate map of the motor transmitting areas is shown in the precentral gyrus, while the somatic sensory receiving areas are in a similar map in the precentral gyrus. Other primary sensory areas shown are the visual and auditory, but they are largely in areas screened from this lateral view.

about the required movement. It can be regarded as the neuronal counterpart of the voluntary command. The surprising feature of the readiness potential is its wide extent and gradual build up. Apparently, at the stage of willing a movement, there is very wide influence on the patterns of neuronal operation, or as we will consider below, on the patterns of module operation. Eventually this immense neuronal activity concentrates on to the pyramidal cells in the proper zones of the motor cortex (Figure 12-3) for carrying out the required movement. I will later continue with the neurological problems arising from these remarkable experiments.

The Unique Areas of the Cerebral Cortex

The evolution of man's brain from primitive hominids was associated with an amazingly rapid increase in size, from 550g to 1400g in two million years. But much more important was the creation of special areas associated with speech (Figure 12-3). We can well imagine the great evolutionary success attending not only the growth of intelligence that accompanied brain size in some exponential relationship, but also the development of language for communication and discussion. In this manner primitive man doubtless achieved great successes in communal hunting and food gathering, and in adapting to the exigencies of life in linguistically planned operations of the community. We now know that special areas of the neocortex were developed for this emerging linguistic performance, which in about 98% are in the left cerebral hemisphere.[10] Usually (in 80% of brains) there is a considerable enlargement of the planum temporale in the left temporal lobe and in the areas bordering the sulcus in the inferior frontal convolution; and this enlargement is developed by the 28th week of intrauterine life in preparation for usage some months after birth. Its development represents a very important and unique construction by the genetic instructions provided for building the human brain.

Sperry's investigations on commissurotomy patients have shown that the dominant linguistic hemisphere is uniquely concerned in giving conscious experiences to the subject and in mediating his willed actions. It is not denied that some other consciousness may be associated with the intelligent and learned behavior of the minor hemisphere, but the absence of linguistic or symbolic communication at an adequate level limits the extent to which it can be discovered. The situation is equivalent to the problem of animal consciousness.

Fig. 12-4 shows in diagrammatic form the association of linguistic and ideational areas of the dominant hemisphere with the world of conscious experience. Arrows lead from the linguistic and ideational areas of the dominant hemisphere to the conscious self (World 2) (cf. Fig. 12-1) that is represented by the circular area above. It must be recognized that Fig. 12-4 is an information flow diagram and that the superior location adopted for the conscious self is for diagrammatic convenience. It is of course not meant to imply that the conscious self is hovering in space above the dominant hemisphere! It is postulated that in normal subjects activities in the minor hemisphere reach consciousness mostly after transmission to the dominant hemisphere, which very effectively occurs via the immense impulse traffic in the corpus callosum, as is illustrated in Figure 12-4 by the numerous arrows. Complementarily, as will be discussed in full later, it is postulated that the neural activities responsible for voluntary actions mediated by the pyramidal tracts normally are generated in the dominant hemisphere by some willed action of the conscious self (see downward arrows in Figs. 12-1 and 12-4).

It must be recognized that this transmission in the corpus callosum is not a simple one-way transmission. The 200 million fibers must carry a fantastic wealth of impulse traffic in both directions. In the normal operation of the cerebral hemisphere, activity of any part of a hemisphere is as effectively and rapidly transmitted to the other hemisphere as to another lobe of the same hemisphere. The whole cerebrum thus achieves a most effective unity. It will be appreciated from Fig. 12-4 that section of the corpus callosum gives a unique and complete cleavage of this unity. The neural activities of the minor hemisphere are isolated from those cerebral areas that give and receive from the conscious self. The conscious subject is recognizably the same subject or person that existed before the brain-splitting operation and retains the unity of self-consciousness or the mental singleness that he experienced before the operation. However, this unity is at the expense of unconsciousness of all the happenings in the minor (right) hemisphere.

MODES OF INTERACTION BETWEEN WORLD 1 : WORLD 2 : WORLD 3

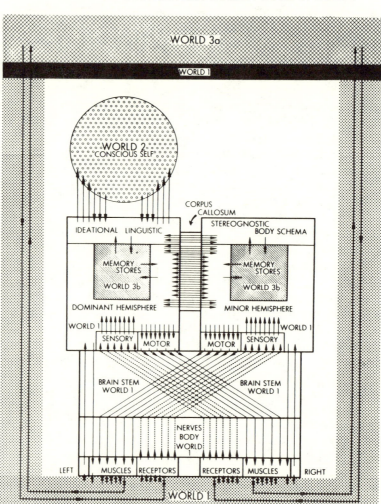

Figure 12-4: Communications to and from the brain and within the brain. Diagram to show the principal lines of communication from peripheral receptors to the sensory cortices and so to the cerebral hemispheres via the motor cortex and so to muscles. Both these systems of pathways are largely crossed as illustrated, but minor uncrossed pathways are also shown. The dominant left hemisphere and minor right hemisphere are labeled, together with some of the properties of these hemispheres. The corpus callosum is shown as a powerful cross-linking of the two hemispheres and, in addition, the diagram displays the modes of interaction between Worlds 1, 2, and 3, as described in the text.

Structural and Functional Concepts of the Cerebral Cortex

The Modular Concept[11]

The excitatory level built up in a module is communicated from moment to moment by the impulse discharge along the association fibers formed by the axons of pyramidal cells.[12] In this way powerful excitation of a module will spread widely and effectively to other modules. There is as yet no quantitative data on module operation. However the number of neurons in a module is surprisingly large—some thousands of which there would be many hundreds of pyramidal cells and many hundreds of each of the other species of neurones. The operation of a module can be imagined as a complex of circuits in parallel with summation by convergence of hundreds of convergent lines onto neurones and in addition a mesh of feed-forward and feed-back excitatory and inhibitory lines overpassing the simple neuronal circuitry expressed in Fig. 8-6 of Chapter 8. Thus we have to envisage levels of complexity in the operation of a module far beyond anything yet conceived and of a totally different order from any integrated microcircuits of electronics, the analogous systems mentioned earlier. Moreover there will be an enormous range in the output from a module—from high frequency discharges in the hundreds of constituent pyramidal cells to the irregular low level discharges characteristic of cerebral cortex in the resting state. The range of projection of the pyramidal cells is enormous—some go only to nearby modules, others are remote association fibers, and yet others are commissural fibers traversing the corpus callosum to areas of the other side, which tend to be in mirror-image relationship.

The Patterns of Module Interaction

Fig. 12-5 is a diagrammatic attempt to illustrate in the limited time span of a fraction of a second the on-going module to module transmission. It attempts to show the manner in which association fibers from the pyramidal cells in a module can activate other modules by projections of many pyramidal axons in parallel. These other modules in turn project effectively to further modules. In this assumed plan of a small zone of the neocortex, the pyramidal cells of the modules are represented as circles, solid or open, according to whether they participate in one or another class of modality operation, e.g., to one type of sensory input for A and to another for B. Main lines of communication between successive modules are shown by arrows, and there is one example of a return circuit giving a loop for sustained operation in the manner of the closed self-reexciting chains of Lorente de No. In addition convergence of the modules for A and B modalities gives activation of modules by both A and B inputs with a corresponding symbolism—dense-core circles. The diagram is greatly simplified because in it one module at the most projects to two other modules, whereas we may suppose it to be to tens or hundreds. There are 3 examples where excitation of modules was inadequate for onward propagation. Thus in the diagram two inputs A and B give only two outputs A and AB. Fig. 12-5 represents the kind of patterning of neuronal activation in the cerebral cortex that was imagined by Sherrington[13]. He likened it to "an enchanted loom, weaving a dissolving pattern, always a meaningful pattern, though never an abiding one, a shifting harmony of subpatterns."

The diagram of Fig. 12-5 is particularly inadequate in that there is no representation of the irregular background discharge of all types of cortical neurones. The modular activation and transmission must be imagined as being superimposed upon this on-going background noise. Effective neuronal activity is ensured when there is inparallel activity of many neurones with approximately similar connections. Signals are in this way lifted out of noise. Thus instead of the simplicity indicated in Fig. 12-5, we have to envisage an irregular seething activity of the whole assemblages of neurones, the signals being superimposed on this background by phases of collusive activity of neurones in parallel either within modules or between modules.

One can surmise that from the extreme complexity and refinement of its modular organization there must be an unimagined richness of properties in the active cerebral cortex. It is postulated that in a situation where the pure ego is operative, there will be changed patterns of modular interaction leading eventually to a change in the spatio-temporal pattern of influence playing upon the pyramidal cells in the motor cortex. The "readiness potential" (Fig. 12-2) bears witness to this cortical activity preceeding the pyramidal tract discharge.

170

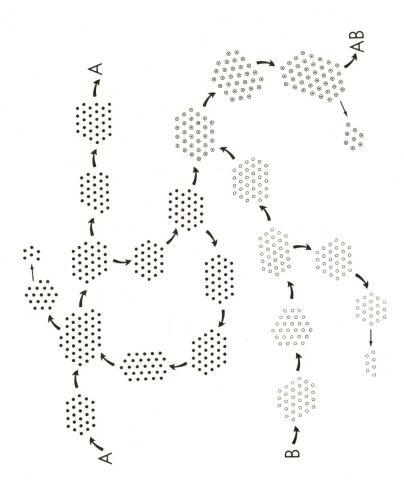

Figure 12-5: In this schema of the cerebral cortex looked at from above, the large pyramidal cells are represented as circles, solid or open, that are arranged in clusters, each cluster corresponding to a column or module as diagrammed in Figs. 12-1, 12-2, where only a few large projecting pyramidal cells are shown of the hundreds that would be in the column. The large arrows symbolize impulse discharges along hundreds of axons in parallel, which are the mode of excitatory communication from column to column. Two inputs, A and B, and two outputs, A and AB, are shown. Further description in text.

171

Evidently we have here a fundamental problem that transcends our present neurophysiological concepts. Some tentative suggestions have been made.[14, 15, 16] It is necessary to take into account the evidence that the conscious self can act on cortical modules only when the cerebral cortex is at a relatively high level of excitation. If the neuronal activity of the cerebral cortex is at too low a level, then liaison between the mind and the brain ceases. The subject is unconscious as in sleep, anaesthesia, or coma. Perception and willed action are no longer possible. Furthermore, if a large part of the cerebral cortex is in the state of the rigorous driven activity of a convulsive seizure, there is a similar failure of brain-mind liaison. Originally it was suggested that the liaison between mind and brain depended on the "mind influences" being able to modify the discharge of neurons that were critically poised at firing level. In the light of the modular concept a more attractive hypothesis would be that the modules themselves are the detector units for causal input from the pure ego. We may give them a function analogous to radio-receiving units.

Thus, the neurophysiological hypothesis is that the casual action of the conscious self modifies the spatio-temporal activity in the modules of the liaison zone of the dominant hemisphere. It will be noted that this hypothesis assumes that the mind has itself some spatio-temporal patterned character in order to allow it this operative effectiveness.

This concept is closely related to those recently developed by Sperry who states:

> *In the present scheme the author postulates that the conscious phenomena of subjective experience do interact on the brain processes exerting an active causal influence. In this view consciousness is conceived to have a directive role in determining the flow pattern of cerebral excitation."*
>
> "Conscious phenomena in this scheme are conceived to interact with and to largely govern the physiochemical and physiological aspects of the brain process. It obviously works the other way round as well, and thus a mutual interaction is conceived between the physiological and the mental properties. Even so, the present interpretation would tend to restore mind to its old prestigious position over matter, in the sense that the mental phenomena are seen to transcend the phenomena of physiology and biochemistry.[17]

Just because World 2 is drawn located above the brain in Figs. 12-1 and 12-4, I do not wish to imply that World 2 is floating above the brain and has an autonomous existence and performance independent of the liaison area of the brain! On the contrary it is, so far as we can discover, tightly linked with neuronal activity there. If that stops, unconsciousness supervenes. As shown by the arrows in both directions in Fig. 12-4, there is an incessant interplay in the interaction between World 2 and the liaison brain, but we know nothing about its nature. This interaction is a tremendous challenge for the future. In this respect we can think of the whole range of psychiatry with such problems as those of the unconscious self, of sleep and dreams, and of obsession. Despite our present ignorance of the precise neurological basis of all these problems of the psyche, we can have hope for some clearer understanding because it is now possible to define the liaison areas of the brain, and postulate that only in certain areas and in certain states of the brain does this relationship occur. This insight, limited as it is, provides hope for more understanding in this most fundamental problem.

Notes

1. E.P. Polten, *A Critique of the Psycho-physical Identity Theory* (The Hague: Moulton Publishers, 1973).
2. E.P. Polten, *A Critique of the Psycho-physical Identity Theory.*
3. M. Planck, *The Philosophy of Physics* (London: G. Allen & Unwin, 1936).
4. K.R. Popper and J.C. Eccles, *The Self and Its Brain* (Heidelberg, Berlin and New York: Springer International, 1977).
5. J.C. Eccles, *The Human Psyche* (Heidelberg, Berlin and New York: Springer International, 1979).
6. H. Feigl, *The 'Mental' and the 'Physical'* (Minneapolis: University of Minnesota Press, 1967).
7. E.P. Polten, *A Critique of the Psycho-physical Identity Theory.*
8. L. Deeke, P. Scheid, and H.H. Kornhuber 1969. "Distribution and readiness potential, pre-motion positivity, and motor potential of the human cerebral cortex preceding voluntary finger movements." *Experimental Brain Research* 7, pp. 158-68.
9. H.H. Kornhuber, "Cerebral Cortex, cerebellum and basal ganglia: An introduction to their motor functions." In: *The Neurosciences: Third Study Program*. F. O. Schmitt ed., (New York: The Rockefeller University Press, 1973).

10. W. Penfield and L. Roberts, *Speech and Brain Mechanisms* (Princeton: Princeton University Press, 1959).

11. In Chapter 7 there has been an account of the modular structure of the cerebral neocortex, and of the communication patterns from module to module. For a more comprehensive treatment see Eccles, 1980, Lecture 2.

12. J. Szentagothai 1978. "The neuron network of the cerebral cortex: A functional interpretation." 201, pp. 219-48.
Proceedings of the British Royal Society

13. C.S. Sherrington, *Man and His Nature* (London: Cambridge University Press, 1940).

14. K.R. Popper and J.C. Eccles, *The Self and its Brain.*

15. J.C. Eccles, *The Human Mystery* (Heidelberg, Berlin and New York: Springer International, 1979).

16. J.C. Eccles, *The Neurophysiological Basis of Mind: The Principles of Neurophysiology* (Oxford: Clarendon Press, 1953).

17. R.W. Sperry 1969. "A modified concept of consciousness." *Psychology Review* 76, pp. 532-36.

Discussion

Long: I see the brain as something which is a physical fact, a phenomenon, a biological component of animals, which is itself subject to precisely the kind of studies which you tell us about. It is clearly an inordinately complicated piece of biology, but still it is obviously revealing itself to further and further studies.

In contrast I cannot avoid a feeling that when I deal with something called the mind or something called the ego, I am dealing with a construct which is a useful, important way of thinking of human behavior, but which differs in a somewhat fundamental way from this biological entity. I would appreciate more of your thoughts on this. Am I right? Are we dealing with constructs and physical facts, and secondly, how does one resolve it?

Eccles: It is of course terribly hard to come to terms with this complex problem. But if we don't, we are, for example, denying our ability to bring about conscious actions, to be responsible for our actions. If everything is simply neural events operating in the neuronal circuits from input to output in the genetically coded structures of our brains together with the changes brought about conditioning, then that is it! We are no more responsible than an animal is responsible.

I am like Karl Popper. I am a common sense philosopher. I believe that the very earliest knowledge we have is from our experiences. On the one hand there is light and color and sound, which we eventually can transmute into meaning and describe in language and so on, and on the other hand there is an immense neural performance in the cerebral cortex that I did not go into. Again, if we so wish, we can deliberately take action into the external world to bring about events. This happens in the way I was trying to show you. Now, more and more we are defining this mind-brain liaison down to special areas of the brain. It isn't just a general brain action. I think it is going to be an action of very specialized regions of the brain.

The next point I want to make is to warn against the idea that the brain is just a bit of ordinary machinery. Some parts of the brain such as the cerebellum can be regarded as neural machinery, but there is the immense and very different structure, the cerebral cortex. As we go up to the cerebral cortex, we are gradually understanding the kind of structure it is. The immensely complicated patterns of neural activity are still far beyond our understanding, being what Sherrington called the enchanted, loom, weaving patterns in space and time. I like to think with Szentagothai that there are modular structures in the cerebral cortex, each with their own incredible dynamical life. They resemble integrated micro-circuits of electronics but are ever so much more so, within each module up to ten thousand cells linked up synaptically in patterns of activity which we don't yet understand. But gradually we begin to realize that in the brain there evolved a structure with dynamic performances of a different order from anything else in nature, from anything else that physics has ever looked at. And we even may imagine that these structures, when in the right dynamical state, could be functioning, if you will pardon the analogy, like antennae out into the mind world, receiving and giving to it.

I think this is a fundamental problem concerning what happened somewhere along this evolutionary story, at least a hundred thousand years ago. Then man attained self-consciousness —knew that he knew. Something had happened, mysteriously, wonderfully, in the evolution of the human brain, to give it these potentialities, which as you are quite right in saying, we still are shocked by. We cannot accept that such a thing happened because we are so immersed in the material world, the physical world, the world of science. But let me tell you, that the whole of science itself is in fact mental. It is World 3. The imaginative, creative, scientific efforts of mankind have given us a philosophy that makes it difficult to understand how minds can work on matter. It has given us the laws as you might say, of matter, and left mind out. This was of course due to Descartes, and it is very good up to a point. I am a reductionist, in my work on science, I am a reductionist just as everyone else is. I want to admit that; but metaphysically I am an anti-reductionist.

Jantsch: I am a bit troubled by the internal system which you pointed out and you trace back to Popper, because it does not link World 1 and World 3 although in a later diagram you did link those two. Here in the first diagram, you just had World 1 interacting with World 2 and World 2 interacting with World 3. And I think that the basic trouble with it is that you have reality on one side and you have what you then describe as objective knowledge on the other side. I think if you conceive it as I do—I arrived at a very similar ternary structure but in a toroidal form with feedback links centering the whole thing constantly—you have no trouble admitting that what is going on between World 2 and World 3 may be subjective, or is really subjective at some level, and is objective at some other level.

I have a paper in which I explore the subjectivity and objectivity question—I think that both are just aspects of the same kind of process. I think that if you just call it objective knowledge like that, it means that you believe, or that you infer that there is one absolute truth, which is eventually to be revealed by science. A much more fruitful idea, I think, involves a continuous process of putting models into the world, into our cultural world which act as myths, and guide our lives for a certain period, but which are flexible and have a whole type of cultural evolution which goes to ever new models, and goes to ever new mind regimes, so to say, and keeps our own action within this cultural world alive. So that as someone, I think John Calhoun has put it, man is constantly a "crisis provoker." But what I would also say then is perhaps this view of seeing at one end of the spectrum as a final objective knowledge, that this comes out maybe also in the view and I did not understand whether you have for instance, very final proof or whether this was a hypothesis that only the linguistic, analytic type of brain function is linked to consciousness. It goes very much against much of the experience which more and more people seek also today—that the holistic experience should not directly be linked to consciousness. I think that in a certain way, we have, at least this is my tentative conclusion, we have a holistic way of relating and we have an analytical way of relating. And there is a whole tradition, very much also in the Far Eastern culture which Dr. Sibatani, for example, has pointed out in his paper. Emptying ourselves of the linguistic and analytical ability gives us the possibility of becoming conscious—you may call it sub-consciously conscious, but conscious in a way that it works

177

and acts on our consciousness—of the holistic view which I think, just as an idea, would tie in then very much also with the notions that the mind is not, as you in the last sentence said, let us say, the universe is not as you say it, mindless; but that we all share, as Aldous Huxley has put it, that we all are mind at large in some way. So that we share in some mind and I think I cannot elaborate this more here, but I think there are certain new results coming out, even in physics, which seem to indicate that there is something like a process of evolution which is not mindless but which goes on from the physical, what we call the inanimate world all the way to the social-cultural world.

Eccles: Thank you very much. I am going to get a bit lost, you know, in all the detailed answering. I think I agree with you almost completely. In my first diagram (Chapter 20, Fig. 12-1) you have pointed out that I had World 2 and World 3 communicating to each other. That is Popper's suggestion. However for the most part the interaction between these two worlds has to be mediated by sense organs, with all the complexities of coding. So there I agree completely with you.

As regards the other main query you made: am I putting consciousness only in the left hemisphere and not in the right? I am putting the ultimate experience of consciousness only in the left hemisphere. All of the processing, however, all of the development of the neuronal operations that eventually become associated with conscious experiences goes on in both hemispheres everywhere. The holistic performance goes on in my minor hemisphere. Otherwise, how could I appreciate music? The physical substrate of music comes into my cochlea and is coded in the auditory nerve fiber discharges and eventually in a most sophisticated manner by neuronal machinery of my cerebral cortex to give me an experience of delight in the analysis of the musical patterns of remembrances and associations. Most of that analysis and synthesis comes about in the minor hemisphere and then it is shot through the corpus callosum to be experienced in the liaison areas of the dominant hemisphere, where it comes through to consciousness. In general I think we agree. I don't believe that consciousness is only linguistic. I believe that we have direct consciousness of pictures, of music, of odors and tactile experiences of all kinds of pain without having to talk about them. I think that is a bad fallacy that some people are expressing today, that you never know about anything until you talk about it. We are supposed to spend all our waking time in talking to ourselves. I disagree with this completely. This is only for primitive people.

Now, what is the other point you made? The mindless universe. I am strongly against pan-psychism. I don't believe that it tells us anything. I think it is based upon a fallacious idea that nothing new can come to exist. Even Sherrington thought this, as did Teihard de Chardin and Julian Huxley—that there is an element of mind in all organized matter and gradually it has become perfected in the evolutionary process, eventually to achieve its great flowering in the human brain. I see no evidence for that. My evidence on the contrary is that of my self-consciousness. For each of us that is the only mind we know. If we did not have self-consciousness, we would not start putting mind into anything. It is only because we find mind in ourselves related to our own brains, that we begin to think about minds in other people. Then of course, if you are unsophisticated, you put minds into the various other manifestations of nature. But this is unscientific. We only know of mind as it is in each one of us, and then by subtle communications we recognize mind in others. That is as far as I am going to go!

Jantsh: Just one point. What about plant communication?

Eccles: Communication doesn't involve mind at all. The whole of biochemistry, the whole of physiology, the whole of biophysics is involved in communication, but it operates simply by physical principles. I am a complete reductionist in all these matters. I am a reductionist with regard to the working of my own brain; only in the respect of the relationship of the liaison brain to the mind world. Am I metaphysically an anti-reductionist?

About all the other questions, I am, of course, not putting up proofs of problems except in some cases which I gave you. Rather I am offering hypothesis in the Popperian manner hoping to be challenged as you have done. That is what we do it for. If we don't define our ideas sharply with diagrams and models, if we only give fuzzy expressions, then I don't believe we can ever make progress. We have to dare to make statements which challenge refutation.

Haskell: You mention something to the effect of PSI—telepathy, clairvoyance, perhaps even precognition. There have been many books published on it, and some experiments actually done with it. Would you please expand your views on that subject?

Eccles: I have in fact been to Duke to see experiments of Rhine and have read widely in the literature. I don't see anything definitive against telepathy. We don't know how brain actions communicate to our own spiritual World 2. We don't know how the World 1 to World 2 communication goes on in our brain. It is conceivable that World 2 could receive from other World 2's but I don't think the experiments have been adequate to prove this extraordinary idea. I would on the other hand keep my options open on it. I don't want to say that it cannot exist because the world has so many incredible events happening in it. For example from our own experiences, we know the creativity and the imagination of man. What are we in fact as human beings? We are indescribably wonderful, beyond our understanding. Therefore, I would say that I would keep my options open on telepathy and I would recommend that if people want to they should be free to work on it and be supported in for it. We have many examples in the past where attempts to investigate problems of an esoteric kind were frowned upon. All kinds of pioneers had to fight for their existence. Not that they have always been right; most of them have been wrong, as for example the astrologers or the vitalists. But I would say that the cost is quite small, and we should be prepared to allow people the freedom to investigate even extremely unorthodox problems.

Bar-Hillel: First, how would you go about corroborating or refuting your conjecture that non-human animals have no awareness of death? Secondly, this primariness of personal experiences and the secondariness of physicalist modes of view, has been an old philosophical tenet, of which you are of course fully aware. It has been called various names, (Phenomenalist views, etc., Eigenphysischer by Carnap in 1928) and has as often been shown to be inadequate as it has been proposed and re-proposed. Do you have any new conceptions to vindicate the view that in some interesting sense the Eigenphysischer and Lebens are primary relative to the other points of view which have been claimed by other people to be primary? Or relative to the views say of the later Carnap in which this whole problem has become a pseudoproblem, so that this talk about primariness and secondariness didn't make much sense any more to him.

Eccles: The first question is one of observation. When you are studying animals, please remember you have to study them in the wild. Do not study domestic pets. In this case even Joan Goodall's chimpanzees have become her domestic pets. Professor Washburn of Berkeley has studied monkey colonies in the wild. He has observed that, as animals get old and injured, they are rejected by the colony. No monkey takes any notice of an injured or dead animal. The point I would make is that you should observe the behavior of animals in the wild state.

There are occasional reports on elephants which could be used to refute my statement, but elephants are domestic animals. You know where this behavior of caring for the sick or dead is reported the elephants are associated intimately with people and they are very intelligent. It is reported that elephants just cover the dead elephants with leaves. But the chimpanzees in Joan Goodall's experiences take no notice in the end of dead chimpanzees and this is certainly true of Washburn's monkeys in the wild. Therefore, I think that you can say that animals are not aware of death. As soon as an animal is dying they reject it. It is no longer interesting to them. They do not recognize it. They never recognize that this too could happen to me. This poignant insight happened to man at least one hundred thousand years ago. When he saw the other members of the tribe dying, he must have gotten the sense that, they are like me. They die. I too can die. I will look after the dead body to the best of my ability in the hope that when I die, it will be done to me too.

The second question was about the primary and secondary. I just think that this is simple neurophysiology. Perceptual physiology wasn't well known by Carnap and his colleagues. They did not study the physiological processes concerned in perception. That is the trouble with so many philosophers who have talked and written books on perception. They do not know about the neural events involved in perception—the coding by the sense organs and the successive analysis and synthesis that goes on in the sensory pathways to the brain and the further integration there. I think this would be my answer, that it is just the inadequacy of scientific understanding that leads to these philosophical problems. If philosophers were much better informed upon the basic physiological events involved in perception, I think they would be quite different in their interpretation about primary and secondary reality. And I should mention that the distinguished physicist Eugene Wigner has made this very same statement, and I am following his concept in talking about primary reality and secondary reality.

Anderson: This is by way of comment to Dr. Eccles to see if you would concur in my observation. It seems to me that your unique use of language as the base of culture is of great importance to us, particularly vis-a-vis the term, "communication," as was brought up by one of our other speakers. In the plant world and more so in the lower animal world communication is on a one-to-one kind of non-transformational basis, where in fact a signal for aggression is automatically met by aggression; whereas in man, language is transformational, that a cue for aggression can by way of our higher brain centers, be transformed into a cue for, if you will, non-aggression, non-conflict, but rather, if anything, to amicability. Therefore, I think it calls for a clear distinction between communication and language to allow for this transformation and greater enhancement of culture as your model seems to imply. Would you agree with that?

Eccles: Thank you Dr. Anderson. Of course I would. That is a very nice expression that you have given to the ideas that I was trying to convey. We are in fact, speaking animals. It is through the subtleties of communication in a linguistic mode that I think man came to become human. I was trying to give you these instances of "Genie" and others, to show you that but for this developed communication, we stay animals. Each human child has to be created anew as a human being, a sophisticated human being, through linguistic communication and other methods too of course. I don't want to exclude artistic form, and sound, as with music. These are all part of human language if we think in a wider mode that includes all of the cultural means of communication. This is the wonderful thing that we have been born to. How grateful we should be to be born now into this marvelous cultural world of ours, rather than to have been born, six thousand years ago in this area, in Japan, in Europe, or in America. What a difference! No, we are the lucky inheritors of this rich human culture, and this makes it all the more important for us, as responsible beings, to see that this heritage is enriched further for subsequent generations. This thought relates to the motto of this conference.

13.

Subjective and Neuronal Time Factors in Conscious Sensory Experience, Studied in Man, and Their Implications For the Mind-Brain Relationship

Benjamin Libet

I propose to confront you with a rather recent experimental discovery of ours that we think has an important bearing on the mind-brain problem. It was made with neurosurgical patients in whom electrodes were implanted for therapeutic purposes. That gave us the opportunity to try to investigate what kinds of neuronal activities might be required at cerebral levels for producing a conscious sensory experience. The particular experimental finding I want briefly to get across to you deals with time factors in the relationship between the neuronal and the subjective events. There were two experimental questions involved. First, when are the neuronal activities adequate to produce the conscious sensory experience after a sensory stimulus is delivered? There is a second, less obvious question that we found had to be addressed, namely, is the timing of the subjective experience the same or different from the time of the neuronal adequacy that is necessary for occurrence of the experience. The answer to the second question appears to bear on the issue at least of psychophysiological parallelism, and in that sense perhaps on identity theory.

We attempt to place an electrode on the lateral surface of the cerebral hemisphere, in particular on the postcentral gyrus, which receives sensory representation of various parts of the body on it. When we electrically stimulate an appropriate site here in the awake human subject, he reports a sensation in the hand or finger area of the opposite side of the body. Now you will notice that the subject does not experience the sensation in his brain where we are stimulating; he experiences it as being referred to a peripheral part of his body. This immediately tells us that there is not an identity between the actual neuronal-spatial configurations that are being activated and the spatial locations of the subjective experience that results from it, because the latter is in an entirely different place altogether. Now we consider the time factors involved. We found that one single electrical pulse was completely inadequate to produce a conscious sensory experience; it requires repetition of stimulation pulses. More surprisingly, the repetition, at least near the threshold levels, had to go on for around a half a second, 500 milliseconds, before the subject would report anything. Using different frequencies of pulses makes no difference to this requirement. If we stopped the stimulus train just short of a half a second, the subject would report he felt absolutely nothing. Additional evidence indicated that there seemed to be a corresponding delay of about 0.5 sec in the subjective experience for this cortical stimulus.

When we stimulated the skin, however, the situation became even more interesting. At the skin one single electrical pulse, as many of you may know, is sufficient to give rise to a sensory experience, even when it's very weak. So the question there becomes, first of all, is there also an actual delay at cerebral levels of up to about 500 msec, before the neuronal responses to that single pulse become adequate? Evidence was developed from two lines of experiments. In one, it was found that a conditioning stimulus, delivered to the cerebral cortex up to 200-500 msec *after* a skin stimulus, could retroactively affect the conscious experience elicited by the prior skin stimulus; this indicated that cerebral process going on for some time after the skin stimulus could still be altered before actual production of the sensory experience. In another line, it was shown that the early electrophysiological indicators of the cerebral cortex responses to a skin stimulus were clearly insufficient to elicit a sensory experience; later components of this electrophysiological complex were necessary. This evidence led to the conclusion that even though a single pulse to the skin is adequate to elicit a sensation, it is in fact followed by a series of events at cortical levels before the neuronal system becomes adequate for the production of conscious experience.

The *subjective* experience for the skin stimulus, on the other hand, seemed to appear with no appreciable delay! I cannot give the details of the evidence for this in the space available. In brief, the evidence was based on the order of the subjective timing of experience for a skin stimulus relative to that for a cortical stimulus (the latter known to require at least 500 msec before it could produce any experience).

Let us summarize the situation. When you stimulate the skin with one single pulse, there are initiated, after a brief delay of 10 to 20 milliseconds, a series of electrophysiological changes recordable at the cortex; these in fact go on for about a half a second or more. The early or primary portion of this is by itself not adequate to produce any conscious experience. In fact, you can produce conscious experience without having the primary response there at all. The apparent delay of up to about a half a second before there is neuronal adequacy for the production of the conscious sensation, is thus paradoxically coupled with the apparent absence of any delay for appearance or timing of the subjective experience that is "produced" by the neuronal activity. To explain this we proposed (a) that the initial primary response of the cortex to the fast message which arrives via a specific projection system, acts as a "time market;" and (b) that, after neuronal adequacy for the production of the sensation is achieved, the experience is somehow referred back automatically to this initial time marker. As far as the subject is concerned, therefore, there would be no delay whatsoever. With different sensory inputs delivered synchronously to different parts of the body, including also visual or auditory, you know you have no jitter or asynchrony in your experiences. They are all, in our thesis, referred back to the initial fast signals for each input case, and thereby appear to be subjectively synchronous.

So we have the proposition, then, that there is a discrepancy between the time of neuronal adequacy, delayed for up to about a half a second before in fact a conscious sensory experience can be produced, and the time of the subjective experience "produced" by this neuronal activity. I'm going to touch briefly on one or two points that relate this discrepancy to the mind-brain relationship. A substantial delay for neuronal adequacy would mean that if you make a quick response to a stimulus, it would have to be made unconsciously. If quick responses are unconscious, that puts a time constraint on what you can refer to as being an act of free will, since free will could presumably be exercised consciously. If by experimental observation, not theory, the subjective experience of an event seems to have a different time base from the neuronal activity that produced it, the concept of psychophysiological parallelism would have to be stretched to encompass this discrepancy. One could argue that this discrepancy is not different in principle from the discrepancy between a subjective referral of an image in space and the neuronal spatial configuration that is responsible for it. But somehow the discrepancy in time bases seems more disturbing. One cannot conclude that it supplies a rigorous disproof of identify theory, which requires a strict psychophysiological parallelism. However, it introduces an experimentally based factor that may affect the relative attractiveness of alternative philosophical views of mind-brain interaction.

Commentary

K.B. Madsen

Fortunately, I have had the opportunity to read Sir Johns Eccles' and Sir Karl Popper's book. I got it just before I went on the airplane from Copenhagen and read it, and there were two pages in that book where Sir John tried to put Libet's experimental results in. What I will do now, as Sir John has not already himself done it, is to try to expose that part of his theory which explains these experimental results. First I must say that I think the mind-body problem is the most important philosophical problem, at least for psychologists, and I think from this conference it is one of the most important problems. But I think there had not appeared real new original theories of philosophers about this problem for many years until Sir Karl Popper's theory appeared. I think it was in 1968 that he first exposed his theory about the three worlds, and this theory is already exposed by Sir John, so I can refer to that. And then I will say that even if it was a new philosophical theory, it was after all a philosophy after Sir Karl Popper's own requirement for a scientific theory. It was not a scientific theory because a scientific theory according to his principles had to be a testable theory, a theory which can be falsified. And I don't think his own formulation of it is so that it can be falsified. So we must call it a philosophical theory in the exposition which he has given. But then Sir John Eccles has in his part of the book transformed this philosophical theory to a real and scientific theory which can be falsified, and I think what you have heard here is one of the things which is testing their theory, and I shall mention another thing.

First I must repeat the three most important hypotheses in the version of the theory which Sir John presents in the latest book. First, what you have already heard, the interaction between mind

189

and brain is going on in the liaison-brain, which is the cortex or the dominant hemisphere of the cortex. That we have already heard.

Second, integration of information in perception is the function of the mind, not of the brain. And this explains the delay of the half second which Libet has found, because it's the function of the mind and not the brain. I cannot avoid referring to a very old experimental fact in psychology, one of the most well-tested areas, classical conditioning. Pavlov and many of his followers have found that a half-second is the optimal time interval between presenting the unconditioned stimulus and the conditioned stimulus. So it seems to be as if there already existed the requirement of some kind of consciousness, say in the dog or whatever animal it is which they experiment with, because it was just the same time interval. That was the second hypothesis.

The third hypothesis could be formulated in this way: The decision and plan of action is of the mind and not of the brain. This is demonstrated or tested by the experiment which Kornhuber has made, in which he found that the delay between the decision, the act of will, and the performance of the movement was 0.8 seconds. That is a parallel to what we have heard here. Now it is the other side of the interaction, and there is a time lag of almost a second, 0.8, and I think it's interesting that the time lag is not the same on the input side as on the output side. The input side and the output side between the interaction of the mind and brain is perhaps not the same, and I should like to hear some comments from Libet and Sir John about this difference in time in these two experiments.

Of course I cannot repeat here all of the experiments which are set forth and exposed in the book as data which is evidence for the theory as a scientific theory. So here you see the results have an important place in a theoretical frame of reference, which again has a place in philosophy.

I have one critical remark, and it's half terminology and half real criticism. I think that the mysteriousness of the interaction between these two worlds, as they are called in Sir Karl Popper's theory, will be reduced by two things: first, instead of calling them two worlds or three worlds, you should call them three levels of the same world. I think many people here would accept the theory if framed in another way. I can't see it would hurt the sense of the theory if you called it three levels of the world instead of three worlds. It will reduce the mysteriousness a little, I believe. These three levels you can conceive of as only *methodlogical* levels or, if you prefer, *onotological* levels. You need not take both steps. The first step is enough to deal with the scientific theory, at least.

In addition to these three levels which can be conceived methodologically and onotologically, you could add more levels because I think that the same problems are coming up in many other places where sciences are working on borderlines. We have already heard today that even inside one science, physics, there is a kind of leap from one level to another, from classical mechanism to the electromagnetic theory. Then of course we leaped from the level of physics to chemistry and from chemistry to biochemistry: and if you go on in the line which Pribram has done from "*The Languages of the Brain*" (1971), you could say that some psychologists at least, work on the levels from neurochemistry, neurophysiology, brain physiology (where the brain is dealt with as a whole) and to psychology in the traditional way (where the person is dealt with as a whole). We then proceed on to the cultural level where the third world in Popper's theory is placed, so I think that there are many such levels in the world but we can think upon it as one world leveled by our sciences, by our methods, and by our conceptual frame of references.

If you wish to formulate a philosophy about your scientific theory you can think upon these levels as levels in the reality; and many of you will recognize this as the systems theorists' approach to the world.

14.

Experimental Transference of Consciousness: The Human Equivalent

Robert J. White

In recent years we have been able to construct a series of brain models that have permitted us to transfer the entire brain of the experimental animal; yet allows the brain to remain capable of high performance at all levels. The majority of these experiments utilized the subhuman primate, but, more recently, both the canine and the rodent have been employed in the surgical engineering design of these isolated brain preparations.

The initial experimental protocols involved first, the design of a unique surgical procedure permitting isolation of the complete brain, both vascularly and neurogenetically; and, second, the construction of a support system to insure viability of the brain outside of its own body. This was accomplished by reestablishing cerebral circulation and by employing a hematologically compatible donor or a miniaturized extracorporeal perfusion system. With both of these extracerebral vascular support systems, the brain was in a truly isolated state and the performance of the organ is continuously monitored using ongoing neurochemical and neurophysiological criteria. While, particularly in the donor supported model, data retrieved from these tracking techniques approached normality in character and value, we were unable to assume that the preparation was, in the final analysis, conscious or aware of its existence.

By definition, to isolate the brain required neurogenic separation and, therefore, not only the spinal cord, but all of the cranial nerves must be severed; as a consequence, the inner organizational matrix of the brain is no longer receiving an inrush of information from the peripheral nervous system. It is exclusively dependent on hormonal secretion via the circulation. Obviously the brain is also unable to "express itself" through nerve pathways and, thus, can only remain in contact via the release of neurohormones into the vascular system.

In recent experiments, in which a single cranial nerve complex was purposefully preserved, for example, the auditory or optic nerve, it was demonstrated that with either sound or light stimulation, the appropriate neuroanatomical connections in the isolated brain remained intact and, when the appropriate areas of cerebral cortex (auditory or visual cortex) were instrumented with surface electrodes appropriate responses were recorded, strongly suggesting the preservation and functioning of these intimate and delicate neural fiber tracts and connections subserving these modalities of sensation. Once again, however, this did not provide evidence that the preparation in the isolated state was capable of processing or appreciating this information.

Detailed neurophysiological investigation utilizing stereotaxically oriented depth electrodes in the brain stem demonstrated preservation of functioning in the reticular activating relay systems. The accumulation of data strongly supported the concept that, under these experimental conditions, the isolated brain, vascularly supported outside of its body, existed in a recreated environment that provided adequacy of substrate delivery. It was therefore very reminiscent of the in situ situation. Furthermore, neurophysiological sampling at a cortical or subcortical level, particularly in the donor supported isolated brain, appeared to meet the criteria of electroencephalogic normality in hundreds of samplings when compared with similar tracings from awake and intact central nervous system animals. Thus, while we have no objective criteria that the isolated brain model, even in the subhuman primate, was conscious, it did appear that its biochemical and neuroelectrical state would be appropriate for the maintenance of an alert condition.

In more recent years, it has been possible to actually transplant the isolated brain into the body (anatomically either in the neck or abdominal cavity) by interposing the organ between the arterial and venous system. Under these circumstances, a significant increase in longevity was, and is, possible. In general, these periods have been of the order of three to seven days. Originally the technology required the use of specially designed vascular cannulae to achieve artery to artery and vein to vein anastomosis, necessitating the continuous use of an anticoagulant state. This often required termination of the experiment because of gradually increasing hemorrhage in the preparation. More recently, with the employment of micro-surgical techniques, the vascular anastomosis has been achieved without the use of cannulae and without the requirement of chronic heparinization. Isolated brain models in the transplanted state are equipped with a survey module permitting continuous recording of cerebral blood flow, arterial-venous chemical analysis, cortical and subcortical neuroelectrical recording and temperature sampling. Again, and with great frequency, brain performances in the transplanted subhuman have approached cerebral performance in the intact animal.

There is, of course, no way that we can argue, in spite of the high level of functioning of the brain in the transplanted model, that consciousness or appreciation of environment change is attained or maintained. In order to achieve evidence of responsivity of the brain in isolation, it appeared to us that it would be necessary to retain cranial nerve function. Toward that end, an entirely new generation of brain models had to be developed. This would require the operative transplanting of the entire cephalon of the body of another animal from which the animal's own cephalon had been removed. This has necessitated the development of unique technology where none existed previously, not only in terms of anesthesia and surgery, but, equally important, the construction of advanced engineering suspension and fixation units. In the initial experiments the employment of vascular cannulae were required to make the vascular connections between cervical vessels (arterial and venous). As in the isolated brain transplantation experiments, continuous heparinization was necessitated to prevent clotting of the connecting tubing and, as a result, the experiments frequently were terminated after a day or two.

More recently, using direct microsurgical anastomosis of the arterial and venous vessels, the transplanted cephalon could be surgically connected with only short phase heparinization (during the actual operation.) Under the design of these experiments, it was now possible to examine the brain within the head with the cranial nerves intact and, at long last, to answer the question as to whether or not, when the brain is transplanted, it retains the capability of consciousness and for appropriate response to external stimuli. While this question has now been answered in a more chronic sequence in the preparations that were vascularly associated through microsurgical anastomosis, even in the early models of cephalic transplantation where cannular connection was employed, that with the emergence from anesthesia it was immediately obvious that *the brain had regained a state of consciousness*!

In the ensuing hours following surgery, a completely awake state supervened and, through the available cranial nerve function, the preparation did respond appropriately to external stimulation! It was obvious that the animals could see and did appreciate movement and, indeed, would track with their eyes objects of interest placed in their visual fields. Responsivity to ordinary stimulation was obvious in that, if a loud sound was produced, the cephalon responded by a facial expression of discomfort. Light pin prick of the facial tissues, likewise, gave evidence of discomfort on the part of the animal.

These preparations could and did masticate and swallow food, as well as appropriately handle fluids employing the expected muscle movements of tongue and oral cavity. Indeed, one had the impression that the animals were "hungry and thirsty" and understood the oral processing of food and liquid with alacrity.

While these behavioral observations might be considered gross, there was no disagreement amongst the examiners that the isolated brain in the cephalon transplantation had achieved consciousness and that its preservation, as reflected in the proper responses of the animal to appropriate cranial nerve stimulation was dependent solely on the maintenance of an adequate circulation and substrate delivery to brain. The sustaining of viability in the unique cephalic transplantation model required a highly sophisticated intensive care unit with detailed programs of management. Maintenance of pulmonary function necessitated continuous mechanical respiratory support, and to maintain appropriate levels of blood pressure, exogenous catecholamine infusion techniques required development.

The most advanced transplant model yet devised requires the preservation of the brain stem at a mid-brain level in the body that is to receive the cephalon. Thus, when the cephalon is vascularly connected with the body, the new preparation is able to initiate its own respiratory activity and provide for self-maintenance of blood pressure.

To date, the obvious problem of tissue rejection has not been addressed although neuropathological examination of the transplanted brain has not revealed any light microscopy evidence of hyper-rejection of tissue. In actuality, the brain tissue stained with hematoxylin and eosin looked quite normal!

While the investigations described in Part I deal exclusively with the transference of cerebral function including consciousness in the experimental animal there is every reason to believe that with additional advances in surgical and instrumentation technology, similar operations could be performed in the human. In some ways, the accomplishments presented in Part I enabling the scientist to perform cerebral transplantation in the subhuman primate actually present a more difficult undertaking surgically than would be the case in the human sphere. Thus, because of the extremely small size of the blood vessels in these animal preparations, as opposed to those available in man, the increase in vascular dimensions would markedly increase the ease of constructing the blood vessel anastomosis. Additionally, considerable anatomical and operative information is available on a human level that would permit solution of the problem of designing a surgical technique for cephalic transplantation in man.

Be that as it may, the methodology, as yet, is not available, nor have we undertaken an attempt at preparing such an operative technique. Obviously, if such an operation were to be considered in man, a great deal of work would have to be undertaken in the area of tissue rejection, not only in terms of the brain itself, but as it would relate to other tissues of the cephalon. (It would be interesting to contemplate the construction of a series of subhuman primate cephalic transplantation experiments in which immunological suppressive drugs were utilized much as in renal transplantation to further extend the longevity of these preparations.)

Additionally, and over and above the operative technique itself, a great deal of research would have to directed toward designing support systems to provide viability of the human model, for surely these patients would require an incredible array of monitoring and maintenance equipment, as well as specially trained physician and nursing personnel. Granting the justification of funding and undertaking the necessary research, there is little doubt that, even at the present time, cephalic transplantation in man is a technical reality. Whether we can justify this socially, philosophically, or theologically, there is no question that it can be done. More importantly, there is no question that such a preparation should and would demonstrate a level of consciousness and cerebral performance that we have come to expect in the subhuman primate model nor is there any reason we should not expect that the intrinsic individuality, personality, emotional structure, intelligence, and memory would not continue to function under these experimental circumstances.

Thus, it is already possible to transfer human consciousness provided the organ that subtends such functioning is retained. It could be argued that all of the other body systems and organs have been primarily developed for and, in a sense, subservient to the concept that brain function must be sustained and that their very existence and design is based on this principle. In other words, the body and its systems are nothing more than a "power pack" for the brain for, in the final analysis, the brain is the tissue substrate for the mind and possibly that which we call the spirit or soul of man.

Science has reached the threshold where *human consciousness can be transferred* provided the organ which supervenes this characteristic is maintained. Whether research directed toward human cephalic transplantation should be undertaken requires extensive review by such fields as philosophy, theology, sociology, and medicine.

Part III

The Biology of Consciousness

15.
Evolution of Consciousness

Karl H. Pribram

The topic before us is "The Evolution of Consciousness." I would like to first recall to you a definition of evolution. Dr. Wescott suggested that evolution means change, and that the change must be in essence either gradual or come in stages. There may be some discontinuities but the discontinuities have to be related to each other in some fashion. The difference between evolution and revolution is that in evolution the stages can be related to each other, and that there is not some major discontinuity in the change. Empirically the problem is to find the missing links that relate stages.

Consciousness is perhaps more difficult to define. Perhaps we can start with the difference between states of consciousness which we have all experienced. We have one state of consciousness when we are asleep and dreaming, another state of consciousness when we are awake (hopefully) attending a conference such as this. There are discontinuities between states, and we cannot remember in one state what occurred in the other. This state specificity of memory and thus of the articulation that defines consciousness applies to many more states of consciousness than just dreaming on the one hand and being awake on the other. Sometimes even different scientific disciplines appear to provide different stages of consciousness in this sense. One of the problems of a transdisciplinary conference such as this is that the articulated consciousness which one discipline gives to an individual limits him, and he cannot somehow get to the other state of consciousness within which someone else is speaking. States of consciousness mutually exclude each other: A salmon spawning does not eat. A salmon eating does not spawn. A behaviorist in psychology does not speak about consciousness at all. He has no consciousness.

There is much talk about altered states of consciousness these days. I don't think there is such a thing; rather, there are alternate states of consciousness. The biochemistry and electrophysiology of the brain seems to have a great deal to do with establishing these states. The idea that a conceptual discipline can determine a state of consciousness may seem a little farfetched when brain biochemistry is concerned to be the root of a conscious state. But in our own work, we've established the fact that the areas of the brain involved in cognitive operations, the so-called association areas, modulate the activities of the biochemical mechanisms. At least the anatomy of the connection has been worked out as has the electro-physiology, so whatever becomes organized cognitively can then change the chemistry of the brain.

These brain mechanisms help define the states of consciousness, but they do not define the contents of consciousness. The contents of consciousness are our perceptions and feelings. What relates the states of consciousness to their contents are what we call attentional processes. We'll hear a great deal about these processes today.

This is not, however, the total range of ways in which consciousness is talked about. One way compatible with the above definitions is the manner of the neurosurgeon. The neurosurgeon is interested in whether the patient is conscious or not conscious. I noted that dreaming is a state of consciousness. How do we know that? We poke a person who's asleep and dreaming and he wakes up. He's not in coma, he's not in a stupor. And so we make useful distinction between consciousness and unconsciousness in that fashion. Freud used the term in a similar fashion: when we have ready access to the determinants of behavior (that is, we know why we did something) we call it consciously determined. If, on the other hand, access is difficult or eludes us, then we call its determination unconscious. This is one set of definitions.

Another set of definitions becomes evident in religion and philosophy. These include the problem of self-consciousness, and the problem of awareness of the self, or what philosophers call intentionality. There is also the difference between being able at one and the same time to be aware of the contents of consciousness and of the process of being aware—i.e., simultaneously aware of one's self and one's environment. That is a second way in which consciousness is defined: people don't always use the term self-consciousness—they simply use the word consciousness to cover this intentional aspect of consciousness.

Finally, there is still another way of talking about consciousness. Sir John Eccles has been talking to us in these terms for a number of years, and often we have not understood him. I'm beginning to understand him now and will label this form of consciousness "transcendental." This definition holds that consciousness extends beyond, and is not just the product of, the interaction through this brain and senses of an organism and his environment. This is the mystic's way of conceiving consciousness. We must not confuse this transcendental consciousness with either the content definition of self-consciousness nor with the state definition of consciousness.

16.
The Evolution of Consciousness

Harry J. Jerison

$\mathcal{T}$he evolutionary biology of consciousness cannot be studied directly for several obvious reasons. First, we know consciousness as an essentially private experience. It cannot be analyzed directly in a group of people, a human population. There is, therefore, no direct information on variations in human consciousness. Variation is the stuff of evolution, and without information about it an evolutionary analysis is impossible. The second source of difficulty follows from the first. If we are to analyze the evolution of a trait we must have some sense of its nature in different species. If we cannot have direct access to the consciousness of another human, how much less likely is it that we will ever have direct access to the consciousness of individuals of nonhuman species of animals?

In making these points, however, I am belaboring the obvious. Their value is primarily in emphasizing the requirement for indirect assessments of consciousness and, thus, of definitions of consciousness that are both acceptable and useful in suggesting indirect measures. I will not plunge into measures and data. The necessary definitions at this time can be much more vague and yet retain some utility.

To begin with, let us recognize that all aspects of life can be viewed as adaptions, that is, as characters or traits that evolved as a way of making animals work more successfully in their normal environments. The consciousness that we know individually is as much a biological adaptation as the hand or eye. I think that I can characterize this consciousness in a way that will help us appreciate its biological role, which I believe is an inevitable one for animals more complex than simple invertebrate species in coping with the challenge of an environment. I would start with the place of the nervous system in coping with information about the environment.

The biological problem raised by the existence of nervous systems that contain more than a few thousand neurons is how to control the responses of a whole animal. Even if the animal worked as a piece of clockwork, with each bit of information from the environment triggering fixed sensory and motor responses and movements of muscles, it would be impossible for the system to work accurately without further organization. The chain of events, which we should call reflexes, would never complete an appropriate response to stimuli if more than a few dozen elements were involved. The difficulty is due to the fact that neurons are built with some uncertainty inherent in their operation. This uncertainty is such that the system would produce impossibly many errors unless the chain of nerve cells in the reflex arc had no more than a dozen or so elements in it.

The solution to the biological problem was undoubtedly achieved by chunking or clumping the information-processing procedure, analogously to the way computer programmers write their programs by putting "instructions" together into subroutines and then calling up subroutines when a complex instruction is needed, rather than attempting to rewrite a complete detailed instruction on every occasion that it is needed. An even better analogy derived from computers is in the way user-languages, such as FORTRAN, have evolved, in which the simplest element in the language is already a complex set of electrical yes-no events as described in "machine-language."

Consider the information-processing problems faced by an "average" mammal such as a cat as it stalks a mouse: let us restrict ourselves to visual information, even though this may be one of the less important channels of information. The visual image of the mouse could be captured without difficulty on photographic film placed at the cat's retina. At the living retina, however, the physical image becomes a remarkably complex, elaborate, and almost innumerable set of events. Literally millions of sensory cells are excited to different degrees and at different times, and the bleaching of pigments in those actually

206

excited at a given time is the source of nerve impulses in addition millions of nerve cells in the cat's eye. Not in what we conventionally recognize as its brain. The neural retina is technically brain tissue, but since it lies outside the cranial cavity it is usually treated as non-brain. A complex pattern of exitation and inhibition is transmitted by several hundred thousand nerve cells in the retina upward into the brain. The "information" in this pattern consists of perhaps 10 events or so per second, on the average, with some neruons passing more than 100 events per second into the first stage of analysis in the brain.

I am not about to treat you to a lesson in elementary neuroanatomy, so let me sum up this issue by noting that before the instantaneous information about the mouse in space is fully analyzed by the cat's brain, before the half second or so of analysis is complete, it is likely that more than 100,000,000 neurons will have been involved (This figure is probably an order of magnitude too low in this estimate). It is inconceivable that a system adapted to process information, the brain in this instance, could work directly on so much information. It would have to be chunked, and there would have to be hierarchies of chunks.

Now let us consider the same cat but other modalities. If the mouse moved it might produce some sound. That would reach some 70,000 sense cells in the cat's ears, and the signals would eventually be processed in millions of neurons in the brain. A comparably complex or even more complex situation exists for smell, and it is likely that we misread the role of this modality. As primates, we are severely crippled in our ability to use olfactory information. Our sense organ is, in a real sense, atrophied, at least when compared to that of other orders of land mammals. (The weak olfactory system of primates will be a central element in later analysis here; it certainly keeps us from understanding intuitively the experience of most other species of mammals.) We must assume comparable chunking and hierarchies of chunks for auditory and olfactory brain and for visual brain.

As a thought problem, let us try to imagine the nature of the chunks produced by the brain as it processes information. Within each modality these can be arbitrarily constrained. The essential requirement would be to have the highest level of chunking produce chunks that would be reasonably stable labels for the source, the environmental source, of stimulation. The whole animal might be thought of as an object that has to move through physical space (with the option of remaining stationary, or freezing in position, a zero-movement among the "movements"). As the animal moves the pattern of neural stimulation must change dramatically even if the environment is entirely stable. The highest-level-chunks must represent the stability of the environment and, where appropriate, the fact of the animal's motion through a stable environment. Now a further problem: the highest-level olfactory chunk, representing stalked mouse against environmental background, and the highest level visual chunk and auditory chunk for the same information-complex are very likely in different parts of the brain. Furthermore, with respect to the neural constraints on processing information there is no necessary relationship among these modality-specific chunks. It is only in the ultimate use of the information, perhaps in guiding a leap by the cat as it catches the mouse, that a unity is or must be developed.

It is obvious what that unity must be. The mass of information, the changes-of-state of many nerve cells, has to be converted into a useful entity, namely a "mouse" that exists in a "world out there." The chunk must represent an object in space. And the olfactory and visual and auditory chunks, though perhaps distinct as smells and sounds, must all refer to the object: the smell of the mouse, its appearance, and the effects of its movements and squeaks.

This constructive act by a complex nervous system is more complex than I have indicated here. The mouse is known against some environmental background. It is in some position in space. In the visual system, space of a sort is inherent in the structure of the system. There are labeled spatial coordinates, essentially x,y, z labels for the points of space, and one assumes that this system (*x, y coordinates given by the retina of the eye; z-coordinate* added in some analytic fashion from stereopsis and from the many other cues for the third dimension of visual space) is also represented by appropriate higher-order chunks.

The fact of time, of the organization of events in time, which appears so natural and elementary to us, is not a simple phenomenon from a neural point of view. Simultaneity is as much of a problem for the psychologist and for the sensory physiologist as it is for the physicist. Certain departures from physical simultaneity—temporal disparties among neural events—may yet be experienced as simultaneity with added character. I have a specific example in mind. If the cat's mouse happened to squeak, and certain neurons in the cat's medulla were activated within 5 millionths of a second of one another, the information would be chunked (or put into a super-chunk higher in the hierarchy) as indicating that the mouse was directly in front of the cat. If the physical temporal disparity between the events in the medulla were, let us say, 1/10,000th of a second, the mouse's squeak (and the mouse) would be experienced as off to one side or other, but not in line with the cat's midline. The squeak would still be a unitary event in time, but it would be displaced in space. The time-difference in the brain would be structured as a spatial deviation—a localization of sound in space.

The reason for developing as much detail as I have is to make a central point for the analysis of consciousness as a biological phenomenon. The point is that reality as we ordinarily under-stand and experience it is not a phenomenon of the outside physical world. Rather it is a construction of the brain, a phenom-enon of what we might correctly consider as the inside physical world of the brain. This is not to be solipsistic on the matter. Our naively experienced phenomenal reality bears a close relationship to physical reality (as understood from sophisticated analysis of the nature of the physical world). But phenomenal reality is very much a construction of the brain, as can be shown by the tricks and failures of experience in illusions, dreams, and hallucina-tions.

My approach to the evolution of consciousness takes the idea of a constructed reality as its basis. To be conscious is first to experience a real world. It is as simple as that. Certain "events" are constructed by the brain as part of experience. These include space, time, and a variety of objects. The puzzle and confusion in the analysis of consciousness is certainly on the role of the self as one of the objects in one's world. I doubt that many would argue that relatively complexly organized animals, such as mammals, do not experience a reality that is at least comparable to the one that we experience. All but a few odd philosophers would agree that my reality is essentially the same as yours in its basic structure, though the events that we experience at any given moment will differ, of course, depending on where we are and what we happen to be doing.

The evolution of consciousness can then be analyzed from at least two perspectives. How do the basic structures of consciousness differ in different species of animals to reflect specific adaptions and unique environmental niches? Second, can we find some hierarchy with respect to the level of organization of consciousness in different species, to characterize some as higher and others as lower? These two questions will occupy the rest of this analysis. The answer to the first is entirely in the context of environmental niche and the available neural apparatus for adaption to the niche. The answer to the second question also concerns the environmental niche and its pressures, but also concerns encephalization—the evolution of more neural tissue and of a more important role for the brain (especially its "higher centers") in more advanced species. The concept "more advanced" can be tricky, and I will try not to trap you in the illogic of the idea of directed progressive evolution.

Consciousness as a Biological Adaption

It may be unfortunate that the word "consciousness" appears here, because the basic adaptation is the construction of a real world within which to behave. That this construction differs in different species has been appreciated for generations. Popularized as *Umwelt* by the neo Kantian biologist, Jacob von Uexhull, the concept is well illustrated in pictures of the same environment as it might be experienced by animals of different species. Obvious examples include the visual world of carnivores, such as dogs, which are relatively insensitive to color and the comparison of this world with the color-rich world of man and other primates. But there are more dramatic and radical examples that may be beyond our ability at representation. The visual world of the horse and rabbit and of most birds is not the proscenium stage that we experience. Rather it is a complete hemisphere or sphere (depending on whether the earth forms a platform or, as a bird in flight, the animal is in the center of an almost complete sphere). We are reasonably certain that these are the visual "real" worlds from reconstructions of the visual field represented on the retina of the eye. The two retinas of these species are at the sides of the head, more or less parallel to one another, and a reconstruction of the visual field covered by the two retinas turns out to involve more than 360 degrees, both in front of and behind the head. Can you imagine living in such a 360-degree physical universe experienced at each instant of time? You probably can, because even in our natural proscenium-stage world, the limited 120-degree extent of visual space is recognized as a limited experience that could easily be extended by turning our heads about. I would ask you to stretch your imaginations here, however, to guess at the world of the horse in which the instantaneously visible includes the world behind the head as well as the one in front of it.

The picture of reality, of conscious experience, is really more complex than these examples suggest. Our world is the peculiarly visual world of a species of primate. It is also richly auditory, especially in the human world of heard speech. But it is an underprivileged world of odors and the olfactory sense. You need only watch your dog as it moves about sniffing at objects and dropping a few drops of urine (if it is male) and thus marking its world. The marks are intelligible to other dogs, so much so that present views are that they give information about specific individuals. The world of knowledge conveyed by scent-marks and scents, so rich for dogs and other canids (wolves, foxes, etc.) is unknown to us except when analyzed with sophisticated scientific procedures. Even then we can be reasonably sure that the gap between our understanding of the message of the dog's urine and the place of the message in the dog's world is as great as the gap between the representation of speech in sophisticated sound-pictures, a sonogram or an oscilloscopic trace, and the place of its message in our lives.

The adaptation involved in the creation of a real world is one that enables an animal to make sense of an otherwise overwhelming load of neural information. The workings of this adaptation can be illustrated by pictures of what the world of experience "looks like." The best illustration of this adaptation may be at the other end of its operation, but the way movements are controlled.

As I write these words, I sit at the typewriter (since that is my habitual way) and my thoughts are eventually converted into marks on a piece of paper. The observable end of this conversion as a biological process is in the movement of my fingers striking keys. Note how complex that analysis has to be. There is the microscopic level, analogous to machine-language or the operation of yes-no devices in a computer, in which millions of neural and muscular events are recordable every second in the fibers running to the musculature of fingers, arm, shoulders and elsewhere. It is obviously impossible to handle instructions to this system by working at this machine-language level. But it would be as serious a mistake to imagine the operation at any of several higher, chunked, levels, such as the movements of individual fingers or even sequences of movements. I can control the motions by ordering: "Move index finger from coordinate position x_1, y_1, z_1, to position x_2, y_2, z_2." Further reduced, I might rephrase the order as a sequence of commands: flex index finger, extend ring finger, etc. Neither of these make much sense and neither is a true picture of the activity or of the instructions. Yet even these false overly reductionist pictures are highly chunked organized versions of commands in the form: i_1, t_1, i_2, t_2, . . . where i refers to a nerve impulse and t to a time and the subscripts are summary statements to identify the position and order of the events. The last is the measurable biological output of the system, but the controls are at a much higher level. If I were typing single letters without further semantic content the instruction would very likely take the form: "type k," the same as the intent to have the letter k typed. The resultant action would involve the ballistic movement of one finger oriented in space with respect to the key on the typewriter for the letter k, and the execution would be through the reduction of "error" in the relative positions of finger and key, coupled with "subroutines" specifying force, etc. That is, a still higher order chunking than noted before, and here it is important to recognize that "finger" and "key" will have been constructed by a brain as elements of a reality in which "events" can take place—all chunks of a higher order. The actual performance, as I sit and type, is one which only I can report with even approximate clarity. I type not as motions of my fingers on the typewriter, unless I attend to these motions. Rather I "speak" to an imaginary listener, and my speech is not through my voice box but through my fingers. If I took time to think of each movement of each finger I would give this up as a bad job. My chunks are larger units, syntactic and lexical units, and I have evidence for that in my errors. A common one for me is: *I no what I'm saying* in place of *I know what*. . . . Clearly my fingers take an acoustic message and can confuse homonyms.

To summarize the biological adaptation, it is one that determines a way to chunk neural information into useable units. The elements of my reality are similar to the elements in yours, and the experience of these elements is similar. Hence we know similar worlds. It is impossible to imagine a radically different world in other animals, even if we imagine intriguing species-typical adaptations. This naive awareness, phenomenal experience, or consciousness is a necessary aspect of information processing, and we are only vaguely aware of it as being special or unusual or a problem.

Human Consciousness and Speech and Language

Just as the reality of a species, as a construction of its brain, must to some extent be unique to the species, so must consciousness be unique to a species. I have tried to suggest the way in which reality is structured as being part of the adaptation of brain as a bodily organ, and I will carry this analysis forward to consider the special adaptations of *Homo sapiens* and their implications for our reality. It is in the uniqueness of our reality that we will appreciate the uniqueness of human consciousness.

Note first that I have argued for consciousness as a general adaptation, an aspect of the chunking of information in (moderately) large brains. I have reported elsewhere a detailed analysis of the evolution of encephalization in mammals as a 200-million year old adaptation that enabled our ancestors at that remove to cope with an unusual environmental niche, and I will summarize that analysis now. It is prologue to the analysis of the evolution of human consciousness.

The problem was to account for the appearance of enlarged brains in the earliest mammals which distinguished them from their immediate ancestors among the reptiles. The "larger" brain was about one gram; the smaller, ancestral brain about ¼ gram. My solution involved the often (and I believe, correctly) assumed adaptations of early mammals as nocturnal animals. Add to this the fact that reptiles of that period were almost certainly diurnal, with highly developed visual systems (and associated chunking of visual information), it was natural to consider the hypothesis that the earliest mammals were "reptiles" that had invaded a new environmental niche, that of life on land at nightfall and through the night.

Without detailing the full analysis, it is sufficient to note that the visual system is much less useful to a nocturnal animal than to a diurnal one. If the species invading the new niche were to conserve as many adaptations as possible it would have to evolve new distance-sensing machinery analogous to the visual sense of reptiles. I considered the likelihood that hearing and smell were elaborated for this purpose in the earliest mammals. I could then show, easily, that to pack a number of neurons into the auditory and olfactory systems that would be comparable in number to those packed into the retina of reptiles would require a significant enlargement of the brain. Thus the enlarged brain of early mammals, the encephalization of these species, could be accounted for as the solution of a packing problem: where to put the information-processing neurons for auditory and olfactory information that would function analogously to those relatively useless neurons of the neural retina.

The full argument acknowledged the persistent role for the retina at twilight (including the evolution of the rod-system of the retina that functions primarily in a dark-adapted eye and is presently a typical mammalian adaptation). Night vision, coupled with audition and olfaction in the early mammals would then be providing information from the same points in space. Organizing that information with code-representations or chunks as "objects" in space and time were clearly useful adaptions that would provide a selective advantage for animals dependent on information about the distant environment. It was possible to argue, further, that the construction of "space" was natural for a visual system structurally organized with spatial coordinates in at least two dimensions. The category "space" would be supplemented in the early mammals by comparable constructions based on the unique elements of the other neural systems—audition and olfaction. The auditory system, with its intrinsically temporal organization (witness the conversion of microsecond differences between physical neural events into spatial displacement for the localization of sound, as described earlier), would in its normal operation chunk events into a construction that we would know as "time." The picture for the olfactory system is more obscure, since, as noted earlier, our intuitions about an olfactory world are necessarily poor.

The essence of the analysis was to account for a novel development in evolution—the enlargement of the brain while other organs of the body remained at an appropriate size—by seeing in the novelty nothing more than a conventional adaptation to an understood environmental requirement. The major point was that the earliest mammals were "reptiles" trying to make a living as animals on land at night. The nocturnal niche was new for reptiles and there was the novelty. The adaptive response was conventional: add neuronal material to process environmental information that can be handled by existing sensory systems. In this "addition" there was a new adaptation: encephalization. I will presently develop the same kind of analysis for human encephalization, a unique phenomenon as far as we know at present for the past 3 million years or so in the history of life on earth.

The facts of the history of encephalization can be stated fairly simply. During the 500 million years or so of known vertebrate life most vertebrate species have had brains that were fairly similar in encephalization, that is, in relative size with respect to their body-sizes. This means that most species were comparable in their ability to process neural information; because encephalization is a measure of general information-processing capacity. This majority of species includes almost all fish, amphibians and reptiles. Birds and mammals have been more encephalized throughout the past 150–200 million years, and I have analyzed the history of early encephalization in mammals in the preceding paragraphs. After the great extinctions about 65 million years ago, there was a major evolution of encephalization in mammalian species, correlated with the reinvasion of diurnal niches. A new evolution of the visual system would have been required for corticalized vision to interact with the auditory and olfactory system at the level of higher brain centers in the neocortex and cerebellum. The primates formed an unusual order of mammals in this respect, much more encephalized than other orders (about twice as much brain per unit body size, on the average) throughout their known history of over 50 million years. The primates probably were encephalized to this extent because of their highly visual behavior, which involved color vision, fancy stereopsis, and perhaps other adaptations of the system. But the primates also were peculiar in their underdeveloped peripheral olfactory systems. The key element now is derived from the anatomy of the latter systems, hence the following recapping of a bit of neurology.

The olfactory system of the brain is a highly elaborate one, scarcely olfactory in the simple-minded sense, but nevertheless treated so by classical neurology because it is connected to the olfactory bulbs. The olfactory bulbs are essentially that "bulbs" of nerve tissue attached to stalks that are nerve fiber tracts, known as the olfactory tracts. These can be tracked into the inside of the brain.

Once inside the brain these tracts connect to enormous systems of cells named collectively as "rhinencephalon" (smell brain), limbic system, or paleocortex. Primates have very small olfactory bulbs compared to the bulbs of other mammals of similar body size. But they are perfectly normal mammals with respect to the rest of the "olfactory" system. In fact, that system is notorious in modern neurobiology as the neural system involved in emotions, motivation, and even in some types of memory—everything except "smell"—hence the discarding of the old term, rhinencephalon.

To skip now from neurology to behavior, I want to reconstruct the niche invaded by that group of primates that included our immediate ancestors, family Hominidae, which branched away from the manlike apes perhaps 15 million years ago. This family is rather well known as of about 3 or 4 million years ago as the australopithecines, whose environment can be reconstructed with some confidence. More, their way of life can also be constructed. They were likely social predators living in relatively open country (rather than forests). It is in that niche or adaptive zone that I have sought to understand the evolution of many of the peculiarly human features of our brain and behavior.

Let us recall, before lunging into this analysis, that we must deal with adaptations to existing environments, not *pre-adaptations* appropriate for environments that might be entered later. The model social predator is the wolf, and we should imagine the ecology and neurobiology of the australopithecines (and their predecessors) in terms of species of primates trying to make a living doing what comes naturally to wolves. The missing element for primates is as easy to think about as the missing visual world for early mammals as "reptiles" in a nocturnal niche. That element is the olfactory sense associated with environmental markers. To appreciate the importance of this lack of effective olfaction, let us see its place in the wolves' niche. In its normal life, a wolf pack may number a half dozen individuals. The pack ranges over a territory that is hundreds of kilometers in extent. Its members can mark the territory with urine, know their friends of the pack, and members of adjacent packs, and navigate the territory with daily treks of tens of kilometers. There is little doubt that an individual wolf retains an excellent mental map of its territory, and the problem faced by a primate attempting a comparable life would very likely begin with the methods for constructing a useful cognitive map to navigate its extended range. I would argue that primates accomplished this without the olfactory and scentmaking skills by adaptations of their auditory and vocal systems for analogous functions. The internal portions of the olfactory system, the existing smell-brain or rhinencephalon, would also participate in the neural adaptation.

In short, I imagine the early primates as "marking" their territory with sounds, recording the auditory label of the sounds, talking to themselves, as it were, about where they were in space and where their positions were relative to other marked positions in space. This speech would be elementary, of course, prelinguistic or protolanguage at best. But it is in this kind of adaptation that I would seek the eventual adaptation that we know as language.

Many puzzles fall into place if we adopt this view. Living languages are tools for communication, but peculiar tools for living animals. For one thing, they are severely hampered by the requirement that they be learned through an elaborate cultural ritual. Strangely (in terms of newer developments in the neurosciences), the learning of language is more like the learning of sensory-perceptual abilities than of communicational abilities, at least in the perspective of general biology. Most animals communicate fairly instinctively with one another with only rare instances of major constraints imposed by early environments. But they must be exposed to normal environments for their sensory systems to develop normally. Another feature of human language is its function as a kind of representation of reality rather than as a method of commanding or eliciting actions from others. It is a cognitive rather communicational domain. Further, human language is controlled by extensive neocortical networks in the brain, as opposed to the paleocortical and subcortical systems that appear to be most relevant for the analysis of the control of communication in other species. Finally, there are important cognitive functions for paleocortical systems, including the involvement of the limbic system in language and of the hippocampus in memory.

The peculiar element in the human construction of reality is the place of language in that construction. Recognizing consciousness as the labelling of reality, the important place of language in our reality must have immediate consequences. Linguistic labels are themselves representations of things, hence their use as a part of reality makes the representational activity, the second-order "object," a part of our reality. To see a table and the word, "table," and to recognize the differences and associations of these "events" in our reality makes our reality representational as well as a world of immediate experience with object. Words (their sounds, appearances, etc.) are as real as the things they represent, and to encompass both realities in our reality certain reflexive features are inevitable. The words about our selves, our bodies, and perhaps most important, our thoughts and memories, are also elements of the reality. (We may not require actual words—brain processes of a comparable sort in the deaf or blind must still occur and contribute to the chunks that become objects and things in our individual real worlds.)

It is evident to me that the evolution of human consciousness must be related first to the evolution of hierarchical structures in the brain's analytic machinery. That aspect of consciousness must be shared with many other species of animals that have even moderately large brains. As processing capacity increased, either through encephalization or the increases in body size, more and different kinds of chunking must have occurred. The peculiar features of human consciousness: self-consciousness, reflexive events or knowing that we know and that others know, must be related to special constructions, special kinds of chunks, in human brains. Given the representational activity of language systems of the brain it seems evident that all of these "higher order" conscious activities would have to follow. They are not so much higher order as specialized and different orders of conscious activity, but like other adaptations of essentially familiar systems (chunking and hierarchically organized systems in this case) their ultimate effects may be difficult to predict or understand. The dominant place of *Homo sapiens* in the present world of nature is an outcome of this adaptation, applied in new ways and thus creating a new environmental niche within which we live our lives.

17.

Was Darwin Conscious Of His Mother?[1]

Diane McGuinness

Darwin and His Descendants

In the *Descent of Man* Darwin sets out the major distinctions between ape and man.[2] For the majority of these distinctions, bipedalism, development of tools, increased intelligence, and social behavior, etc., Darwin attributes the selection process solely to hunting and warfare, going so far as to conclude that benevolence and empathy are a direct result of male cooperation during war.

Continued speculation about factors leading to human evolution has not changed since Darwin. Washburn and C. Lancaster derive their theory on sharing from the hunt.[3] Shepher, writing in 1978 in *The Journal of Social and Biological Structures*, concludes after reviewing many theories that the evolution of pair-bonding derived from the transition to hunting.[4] This in turn led to larger brains, a consequence of tool-making, (causing larger skulls) earlier parturition, wider hips and long lactation, sexual specialization, and less muscular, more cuddly females!

Apart from one or two authors, such as J. Lancaster and Morgan, evolutionary theorists seem convinced that male specific behavior provides the only relevant clues to man's evolutionary descent. Because of this onesidedness the theories are remarkably contrived and unconvincing. To remedy this state of affairs I wish to explore the possibility of developing a model based largely on female-specific behaviors.

The truth is no doubt somewhere in between, but as will be seen, natural selection based upon female aptitudes gets us considerably further from the apes than selection based exclusively on male aptitudes. This approach also has merit from a genetic point of view. Females have two X chromosomes. Genetic information from *either* chromosome can be passed on to offspring of both sexes. Information from the male Y chromosome, however, can only go to one sex. No information about Y chromosomes is ever passed on to females. Thus, females maintain the dominant gene pool, sharing their *female* characteristics with both sons and daughters. As will be seen, this genetic arrangement is a direct parallel of behavioral distinctions.

The Puzzle of the Enlarging Brain

The major dilemma in the attempt to understand man's origins is related to *why* and *how* the brain began to change in size so dramatically. Man's nearest genetic relative, the chimpanzee, has a body weight of 45 kilograms and a brain size of approximately 400cm^3. This is a ratio of 1 kg to 8.75 cm^3. Homo sapiens' body weight/brain size ratio is 1 kg to 22 cm^3 (57 kg to 1230 cm^3). The most important clues to the nature of this transition lie not only in the difference in mass of tissue, but in specific areas of development. The most prominent distinction is found in the fourfold increase in the size of the cerebral mantle. Both posterior and frontal cortical areas are grossly enlarged, and in humans the left hemisphere is larger than the right. This difference between the hemispheres is not found in the apes.

Bipedalism and use of tools, long considered to be fundamental antecedents of the changing brain, have largely been ruled out as salient contributors to man's evolution. Bipedalism and tool use occurred long before the radical change in brain size. Observations from Darwin's period to current studies by Goodall show that apes frequently use tools for a number of purposes.[7] The discovery of a "home-base" for primitive man prompted a theory which suggested that we evolved *because* of discovering how to stay in one place and share food instead of foraging. However, the establishment of home bases has been shown to precede the change in the size of the brain. Bones, stone artifacts and crude tools have been found in small contained sites estimated as well over two and one-half million years old.

Nor is hunting the answer. Apes occasionally "go hunting" if they accidentally come across game while foraging. They will grab whatever weapons are available in the form of branches, stones, etc., and attack the animal and consume it on the spot with enormous excitement, agitation and vocalizations. A number of lower mammals hunt successfully without the need for large brains.

Despite the legend of man-the-hunter handing down his genes to his sons and thus passing on skill in aimed throwing, there is simply no evidence to support this notion as a model for evolution. Hunting was and is a sporadic endeavor. Apes throw quite well. Wolves hunt in packs, cooperatively, without the need for language that some have proposed derived from hunting expeditions. In fact, studies have shown that *silence*, not speech, is essential to the successful hunt.

Washburn and C. Lancaster, in an intriguing hypothesis, proposed the theory that *sharing* became important because of geographical and climatic factors. They interpreted this insight, however, in a straight Darwinian tradition. Sharing is presumed to be derived from *hunting*;[8] though there is little logic in this assumption. In most hunter-gatherer societies the majority of food is obtained through gathering. In modern day hunter-gatherer tribes, gathering is the primary source of food. The gatherers, Bushman women, living in desert conditions, will walk up to 10–15 miles a day in search of small plants and insects, carrying them back to the home base. Because of the difficulties with this hypothesis, J.B. Lancaster proposed that *gathering, carrying* and *sharing* are the critical factors in our evolution.[9] She suggests that sharing began as a cooperative endeavor by females. One of the most elementary distinctions between apes and men is not the proclivity for hunting, but the fact that apes are hairy and we are not. Young apes are transported by clinging to their mother's fur. Human mothers, being hairless, have to *carry* their infants. Whatever clues may be found to solve the riddle of our hairlessness, the fact remains that human beings carry their children, and this has a multitude of consequences. The propensity for carrying is available even in monkeys through ventral-ventral contact between mother and infant. In studies on Rhesus macaques carried out by Gary Mitchell and associates at the University of California at Davis, it was found that pairing infants with males produced bonding largely through play behavior.[10] There was an almost total absence of ventral-ventral contact between infants and their male "mothers."

Here is the hint then, that one of the more radical shifts in evolution may have had something to do with the female: her need to carry her child, the reliance of the tribe or troupe on her skills in gathering food, and her ability to share in both the gathering and the distribution of food. The bones of a theory proposing that evolutionary changes leading to Homo sapiens was produced somehow through selection of female specific behaviors is given more flesh when considering the differences between apes and men.

Differences That Make a Difference

There are four primary differences between humans and the apes, all of which combine to produce the elements and artifacts of human culture. As will be seen subsequently, all of these differences are female-specific aptitudes. The first is language, the second a vastly superior memory and the third, self-awareness, or context dependent behavior. The final difference is a vast superiority in sequencing fine-motor behavior. In almost all other respects involving the sensitivities of sensory systems, strength, agility and so forth, apes and men are remarkably similar. As each of these differences reflects a refinement of an aptitude, not merely the possession of that aptitude, they rely on changes in *cortical* tissue.

Apes, of course, do share all of these abilities but to an exceedingly lower degree. The pioneering studies of the Gardners and those of David Premack have illustrated that chimpanzees are able to master certain aspects of language using signs or tokens, specifically nominalization and a rudimentary form of sequencing signs and symbols.[11],[12] The Gardner's chimp, Washoe, has subsequently invented "words" by combining two signs into a novel relationship. There is considerable debate, however, that the ape's capacity for language contains an ability to master syntax and any grammar with semantic connotations. No ape has ever been taught to utter human sounds beyond a few words, suggesting that the brain region governing the fine motor –control for the vocal apparatus is undeveloped. Fine-motor control of all types is noticeably lacking.

Apes must remember in order to master language, but their memory span is short. Immediate memory involving the processing of a number of items at one time is directly related to span of attention. Maintaining items in awareness, or paying attention

involves the ability to remain undistracted by irrelevant information. The outcome of processing efficiency is a more stable and
functional use of coding strategies and hence retrieval from a
permanent memory store. As noted above, apes use objects as
tools, but generally discard them when they have obtained their
goal. Remembering specific objects and noting their permanence
is essential to the development of an understanding of object
relationships in the physical world. It leads ultimately to a sense
of time and place. A highly developed memory for time and place
is essential to a species who searches for specific foods at specific
seasons and can bring food back from remote locations to a home
base.

The remaining psychological distinction is the human's capacity for self-awareness or the ability to view the self in the context of
others. Self-awareness or self-consciousness therefore leads to
context—sensitive behavior, specifically to the ability to imagine
oneself in situations or states observed in others. This is the
beginning of empathetic understanding, the beginning of rule
governed behavior, and of values. It is the preliminary requirement for *sharing*. The implications of this form of consciousness
will be considered later in this paper.

Female Influence on Evolution

Current data reveal that almost all of the abilities outlined above
are female specific aptitudes.[13] One, female ability in language
skills of all types is well documented. Females speak earlier, use
longer words and more words per utterance than males, and this
facility continues into adulthood. Two, females also have superior
memories for both visual and auditory information. Three, females are context sensitive. They analyze information *in the
context* of each specific situation (one of the reasons, perhaps,
that women are always accused of changing their minds). This is
particularly relevant in social settings where female empathy has
been documented at all ages. Four, females are fine-motor special-
ists, particularly for rapid sequencing of movement, and show
fewer deficiencies than males in all forms of speech production,
including less stuttering or inability to pronounce certain combinations of sounds.

Not only are these sex differences found in humans, but the
seeds of these differences exist in all non-human primate species.

It may not only be because of female apes having a more docile nature that most "talking" apes are female. Patterson reports that by age 5½ Koko had acquired 450 signs. Her playmate Michael, at the same age, signed only 35.[15]. Female non-human primates are more socially oriented, more empathetic and emit vocalizations that are more often used to signal contact or to calm other troupe members. Male vocalizations are almost all antagonistic, accompanying gestures of threat. Females in most non-human primate species do the major portion of grooming, and in some species are the only groomers. Primatologists have suggested that the presence of grooming is the major indicator that a socially cohesive group exists.

In hard times the non-human primate female preserves and protects her young; the male preserves himself. The skill needed to care for others and maintain life becomes essential to a social unit. Foraging for oneself does not support a social system. In terrestrial primate colonies, once the males are old enough, they are pushed out by their mothers and find themselves on the periphery of the colony. Females and their daughters remain on the inside of the colony. This arrangement works well when all that is required is a loose arrangement to protect a large territorial domain. In a situation where sharing becomes the means of survival and cooperative behavior is essential, the food supply would inevitably be controlled by the females. The female would thus determine who survived and who did not. Infants of clever females adept at cooperative endeavors, aided by some form of gesture, or rudimentary speech, with excellent memories for place (the source of the food supply) and time (knowledge of seasons) would be the successful mothers. Sons of these mothers would survive. Sons of mothers who were inept, uncooperative and lazy would, along with their mothers, be driven out or starve.

Ultimately a type of cooperative interaction between the sexes would arise, with males maintaining and patrolling the territory, attempting to bring in food from hunting, and females providing the major sustenance within it. It is possible that the initial cooperation between the sexes came about through mother-son interactions, and only subsequently through unrelated male-female pairs. Though the division of labor with specialist functions for each sex is already present in non-human primate colonies (even pair bonding is observed in species like the Gibbon), what is lacking is sharing the food supply. Those primitive peoples more able to share and cooperate, more able to value skills which could maintain a troupe, and more able to specialize in order not to waste energy, would become the most effective species.

A New Male: A Conflict of Empathy and Territoriality

Cooperation, awareness of self in the context of others, extended memory, the evolution of language to establish an effective means of organizing work parties, monitoring the young, sharing out food by learning to count—all have implications for male behavior. The genes that effective mothers pass on to their sons cause behaviors that become integrated with male-specific activities. Two of these male activities are rituals of dominance and the manipulation and construction of tools and weapons. In some ways these are related. Darwin was the first to propose that the drastic change in the shape of the adult human skull, with its small jaw and teeth, came about through the invention of weaponry. Weaponry obviates the need for what Washburn C. Lancaster have described as the "anatomy of bluff." Like Darwin, they were puzzled by the presence of huge teeth in male but not female apes.[16] Apes are largely vegetarian, and females are as well nourished as males. Large incisors appeared to have no function.

The anatomy of bluff involves muscle mass and size as well as a number of specific muscle groups around the face and skull, permitting certain facial gestures of threat that function to promote dominance. Although intra-species aggression is exclusively male (Moyer calls this inter-male aggression),[17] females do have a function in establishing male dominance positions. Evidence from observations of a colony of Rhesus macaques in Oregon, shows that dominant males tend to be the sons of dominant females. The form dominance takes in the females is the observed ability to stand up for her young against threat from other mothers and juveniles. Confidence, it appears, is part of the dominance game.

With the discovery that weapons can function to promote dominance, males skilled in the manufacture and wielding of weapons would predominate and contribute to the gene pool. In times of hardship and danger, a cooperative use of weapons becomes useful and necessary. Weapons are used in hunting and in fending off invaders. Cooperative hunting with weapons and cooperative warfare or defense against attack requires *planning*. Skill in strategic warfare involves the same brain system, namely the frontal lobes, that cooperative, context-sensitive behavior involves. Thus the female capacity for cooperation and planning, passed on to her sons, combines with strength, agility, dominance, manufacture of weapons—all male specific aptitudes.

In advanced civilizations these skills and abilities have increased enormously. Yet we still find a continual shift between the female principle and the male principle—communal life, respect for other's needs and empathy, vie with territoriality, dominance and power and an emphasis on the individual emerging from the ranks through competition. How then does this interplay emerge in human consciousness?

The Evolution of Self-Consciousness

Consciousness, the ability to pay attention, to be aware of one's surroundings, is a characteristic of all mammals. What is open to debate is whether or not other species besides the great apes and man have achieved self-consciousness. The classic test of self-consciousness has been the ability to recognize one's self in a mirror. Dogs and cats do not appear to do this. Yet social animals like dogs and wolves work cooperatively and appear to distinguish self from other. Domesticated dogs respond to human demands by signalling what appears to be similar to a sense of guilt following a misdemeanor. A dog is aware that *he* and not another has produced an unacceptable act. Thus it seems that all social animals may possess some rudimentary form of self-consciousness.

What then is unique to man? And how seriously should one consider the assumption raised by Julian Jaynes that self-consciousness only arose when man could distinguish his thoughts from the voices of Gods?[18]

It is my contention that human self-consciousness has taken two forms. One form has its roots in cooperative endeavors characteristic of all social mammals. It goes beyond this in the heightened awareness of context dependent behavior. Situational factors govern what is appropriate and what is not. Context-dependent sensitivity predicated on social systems leads to an ever increasing refinement in the ability to read social signals, to interpret acts, to assist another and to exhibit empathy. As noted above, the ability to share, to take turns, to determine what is *fair*, stem from female-specific aptitudes. The rudiments of these skills are found in all non-human primates in the act of grooming.

Once language is achieved, self-consciousness becomes a dominating force. First, it allows one to distinguish verbally between self and other. Secondly, language provides a new domain for thought, the domain of pragmatics. Whereas semantics and syntax involve cues and rules for establishing the meaning of objects and events, pragmatics enable one to determine *intent*. In recent research on mother-infant interactions, Bruner and his colleagues have discovered that a primary focus for training an infant's speech is forcing the child to specify intent. The mother responds to a request by an attempt to determine its sincerity.

> Requesting requires an indication that you want *something* and *what* it is you want. In the earliest procedures used by children it is difficult to separate the two. First the child vocalizes with a characteristic intonation pattern while reaching eagerly for the desired nearby object—which is most often held by the mother. As in virtually all early exchanges, it is the mother's task to interpret, and she works at it in a surprisingly subtle way. During our analysis of Richard when he was from 10 to 24 months old and Jonathan when he was 11 to 18 months old, we noticed that their mothers frequently seemed to be teasing them or withholding obviously desired objects. Closer inspection indicated that it was not teasing at all. They were trying to establish whether the infants really wanted what they were reaching for, urging them to make their intentions clearer.
>
> When the two children requested nearby objects, the mothers were more likely to ask "Do you really want it?" than "Do you want the X?" The mother's first step is pragmatic, to establish the sincerity of the child's request.[19]

Note that this joint activity is carried out between *mothers* and their children, not by fathers. In fact, McGlaughlin has shown in studies on game playing employing mother-child and father-child interactions, that only mothers attempt to determine the exact level of understanding of their child.[20] This tuning process by the mother shows clearly her empathetic aptitude and her insistence that the child become aware of the nature of his/her endeavors and goals. The child becomes self-aware, *self-conscious*, through the verbal interchange of specifying intent in the context of the situation. Context sensitivity arises from a female specific ability to force linguistic competence and precision on her offspring.

The second form of consciousness is referred to by Jaynes in *The Origin of Consciousness in the Breakdown of the Bicameral Mind.* Whether or not one accepts Jaynes' view that early man was unable to distinguish his own ideas and thoughts from the "voices" of the Gods, Jaynes has documented a radical shift in consciousness during the period of the early Greeks. This shift is a shift towards individualization, and I contend that it is a shift toward a male self-consciousness. It is no accident that this period saw the beginning of monotheistic religions and the birth of a new belief in the power of the individual. The concept of self *against* the others, self as unique, apart from nature and capable of controlling nature, is the beginning of man's conquest of his environment. Man *against* the world, *against* the universe, is an extension of the principle of dominance and it marks a crucial turning point in our cultural evolution. Primitive tribes consider they are part of the natural world, brothers of the animals and trees. Once one recognizes that one can take charge of nature, determine its structure and change its face, one begins the long road to scientific discovery, technology and mastery of the secrets of the universe. Consciousness of the self as *unique*, rather than merely as other, is a male consciousness and is a powerful force for change.

The ultimate question then is what *value* do we put on male and female forms of consciousness and how can these forms be brought into harmony?

Notes

1. This paper was originally presented at ICUS, 1977.
2. C. Darwin, *The Descent of Man* (London: John Murray, 1871).
3. S.L. Washburn and C.S. Lancaster, "The Evolution of Hunting." In: R.B. Lee and I. De Vors, eds. *Man and Hunter* (Chicago: Aldine, 1968). "The Evolution of Man." *Scientific American*, 1978, 239, Sept. p. 194.
4. J. Shepher 1978. "Reflections on the Origin of the Human Pairbond." *Journal of Social and Biological Structures*, 1, pp. 253–64.
5. J.B. Lancaster, *Primate Behavior and the Emergence of Human Culture* (New York: Holt, Rinehart & Winston, 1975). "Carrying the Sharing in Human Evolution." *Human Nature*, 1978, 1, February.
6. E. Morgan, *The Descent of Woman* (New York: Stein and Day, 1972).
7. J. Goodall, "Continuities Between Chimpanzees and Human Behav-

ior." In: G. Isaac and E. McCown, eds. *Human Origins: Louis Leakey and the East African Experience* (New York: W. A. Benjamin, Inc., 1976) p. 483.

8. S.L. Washburn and C.S. Lancaster, "The Evolution of Hunting." In: R.B. Lee and I. De Vors, eds. *Man and Hunter* (Chicago: Aldine, 1968).

9. J.B. Lancaster, *Primate Behavior and the Emergence of Human Culture* (New York: Holt, Rinehart & Winston, 1975). "Carrying the Share in Human Evolution." *Human Nature*, 1978, 1, February.

10. G. Mitchell, "Parental Behavior in Non-human Primates." In: J. Money and H. Musaph, eds. *Handbook of Sexology* (Amsterdam: Elsevier, 1977).

11. R.A. Gardner and B.T. Gardner 1975. "Early Signs of Language in Child and Chimpanzee." *Science*, 187 (4178), pp. 752–53.

12. D. Premack 1970. "The Education of Sarah: A Chimp Learns the Language." *Psychology Today*, 4, pp. 55–8.

13. D. McGuinness, "Sex Differences in Perception and Cognition. In: B. Lloyd and J. Archer, eds. *Exploring Sex Differences* (New York: Academic Press, 1976). K.H. Pribram, "The Origins of Sensory Bias in the Development of Gender Differences in Perception and Cognition." In: M. Bortner, ed. *Cognitive Growth and Development: Essays in Memory of Herbert G. Birch* (New York: Brunner/Mazel, 1978).

14. F. Patterson 1978. "Conversations with a Gorilla." *National Geographic*, 154, October, p. 438.

15. E.A. Missakian 1973. "The Timing of Fission Among Free Ranging Rhesus Monkeys." *American Journal of Physical Anthropology*, 38, pp. 621–24.

16. S.L. Washburn and C.S. Lancaster 1978. "The Evolution of Man." *Scientific American*, 239, p. 194.

17. K.E. Moyer, *The Psychobiology of Aggression* (New York: Harper & Row, 1976).

18. J. Jaynes, *The Origin of Consciousness in the Breakdown of the Bicameral Mind* (Boston: Houghton-Mifflin, Inc., 1977).

19. J.S. Brunner 1978. "Learning the Mother Tongue." *Human Nature*, 1, pp. 42–9.

20. B. McGlaughlin, C. Schultz, and D. White, 1980. "Parental Speech to Five-Year-Old Children in a Gameplaying Situation." *Child Development*, 51, pp.580-82.

18.

Human Evolution: His and Hers

R.W. Wescott

Before dealing with the broader question raised by Dr. McGuinness—that of the male and female components in our developing human consciousness—I should like to deal first with the narrower one: that of Charles Darwin's awareness of his mother, Josiah Wedgwood's daughter Susannah, who died when Darwin was 8 years old. Darwin had, in fact, so little memory of her that he did not even mention her in his autobiography.[1] For some years before her death, Susannah Darwin had been an invalid. Her son's mental avoidance of her may have represented an effort on his part to reject illness as a lifestyle. If so, the effort clearly backfired, since he spent much of his adult life housebound by ill health of obscure origin. A Freudian would no doubt label Darwin's chronic indisposition psychogenic and attribute it to the unconscious guilt he felt over his unfilial behavior.

In a larger sense, Darwin may have been representative of the attitude of scientists toward women. Since most scientists were —and still are—men, a predictable element of androcentricity has crept into their thinking about most subjects susceptible to sexual bias. Certainly human evolution is one such subject. Because men have historically been the leaders in the conversion of horticultural society into urban society, our behavioral scientists too readily assume that males have guided females into each new phase of their joint evolution. We know, however, that male initiative has not inevitably characterized our simian cousins in times of collective behavioral reorientation. Among Japanese macaque monkeys, for example, it is juvenile females who have recently pioneered in the introduction of both food-washing and hot-spring bathing to the behavioral repertory of their troops.[2]

It may be, then, that some of the puzzles of human evolution can be better solved by positing female leadership at certain stages in our collective development than by clinging to the habitual assumption that males introduced every major change which our lineage has undergone. A case in point is what Dr. McGuinness calls "the riddle of our hairlessness," which the conventional wisdom, as represented by Sherwood Washburn, explains as an adaptation to the male hominid's new Pleistocene career as a pack-hunter.[3] Washburn's reasoning is that we lost our ape-fur because it impeded rapid heat-dissipation in the long-distance chase. The difficulty with this argument is that it is directly contravened by another anatomical conundrum—the fact that we, alone among the primates, have a substantial deposit of subcutaneous fat, which acts to retain body heat rather than to facilitate its dissipation!

The resolution of this paradox, which was suggested by Sir Alister Hardy is that the Pliocene hominids, between 3 and 12 million years ago, went through an aquatic stage, in which they lost their fur (as had the dugongs and dolphins) in a way that facilitated swimming, but gained an underskin fat layer (like that of most marine mammals) which protected them from chilling.[4] Elaine Morgan adopted Hardy's thesis and expanded it, explaining our large noses, busts, and buttocks as adaptations to life in shallow water, along with bipedality, a preference for pebble tools, and the practice of ventral coitus.[5]

What Morgan never states explicitly but seems (quite clearly, to me) to imply is that women not only "took the Pliocene plunge" before men but embraced the aquatic life more fully than men, with the result that women even today remain smoother and more streamlined in bodily contours than do their male counterparts.

Well before the Hardy/Morgan Hypothesis was advanced, various theorists, taking note of our exceptionally large brains and gracile bone-structure, had, in effect, defined human beings as fetalized and domesticated apes. If we accept the view of Hardy and Morgan, we may have to expand this definition to describe ourselves, additionally, as aquaticized and feminized apes.

The degree to which wide-spread myths and legends can or

should be correlated with known and inferred paleontological facts remains a question. But, were I to attempt such correlations, I would associate the Garden of Eden tradition with the Miocene Epoch, about 12 to 25 million years ago, when our dryopithecian forebears enjoyed a richly frugivorous forest diet; the matriarchal tradition with the Pliocene Epoch described above, when drought shrank the forests but carnivores made the savannas dangerous, inducing our ramapithecian ancestors to undergo collective baptism; and the Nimrod tradition with the Pleistocene epoch, about 3 million to 10,000 years ago, when glacial and pluvial conditions spawned the large herds of ungulates and proboscideans which made big-game hunting and trapping easy.

There are few of Dr. McGuinness' arguments to which I respond in a sex-stereotyped way. Yet one such is her contention that women are more social than men. I can accept this only if I am permitted to substitute the compound "micro-social," meaning familially social, for the word "social." For I would say that, although women tend to be more empathetic toward members of their immediate kin-groups then men do, men tend to be more responsive toward members of the external community than women do. In this sense, men are, I would say, more "macro-social" than women. Putting the matter differently, we might state that the interpersonal attention which women are inclined to direct toward a small number of close associates, men are inclined to direct toward a larger number of more distant associates. The overall sociability of each sex, though comparable in quantity, would then differ only in focus.

I am inclined, however, to agree wholly with Dr. McGuinness' assertion that "consciousness of the self as unique, rather than merely as other, is a male consciousness and is a powerful force for change." The non-hominid primate precondition for such consciousness may well be the strong tendency for juvenile males, expelled from the troop upon reaching adolescence, to live either in solitude or in "bachelor bands" for a time before finding other troops to attach themselves to at a more adult level. A sense of unique selfhood, on the other hand, is probably not only distinctively human but comparatively recent, dependent on the abandonment, by adherents of the doctrinal religions of the last three millennia, of the totemic view of man as embedded in nature.[6]

Dr. McGuinness' last question—"What value do we put on male

and female forms of consciousness, and how can these forms be brought into harmony?"—is crucial. During the past five millennia, our agricultural, urban, and industrial civilization has evaded this question by taking it for granted that, where male cultural initiative is paramount, male consciousness must also be paramount. Under these circumstances, female consciousness tends to be regarded as constituting, at best, an imperfect approximation of male consciousness. Today, however, when miniaturization and computerization are rendering masculine muscle increasingly superfluous, patriarchal presumptions are increasingly unconvincing. Broadly construed, that "unity of the sciences" to which all of us are committed seems to me to require not only that we relate disparate disciplines to one another but also that we seek to integrate male with female ways of knowing. To do less would be to settle for a monocular view of a world for which we are coming to realize that we need, at the very least, fully stereoscopic vision.

Notes

1. Sir Francis Darwin, *Charles Darwin's Autobiography* (New York: Schumann, 1950).
2. Atsuo Tsumori, "Newly Acquired Behavior and Social Interaction of Japanese Monkeys," in *Social Communication Among Primates*, Stuart A. Altmann, ed. (Chicago, IL: University of Chicago Press, 1967).
3. Sherwood L. Washburn, *Ape into Man* (Boston, MA: Little Brown, 1974).
4. Alister C. Hardy. 1960. "Was Man More Aquatic in the Past?," *The New Scientist*, Vol. 7, pp. 642–5.
5. Elaine Morgan, *The Descent of Woman* (New York: Stein and Day, 1972).
6. Roger Wescott. 1969. "Language, Taboo, and Human Uniqueness," *The Bucknell Review*, Lewisburg, PA, pp. 28–30.

19.
The Mechanism of Knowledge: Limits to Prediction

J.W.S. Pringle

I shall approach the central theme of this paper by means of a diagram (Figure 19-1, solid lines) summarizing some of the intellectual problems that have troubled mankind. There are no doubt many others, but I don't think there will be much doubt that these problems are very much discussed and that they have not been resolved. Thinking men and women everywhere consider and discuss these problems and have done so for a very long time without, in my opinion, making much progress in their understanding.

This word "understanding" seems to me to lie at the root of all the problems. Fourteen years ago, when I was preparing my Inaugural Lecture at Oxford University, it occurred to me that maybe we have been trying to do the wrong thing. That great physical scientist, Sir Arthur Eddington, once wrote that we have no need to define knowledge.[1] I cannot agree. What we are trying to do in all these problems is to establish a state of interrelatedness between our brains, which are the medium for our thinking, and our observation and interpretations of phenomena outside ourselves. So we ought not to be surveying the problems from a pedestal external to them, but ought to take as our material for study the system of ourselves studying and considering things. So Figure 19-1 is completed with the portion drawn with dotted lines, by the insertion of the human brain interacting with the problems. This at once looks more promising, since it becomes obvious that the block to progress may lie in our failure to understand how the human brain works. If we knew how the human brain worked and what was the physiological process that is correlated with our conscious thoughts, then we might be able to judge whether the problems are soluble or not. If they are not then we could stop worrying about them and get on with things that are practicable.

Now I am no more an expert in the functioning of the brain than I am an expert in modern physics or philosophy. I am a zoologist and I suppose that the one field of which I can claim to have some understanding is the process of evolution. My thinking on this subject has developed from considering the process of evolution by natural selection and as this is a rather unusual starting point from which to consider either brain physiology, psychology, modern physics or philosophy, it is just possible that I may have something worthwhile to say.

In 1951, I published a paper with the title "On the parallel between learning and evolution."[2] The argument went as follows. It is common ground among biologists that as organic evolution proceeded, the structure of animals became more complex. What, however, does this mean? If one examines critically the concept of complexity, it is clear that it is a term that can validly be ascribed only to statements about things, not about the things themselves without some further qualification. It certainly appears to be necessary to make more complex statements in order to describe the structure of higher animals than of lower animals, but is there any way in which it can be valid to state that the animals themselves are more complex. I suggested that, in relation to structural complexity, the necessary further condition was that repeated observations should require statements with the same degree of complexity; that is, that the structural features should have some order or permanence in time.

Things that one can describe as structures must have some permanence in time, but this permanence can be a dynamic steady state, as in a lenticular cloud which stays in one place although the wind blows through it. The process of evolution by natural selection preserves thermodynamically improbable states of organization in the molecular complexes of which organisms are composed. The stability derives from the ability of certain

Figure 1

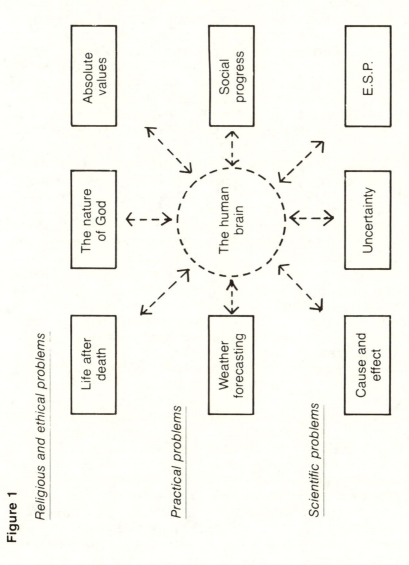

molecular assemblies to replicate: that is, to produce more states of organization like themselves. The whole process of evolution occurs because certain molecular assemblies have this property of replication and because the replication is slightly imperfect. Assemblies which survive longer or which replicate more rapidly under the given conditions are preserved in competition with other assemblies for the available raw materials. This is the process of evolution by natural selection of intrinsically variable replicating molecular assemblies. The most recent semi-popular discussion of the subject is a book by Richard Dawkins entitled, "The Selfish Gene."[3]

Now it appears to students of animal behavior that complexity also increases when the phenomenon of learning takes place in animals. Learning is the modification of behavior which occurs due to events during the lifetime of the animal. All animals possess a behavioral machinery which is part of their genetic inheritance and has been naturally selected with due regard to events happening during the life-times of their ancestors. This is the innate component of behavior which provides the background upon which the learned changes take place. I explored the different manifestations of the process of learning as classified by Thorpe and it became clear that more complex statements were indeed required to describe the final state of affairs than the state before the learning had occurred.

Is it then possible to transfer the concept of complexity from the description of the time pattern of animal behavior to the time pattern itself? Not, obviously, by using the same criterion of permanence in time, because a time pattern is what is being described. I suggested that the criterion to adopt is permanence in space; that is, that simultaneous observations in different places should yield descriptions with the same measure of temporal complexity.

I then tried to see if one could find a type of process which would show an "evolution" of time patterns with the same characteristics as organic evolution except that the parameters of space and time were interchanged. It was necessary that the process should show the essential features of natural selection of intrinsically variable replicating phenomena; otherwise it would not evolve. The simplest time pattern is a sinusoidal oscillation, which has only one frequency component. Loosely coupled sinusoidal oscillators have a tendency to lock to the same frequency if their natural frequencies of oscillation are sufficiently close together. The interaction is, however, symmetrical and this is not a satisfactory model since there is nothing in the nature of selection, that requires some asymmetry. The genes which survive in a population are those that have better means of propagating themselves than do other genes. If, however, the oscillations are non-linear, then when they lock in frequency the interactions are asymmetrical (Figure 19-2). An oscillator O_1 whose natural frequency is swept through the natural frequency of oscillator O_2 has more effect on the frequency of O_2 if its own natural frequency is increasing than if it is decreasing; its own oscillation frequency is displaced less when its natural frequency is increasing than when it is decreasing. The effect is particularly obvious in the case of relaxation oscillators, which are extremely non-linear. If now one adds the further postulate that, when an oscillator has been forced through the synchronization process to oscillate at a frequency different from its natural frequency, its natural frequency is changed in the same direction, then there is a "replication" of a time pattern. In a population of such oscillators, those that sweep through another frequency in the upward direction will gradually "capture" those through whose natural frequencies they sweep and there will subsequently be more oscillators in the population with that natural frequency. The total population with a particular time pattern has replicated in the space occupied by the population.

This looked promising and I therefore went on to two further discussions. First, to what extent could the detailed features of the learning process in animals be explainable on the basis of a model in which the information was contained entirely as time patterns? I showed that all the five forms of the learning process described by Thorpe could, indeed, be modelled in this way and that, for example, the particular relationships between stimuli found experimentally in conditioned reflexes would be expected in the models. Secondly, I considered whether there was any evidence for self-sustaining oscillators in those parts of the brain where it is thought that the learning process takes place, and what was the most plausible neural mechanism of such oscillators. Since much more evidence is available now than was available in 1951, I will expand this part of the argument.

Much of the literature on this subject does not use the language of the animal behaviorist who talks about learning, but refers to

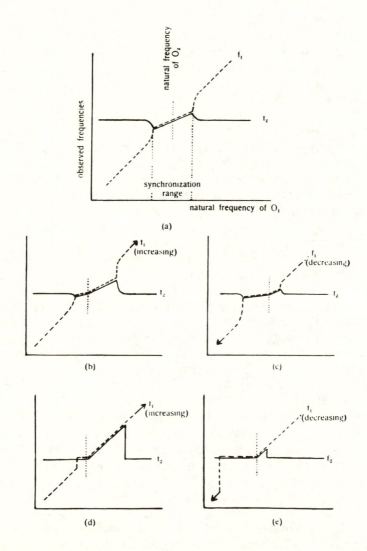

Figure 19-2: Diagrams, based on experiments with electronic oscillators, to illustrate the phenomenon of synchronization. The graphs show the observed frequencies f_1 and f_2 of two coupled oscillators. O_1 and O_2 as the natural frequency of O_1 is varied.

a) Linear oscillation

b) Non-linear oscillation: frequency of O_1 increasing.

c) Non-linear oscillation: frequency of O_1 decreasing.

d) Relaxation oscillation: frequency of O_1 increasing.

e) Relaxation oscillation: frequency of O_1 decreasing.

memory. This is the same thing, since when behavior depends on the previous experience of the animal, it can be considered to have acquired a memory of the previous events. The most important type of evidence that memory must involve time patterns is that it is not localized in space, although this is not usually explicitly recognized. Professor Eccles summarized one of his contributions to a symposium as follows, "We may summarize this discussion of the structural basis of memory by stating that memory of any particular event is dependent on a specific reorganization of neuronal associations (the engram) in a vast system of neurons widely spread over the cerebral cortex. Lashley has convincingly argued that the activity of literally millions of neurons is involved in the recall of any memory. His experimental study of the effects of cortical lesions on memory indicates that any particular memory trace or engram has multiple representation in the cortex. Furthermore, Lashley concludes that any cortical neuron does not exclusively belong to one engram, but on the contrary, each neuron and even each synaptic junction would be built into many engrams. We have already seen that the systematic study of the responses of individual neurons in the cortex and in the subcortical nuclei is providing many examples of this multiple operation."[4]

In the input channel for information from sense organs, there clearly is spatial localization. Each sensory nerve carries information about one sensory quality. Similarly in the output channels, each motor nerve fibre carries the commands to a particular muscle. But as physiologists study the ascending nervous pathways through which information passes on its way from the sense organs to the cerebral cortex, the localization gets less and less precise at each synaptic layer, so that finally a very large number of cortical neurons are influenced by a message in any given sensory channel. Again on the output side, the further back one goes in the motor pathways, the more does any local excitation produce output in several muscles. There are large areas in the human cerebral cortex called by Penfield "the uncommitted cortex" which have no function that can be defined in terms of localized effects. Yet the information is not lost in this whole process. The logical conclusion is surely that the information is being transformed into some other form, such as a pattern in time rather than in space, and back into spatial patterns on the way out again. Eccles talks about "spatio-temporal patterns" being important; I suggest that one should leave out the "spatio-" altogether.

Experimental evidence about the nature of spontaneous oscillatory activity in cortical neurons is intrinsically difficult to obtain, because of the fact that any recording system must be spatially localized. The electroencephalogram is the record of electrical activity as recorded with electrodes placed externally on different parts of the head; this does indeed show spontaneous oscillations which have been much studied in an attempt to correlate particular frequency components with states of cerebral activity as described subjectively or observed behaviorally. The fact that anything at all can be recorded with superficial electrodes from a brain containing about 10^9 neurons implies that a great deal of synchronization must be taking place. Records using microscopic electrodes inside individual cortical neurons are dominated by the discrete impulses which are the way in which information is transmitted without loss down the long axon connections between cells some distance apart and are not the components contributed by each cell to the overall electroencephalogram. The individual component potentials are very small continuous fluctuations in membrane potential which are so small that they are almost undetectable against the noise background of the recording apparatus. So with our present techniques it is probably impossible to determine the exact nature of the oscillators whose frequency of activity may be carrying the information at the time when it is subject to the analytical processes involved in learning phenomena, particularly as, if there is indeed no significant spatial localization, the particular structures which are manifesting the significant frequencies of oscillation may be changing from instant to instant. Waves of electrical activity at a particular frequency do pass over the surface of the cortex.

I suggested in 1951 that the unit of rhythmic activity consists of a closed loop of neurons which oscillates because of a small amplification and phase shift introduced by each neuron. Since each cell in the cortex has synaptic connections to a large number of other cells, the spatial localization of such a loop oscillator will be extremely plastic, depending on the amplification and phase shifts of every cell in the network. One cell can be a component part of more than one oscillating loop at the same time, providing the means for coupling between them. The change demanded by my model when a neuronal loop has been forced to oscillate at a frequency other than its natural frequency, by synchronization to a driving oscillator, is a small change in the amplification or phase shift contributed by the cells. There is no need to postulate any change in the pattern of connectivity between cells and the model is therefore different in essentials from all models of memory which involve synaptic growth or regression. I have been surprised at the way in which neurophysiologists seem to take it almost as an axiom that memory must necessarily involve a change in synaptic connections in the central nervous system. A model in which the information is represented as a complex of time pattern with no spatial localization makes this assumption unnecessary.

I just do not know how to proceed to test further the value of a model of this sort and it is in the hope of obtaining some suggestions and help that I have described the model rather fully. Dr. Brian Goodwin, who has considered oscillating systems in the biochemical machinery of cells, has suggested that it may be possible to develop a sort of statistical mechanics of interacting oscillators and he has even defined macroscopic parameters of such a system which bear some similarity to the parameters of temperature and free energy of classical statistical mechanics, coining for them the adjective *"talandic"* from the Greek world for oscillation.[5] This sort of thing is well beyond my capacity.

Consciousness

The earlier part of this paper restates in outline a hypothesis about the physiological mechanism by which the associative processes of the central nervous system take place and locates the memory trace within a large number of neurons instead of in the synaptic connections between them. In the rest of the paper I shall make some highly speculative suggestions which depend on the general correctness of the hypothesis. If the hypothesis is false, these suggestions have no value; if it is correct, they constitute a possible way of making progress with several problems which have hitherto defied scientific analysis. The first of these problems is the nature of consciousness.

Professor Penfield, as a result of his experience as a surgeon operating on the brains of conscious patients, has written "Consciousness is not something to be localized in space. Nevertheless, if we assume that it is a function of the integrated action of the brain, there is placed before us a challenging problem of physiological localization."[6] Penfield is unable to escape from the assumption that some form of localization must be necessary and is driven to involve a sub-cortical region of the brain. I would like to make a concrete suggestion, which cannot be more than a speculation but which might be testable. It is that consciousness occurs when complex time patterns spread over a sufficiently large region of space. The physiological correlate of consciousness does not need to be localized at all, since the information which a conscious thought contains is represented in the brain as a time pattern. The clarity and preciseness of the conscious thought could correlate with the extent of spatial spread of the time pattern, and "vague" or imprecise thoughts—half-thoughts —could correlate with time patterns which do not have a large enough spatial spread.

Now it is sometimes suggested that only half of the human cerebral cortex containing the speech center, normally the left side, is capable of conscious thought. Normally the two sides of the cortex are extensively connected together by nervous tracts so that the whole functions as a single unit, but in patients in whom these tracts have been severed, Sperry in particular has described how the patient is only able to describe objects presented in the half of the visual field which projects on to the left cortex.[7] Correct motor movements can be made in response to stimuli presented to the other half of the visual field and these may depend on previous experience, but the patient is not conscious of what he is doing, in the sense that he cannot later describe in words what he has done. Conscious thought need not, however, be accompanied by actual speaking and conscious patients whose speech center is stimulated electrically are still capable of thought although they cannot speak while the electrical stimulation lasts. A thought is clarified and made more precise by describing it in words, but it exists in some form before it is spoken. I know of no better statement of this than a little known poem by an anonymous author that I will quote in full. It was published in 1949 in the Oxford Magazine over the signature "X" and was entitled "Words."

> I lag behind, my words go on before
>   And tell me what I did not know I knew,
> And yet I knew it, but I know it more
>   When I have said it too.

Dark mystery of words that can reveal
  Even to the speaker what were else obscure,
Can on the soul's dim searching set a seal
  And mark them clear and sure.

Deceiving mystery of seal and word:
  The inarticulate escapes them still:
The caged is not the glancing, half-seen bird:
  You have not yet your will,

You must go on to seek the bird you sought,
  Yet count as gain, as gain unpriceable,
This which the mystery of words has caught,
  Which sings, is beautiful.

I leave the subject of consciousness with this suggestion. It is conceivable that the hypothesis might be testable by stimulating the surface of the cortex with a sufficiently complex time pattern, with particular phase relationships between different regions. If there is no spatial localization, it should not matter just where the stimulus is applied, since the information is in the time pattern.

The Evolution of Consciousness

In large parts of the nervous systems of many animals, there is probably complete functional localization, even to the extent found in insects where a single cell always serves one particular function. There is also no reason why the particular mechanism for learning proposed above should be the only mechanism found in the nervous systems of animals. It is only in the vertebrates and especially in the mammals that we have *evidence* of the gradual loss of localization that occurs in ascending pathways. It is by no means unthinkable that this particular method of analyzing sensory information is peculiar to the vertebrates, which show more plasticity of behavior than most invertebrates and rely more on learning during the animal's own lifetime and less on innate patterns of behavior inherited from previous generations. Alternatively, it could be that we do not yet know enough about other types of animals to have found evidence for loss of localization. A corollary of the hypothesis put forward in the previous section would be that only those animals are conscious in which the transformation of spatial information into time patterns proceeds to a sufficient extent. Furthermore, there could be degrees of consciousness depending on the extent to which the time patterns achieve spatial spread. A zoologist does not readily accept the emergence of a new character suddenly in evolution. I myself prefer to think that consciousness evolved gradually and that it developed particularly in man when his vocal apparatus developed to the point where it could be used for symbolic expression. The speech center may be unique in that it is located in the cerebral cortex and provides a direct organizing output for the cortical processes; centers for the group control of other, innate movements are located in evolutionarily lower parts of the brain.

Human evolution is peculiar in that the original process of genetic selection has been largely superseded by cultural selection involving the formulation of ideas in the brain and their replication through the population by means of the spoken and written word. This is a much more rapid process than genetic evolution and it demands that there be a form of natural selection different in essentials from the original one. The natural selection of time patterns in the brain could be such a mechanism and something ought to be discoverable about the operation of the process by adapting the knowledge that we have of the dynamics of natural selection.

Emotions

We do not start our thinking lives with an unbiased reasoning machine in our brains. In our adult mental processes as in our adult structural organization, our starting point is the organization that we have inherited in our genetic constitution and in our individual developmental history. In the model that I have suggested, the initial time patterns for any thought, the input channels which determine the conditions in which the temporal selection process takes place and the output channels through which the selected time patterns are re-expressed in spatially localized movements are all part of the given situation for any individual brain. There is, I understand, some evidence that the neural circuits involved in long-term memory are different from those involved in short-term memory and that the establishment of new long-term memories can be prevented by localized lesions without affecting consciousness and short-term memory. Emotional states probably involve the coupling into the cortical circuitry of still more primitive regions of the brain so that the time patterns and the resulting conscious states of mind incorporate other than purely logical determinants.

When we are presented through our sense organs with a situation, we are consciously aware of a mental process that we describe as coming to a conclusion about the action that we will take. We are aware of trying to take into account in arriving at the conclusion, our previous long and short-term memories and our emotions which may introduce bias as between alternatives. What sort of physical processes are involved in this mental process? I suggest that a way of looking at the problem is to treat the sensory input, the memories and the emotional bias as the "environment" within which a process of selection takes place. Coming to a conclusion represents the establishment of a new dynamically stable equilibrium which then determines the output results.[8] In my model the new equilibrium is the new set of time patterns which result from the synchronization process. The more far-reaching is the conclusion, the more have the complex time patterns representing the initial state been resolved into a simpler set of time patterns. Since no new information is generated by this process, the new state of organization is consistent with the original state. I suggest that our mental satisfaction depends on the extent of the process of resolution and that we call this pleasure when the initial state of the "environment" contained a large component from the innately determined input. Certain inputs will be mutually incompatible and no simpler dynamic equilibrium will then result; if the sensory input is incompatible with the innately determined inputs, then the situation is unpleasant, cannot be resolved and is avoided if possible in the future.

I hope that the previous paragraph makes clear the way in which I think some of these problems can be tackled. It is almost impossible to avoid the use of terms whose meaning is incompletely defined and this means that there may be flaws in the logic. If so, I should be glad to have them pointed out. If not, then I hope I have established that concepts derived from the study of natural selection could have value in considering human mental problems.

Uncertainty and Purpose

Our thought processes do not stop when there is not sensory input. Volunteers undergoing prolonged sensory deprivation usually develop, after two or three days, states of extreme mental awareness and their thought processes are liable to become uncontrolled to the point where they become intolerable.

My model leaves room for the possibility that quantum uncertainty can be the "cause" of changes in the time patterns through the ability of the brain mechanism to amplify the effects of thermal fluctuations in individual cells. The possible role of "random" phenomena has been explored by Gomes in the context of the problem of free-will but, as Mackay has shown, it is probably irrelevant to this. What is relevant here is the fact that uncertainty on a micro scale need not lead to macroscopic uncertainty in a mechanism that is dominated by selection. In organic evolution, mutations are random in their occurrence in time but they provide the background against which evolution takes place and, apart from exceptional circumstances, it is the forces of natural selection which determine the direction of evolutionary change. Normally in the brain, the sensory input establishes "environmental" conditions sufficiently precise to ensure that the effect of thermal noise is negligible. Sensory deprivation, however, produces a condition when the state of brain organization can drift, using the term in the same sense as it is used in organic evolution. The fact that the uncontrolled mental states that occur under these conditions are unpleasant suggests that the effect of random drift may then be sufficient to override the innate determinants.

In organic evolution, the negative feedback involved in natural selection can give the impression of purposefulness. Animal communities evolve so as to appear to be "trying" to make the best use of their environment. Purpose in human mental processes could have the same origin and be due to the selection of time patterns that accompanies the reaching of a conclusion or decision. Ethologists call this type of process "insight learning" and speak of it as involving an internal process of trial and error, operating on some formal representation of the external world in the brain of the animal and making it unnecessary to go through an actual process of trial and error by overt behavioral acts, so avoiding the dangers inherent in failure. It is because of the much

248

greater rapidity of the selection of time patterns that this mechanism is superior to other alternatives, making man the dominant form of life on the planet.

Predictability and Understanding

We can now return to the basic thesis of this paper, that many intellectual problems can only be understood on the basis of an interaction between the human brain and the external world (Figure 19-1). Let me deal with practical problems first.

Because the speed of the internal selection mechanism of the brain is so much faster than any process in nature that involves selection, the human brain can hope to make predictions about the future course of events, provided that it can set up within itself a formal representation of all the factors which condition that selection process in the external world. The difficulty arises from the fact that in many such natural situations, there is a near infinity of factors which are capable of influencing the natural selection that occurs, and that some of these factors are themselves the result of a selection process. Drift in an evolutionary development occurs when conditions are such that the intrinsic variability of micro phenomena is magnified to a macroscopic scale without the restraining influence of limiting factors. Ultimately, there is always a limit on the magnification process but if the restraints are reduced, as in organic evolution in the fresh colonization of a new habitat, then drift occurs and the situation is fundamentally unpredictable. It is a moot question whether or not true drift occurs in synoptic meteorology, due to the inherently unstable conditions of atmospheric circulation along the polar front. The exact time and place of formation of an individual cyclonic circulation may be theoretically unpredictable, since even if an exactly similar formal set of conditions was set up in the human brain, the evolutionary development in the two cases might be different. The same may be true of social progress, since here many of the conditions which determine the natural selection are human brains themselves performing "evolutionary" decisions. In such situations, the best that can be hoped for is a statistically probable prediction, but even this may be doubtful, since statistics hold good only for ensembles of similar units. Since in both the examples chosen for Figure 19-1 some of the most important predictions are those relating to a particular time and place, complete predictive certainty may be unattainable.

Rather different considerations apply to the religious and ethical problems of Figure 19-1. Here we are trying to decide the validity and degree of understanding which can be expected of abstract concepts which are themselves the product of our thinking processes. It is worth considering why we establish these concepts in the first place. This can, I think, only be answered in relation to our past evolutionary history as social animals, which has determined the starting organization of the brains which we use for the processes of thought. One can ask the question: what survival value was conferred on man by the selection of a human brain machinery which leads to the formulation of such concepts? This is a problem for social anthropology, but it may be that any mechanism that has evolved with the function of performing insight learning must formulate such concepts when it reaches a certain degree of perfection just because its inherent tendency to try to forecast the future and to make the assumption that all external events have a cause, as a basis for its predictive activities. Our search for absolute values could stem from this feature of the brain mechanism which makes a single concept a more stabled state than a mixture of two concepts; if my model of the brain mechanism is correct, this is ultimately a problem in talandic thermodynamics.

The problem of why we try to perform certain feats of mental analysis is, of course, different from the problems themselves. I suggest that the former is scientifically more interesting; at any rate, to a biologist, it appears to offer more chance of solution, and it is always possible that if and when we know why we try to do certain things it may be easier to do them. I am not myself very hopeful of this, but it is the only suggestion I can offer to the search for absolute values which is the title of this conference.

Coming finally to the scientific problems, the question to be answered is whether our knowledge of the mechanism of the human brain does or does not suggest that we may ultimately be able to understand the phenomena. I think that progress will be made with this only if my model of the functioning of the brain proves to be useful and if someone else thinks it worthwhile to explore more fully some of its implications, particularly from a mathematical standpoint.

Notes

1. A. Eddington, *The Philosophy of Physical Science* (Cambridge: Cambridge University Press, 1949).

2. J.W.S. Pringle 1951. "On the parallel between learning and evolution." *Behaviour*, 3, pp. 173–213.

3. R. Dawkins, *The Selfish Gene* (Oxford: Oxford University Press, 1976).

4. J.C. Eccles, ed. *Brain and Conscious Experience* (Heidelberg, Berlin and New York: Springer International, 1966).

5. B.W. Goodwin, *Temporal Organization of Cells* (New York: Academic Press, 1963).

6. J.C. Eccles, ed. *Brain and Conscious Experience.*

7. J.C. Eccles, ed. *Brain and Conscious Experience.*

8. J.W.S. Pringle, *The Two Biologies* (Oxford: Clarendon Press, 1963, p.26).

Commentary

B.D. Josephson

Professor Pringle has presented us with a fascinating discussion of the possible mechanisms involved in understanding, and of the deeper question of what influences these mechanisms may have on the possibility of our being able to resolve certain long standing and very difficult problems in the future. In my commentary I should like to give first some of my own thoughts on the question of understanding, and then return to discuss Professor Pringle's ideas in detail.

It may be useful for us to divide the process of understanding into two parts, namely the understanding itself and a process which we may call *learning to understand*. Let me illustrate the difference with a particular example, involving students attending a lecture course on quantum mechanics. Someone who knows quantum mechanics can fairly readily follow a derivation such as that of the spectrum of hydrogen. This is an example of what I call the understanding itself. Now before a person can perform this act of understanding he must first of all have grasped certain essential ideas—those special ideas which distinguish quantum mechanics from its predecessor classical mechanics. Such a process of grasping essential ideas may fairly be called learning to understand, since firstly it involves learning and secondly its result is an ability to understand.

The process responsible for the really major advances in science, and the process to which Professor Pringle chiefly addressed himself in his talk, is the one of learning to understand. To give an example, it was the learning and acceptance by scientists of Einstein's concept that space and time are not absolute but depend on the observer that allowed them to develop all the consequences of special relativity: one key idea permitted an enormous number of phenomena to be discovered and understood. The problems to be considered now are, what similar advances may lie ahead in the future, and how (following Professor Pringle's theme) is our ability to make such advances dependent on the way our brains function?

Here is one more point I should like to make before I comment on detailed mechanisms. This is to the effect that both a person's ability to discover a new idea and his ability to understand one are very much affected, often adversely, by his previous prejudices and beliefs. A classic example from the past relates to the law of conservation of parity in physics (the assertion that the laws of nature make no distinction between left and right).

Until about twenty years ago the idea that the laws of nature did not distinguish between left and right was such a firm belief among physicists that it was not considered necessary to test the belief by experiment, while the slight experimental evidence that the symmetry assumptions was not true was disregarded. Eventually certain phenomena caused Yang and Lee to re-examine the situation. They concluded that for certain kinds of process evidence for conservation was lacking. Following this, measurements showed that for these processes the assumption of parity conservation was indeed false. From such examples we can conclude that however much the design of the human nervous system may make possible in principle grand synthesis such as those of quantum theory and relativity, the ability of an individual to make use of such a capability in practice may be reduced considerably by his tendency to adhere quite rigidly to his previously acquired beliefs. I shall return to this problem later.

I should now like to comment on some details of Professor Pringle's discussion of mechanisms of understanding. He described a model involving a system of coupled non-linear oscillators, which had the capacity of undergoing evolution. Such a kind of model is one I find quite attractive, though I do not believe that it is the whole story.

It is important to realize that the process of grasping a new idea, the one I have called learning to understand, consists in fact of two parts, one of discovery and one of memory. Understanding can be regarded as discovering a point of view from which the solution to a problem becomes transparently clear, and the remembering how one came to that viewpoint. Without subsequent acts of memory and reconstructions, many moments of illumination may be experienced to no avail. I would suggest that Pringle's mechanism of coupled oscillating systems or something similar could account for the processes of discovering a new viewpoint and exploring its potentialities, but that long-term storage to make the understanding permanently available is probably due to the conventional mechanisms involving synaptic modification. The latter mechanisms seem to me to be much more suitable for providing the necessary stability of memory.

The detailed working out of Pringle's proposed mechanisms for understanding must doubtless be very complicated. It is possible that the ideas of Prigogine,[1] relating stability in dissipative systems to states of minimum entropy production, may well prove to be the key to understanding what is going on.

I should like to give now some personal opinions on our prospects of understanding the particular problems listed by Pringle (in his Fig. 19-1). I shall leave aside those problems designated as practical problems, since it seems to me that in these cases the difficulties are not primarily those of coming to an understanding. In the other cases, however—the religious, ethical and special scientific problems—I suspect that the prime difficulty is not in the inherent capacity of our brains to solve the problems but in the effects of our previous conditioning. We are in a similar situation to that of those physicists who could not bring themselves to question the assumption that parity in physical processes was conserved.

What are the beliefs that may be holding up understanding in our present situation? I will make two suggestions as to what some of them may be. One, which has relevance concerning the possibility of ESP and other psychic phenomena, is what could be called the myth of the perfect reproductability of natural phenomena. Present scientific method rests on the assumption that one can design experiments such that similar conditions will always produce similar effects. We already know that such an assumption runs into difficulties in the quantum domain; perhaps trying to force such an assumption upon the world at large may be causing us to miss some crucial aspect of reality.

A second possibility limiting belief is the almost universal working rule of scientific workers that no natural phenomena, even those of human behavior or of evolution, should include religious concepts such as the existence of God as a component of their explanation. As far as I am aware, present-day physics does not in any way exclude the possibility of some configuration of matter or energy having the qualities normally ascribed to God, any more than it would exclude the discovery tomorrow of a new kind of charmed particle. It is true that science has not yet found it necessary to postulate the existence of God, but this can reasonably be ascribed to the fact that science has not yet been able to study the situations in which God might be expected to assert an influence with adequate precision.

Finally, I should like to discuss the question of whether there are any specific actions which might be able to allow us to make better use of the problem-solving capability of the brain of man.

Descriptions by creative thinkers have indicated that getting an original idea involves a special state of consciousness, in which the person is aware of the problem to be solved and of that part of his knowledge which pertains to the general nature of the prob-lem, but he has suspended his beliefs or prejudices as to what the solution to the problem might be. It has been suggested that certain techniques such as biofeedback and meditation can enhance the ability to produce such a state. At the moment the situation is not completely clear, but should systematic enhance-ment of creativity prove to be possible to any significant extent, we have in prospect a situation in which original scientific theories may be frequently produced which are not the direct descendants of any previous theories, and enter the minds of their creators simply because they are the correct answers to those problems most in need of solution at that particular time.

Notes

1. P. Glansdorff and I. Prigogione, *Thermodynamic Theory of Structure, Stability and Fluctuations* (New York: Wiley, 1971).

20.

Culture: The Creation of Man and the Creator of Man

Sir John Eccles

Philosophical Introduction—The Three Worlds

Before discussing the brain-mind problem it is essential to give an account of the philosophical position which forms the basis of my discussion. I have written at length on this in my book *Facing Reality*.[1] The philosophy is developed from the fundamental contributions of Sir Karl Popper in defining the three worlds which subsume the whole of reality, in developing their philosophical status and in describing their interaction.[2] Both Sir Karl and I are thus trialists and trialist interactionists. Many examples of the explanatory power of these new concepts follow.

The scope of the three worlds can be seen in the tabular classification of Fig. 20-1, which indicates that Worlds 1, 2 and 3 take care of everything in existence and in experience.

In Fig. 20-1, World 1 is the world of physical objects and states, comprising the whole cosmos of matter and energy, all of biology including human brains, and all artifacts that man has made for coding information, as for example the paper and ink of books or the material base of works of art. World 1 is the total world of the monist materialists. They recognize nothing else. All else is fantasy.

World 2 is the world of states of consciousness and subjective knowledge of all kinds. The totality of our perceptions is found in this world. But there are several levels. In agreement with Polten,[3] I tend to recognize three kinds of levels of World 2, as indicated in Fig. 20-2, but it may be more correct to think of it as a spectrum.

The first level (*outer sense*) would be the ordinary perceptions provided by all our sense organs, hearing, touch, sight, smell,

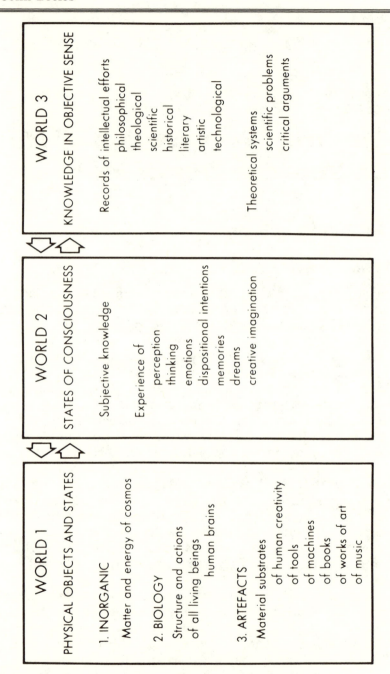

Figure 20-1: Tabular representation of the three worlds that comprise all existents and all experiences as defined by Popper (1970).

and pain. All of these perceptions are in World 2, of course: vision with light and color; sound with music and harmony; touch with all its qualities and vibration; the range of odors and tastes, and so on. These qualities do not exist in World 1, where correspondingly there are but electromagnetic waves, pressure waves in the atmosphere, material objects, and chemical substances.

In addition there is a level of *inner sense*, which is the world of more subtle perceptions. It is the world of emotions, of feelings of joy, sadness, fear, anger, and so on, and includes all memory, and all imaginings and planning into the future. In fact there is a whole range of levels which could be described at length. All the subtle experiences of the human person are in this inner sensory world. While private to the individual, it can be revealed in linguistic expression, and by gestures of all levels of subtlety.

Finally, at the core of World 2 there is the *self* or *pure ego*, which is the basis of our unity as an experiencing being throughout our whole lifetime.

This World 2 is our *primary reality*. Our conscious experiences are the basis of our knowledge of World 1, which is thus a world of *secondary reality*, a derivative world. Whenever I am doing a scientific experiment, for example, I have to plan it cognitively, all in my thoughts, and then consciously carry out my plan of action in the experiment. Finally I have to look at the results and evaluate them in thought. For example, I have to see the traces on the oscilloscope and their photographic records or hear the signals on the loudspeaker. The various signals from the recording equipment have to be received by my sense organs, transmitted to my brain, and so to my consciousness, then appropriately measured and compared before I can begin to think about the significance of the experimental results. We are all the time, in every action we do, incessantly playing backwards and forwards between World 1 and World 2.

And what is World 3? As shown in Fig. 20-1 it is the whole world of culture. It is the theme of this lecture that World 3 was created by man and that reciprocally made man. The whole of language is here. All our means of communication, all our intellectual efforts coded in books, coded in the artistic and technological treasures in the museums, coded in every artistic and technological treasures in the museums, coded in every artifact left by man from

259

primitive times—this is World 3 right up to the present time. It is the world of civilization and culture. Education is the means whereby each human being is brought into relation with World 3. In this manner he becomes immersed in it throughout life, participating in the heritage of mankind and so becoming fully human. World 3 is the world that uniquely relates to man. It is completely unknown to animals.

Following the thought of Popper we can say that the self or ego is the result of achieving a view of ourselves from the outside, as we emerge from the solipsism of babyhood. In that way we each place ourselves in our bodies in the spatial domain and with a time sequence dependent on memories that bridge the diurnal gaps that sleep gives to the stream of consciousness of each of us. The concept each of us has of our own ego is dependent on our intuitive acceptance of the World 3 in which we are immersed in all our cognitive life, which would include all perceiving, thinking and communication.

Sir Charles Sherrington has written in his own exquisite style on the ego or self.

> "Each waking day is a stage dominated for good or ill, in comedy, farce or tragedy, by a *dramatis persona*, the 'self.' And so it will be until the curtain drops. This self is a unity. The continuity of its presence in time, sometimes hardly broken by sleep, its inalienable 'interiority' in (sensual) space, its consistency of view-point, the privacy of its experience, combine to give it status as a unique existence."[4]

A frequent objection to the concept of the ego or self is that its perception involves an infinite regress. This criticism arises from a misunderstanding. Reference to Fig. 20-2 shows that the conscious experiences listed under the categories "outer sense" and "inner sense" are perceived by the ego or self. In contrast, the ego or self is experienced, not perceived. Following Kant, we can make the distinction by saying that the self or ego is apperceived. As Polten states:

> "The ontological basis for the difference between apperception and perception is that the pure ego is a mental thing in itself, whereas the mental phenomena of inner and outer sense are appearances.

WORLD OF CONSCIOUSNESS

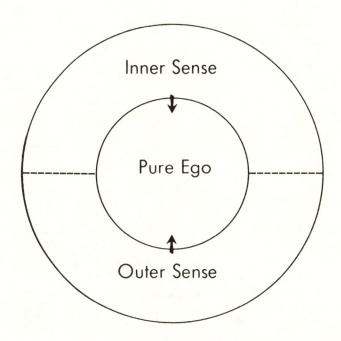

Outer Sense	Inner Sense	Pure Ego
Light	Thoughts	The self
Color	Feelings	The soul
Sound	Memories	
Smell	Dreams	
Taste	Imaginings	
Pain	Intentions	
Touch		

Figure 20-2: World of consciousness. The three postulated components in the world of consciousness together with a tabulated list of their components.

For that reason, too, subject and object merge in the act of the pure ego's self-observation, while inner and outer data are the pure ego's objects."[5]

Sherrington develops a comparable theme in relation to a voluntary motor act.

"This 'I' which when I move my hand I experience as 'I-doing,' how do I perceive it? I do not perceive it. If perception means awareness through sense I do not perceive the 'I'. My awareness and myself are one. I experience it. The 'I-doing' is my awareness of myself in the motor act. . . . This 'I' belongs more immediately to our awareness than does even the spatial world about us, for it is directly experienced. It *is* the 'self'."[6]

The Evolution of Culture

As we survey the cultural story of mankind the most remarkable discovery is that there were eons of incredibly slow development.[7,8] There was an immense time lag between man's development of a large brain and his significant progress in cultural evolution, *i.e.*, in the creation of World 3. For the greater part of the immensely long Paleolithic age, some 500,000 years, all we know is the slow development of stone tools—from flaked pebbles to the very gradually improved hand-axe. It is generally believed that this almost unimaginable slowness demonstrates that man was greatly handicapped by not yet having an effective communication by speech.

Evidently, as recognized by Dobzhansky and Popper, immense and fundamental problems are involved in the evolution of the brain that occurred as man was gradually developing his means of communication in speech.[9,10] One can imagine that speech and brain development went on together in the evolving process and that from these two emerged the cultural performance of man. Over hundreds of millenia there must have been a progressive development of language from its primitive form as expressive cries to a language that became gradually a more and more effective means of description and argument. In this way, by forging linguistic communication of ever increasing precision and subtlety, man must gradually have become a self-conscious being aware of his own identity or selfhood. As a consequence he also became aware of death, as witnessed so frequently and vividly in other members of the tribal group that he recognized them as beings like himself. We do not know how early in the story of man this tragic and poignant realization of death-awareness came to him, but it was at least a hundred thousand years ago, as evidenced by the ceremonial burial customs with the dead laid in graves with antlers, weapons, ornaments, etc.

It was not until the Upper Paleolithic era that man seemed to have achieved a new awareness and sense of purpose—as witness the remarkable progress in a few thousand years, relative to the virtual stagnation of the previous hundreds of thousands of years. As one can readily imagine, by a language that gave clear identifications of objects and descriptions of actions and, even more importantly, the opportunity of discussing and arguing, man was lifted to a new level of creativity. We can presume that because of this linguistic communication man was enabled to progress in the development of the large variety of stone tools with greatly improved design, which is the most important characteristic of the upper Paleolithic age.

But the most fascinating insight into the artistic creativity of Upper Paleolithic man is given by the cave paintings of southern France and northern Spain. When I saw the marvellous paintings of Lascaux, I was overwhelmed by the feeling that these artists had highly developed imagination and memory as well as a refined aesthetic sense. Undoubtedly they had a fully developed language so that they could discuss the techniques they employed and the ideas that inspired them. One has the impression that, at this period of about 15,000 B.C., man was very richly contributing to the world of culture. At the same time there were carvings and modellings of animals and of archetypal female figures that probably are representative of Mother Goddesses. Many would achieve distinction in modern sculpture exhibitions!

In the subsequent Mesolithic age man developed and perfected hunting methods and also clothing and housing, but artistically it was disappointing after the great achievements of the later Paleolithic. This technological Mesolithic period beginning in 10,000 to 8,000 B.C. was relatively brief.

The Neolithic age of settled farming communities began as early as 7,000 B.C. in Jericho and at 6,500 B.C. at Jarmo in Mesopotamia. The settled towns and villages of the Mesopotamian region soon became remarkable for their substantial houses and for the fine pottery and weaving. These developments were possible because of the prosperous farming with crops of barley and wheat and with domesticated animals, sheep, ox, goat, pig and dog. In addition the stone tools were finely made with polished surfaces. The pottery clearly reveals that Mesopotamian man was guided by an aesthetic sense. The decorative patterns of Hasuma and Jarmo were in part abstract, but also, as with the Samarra pottery of the 5th millenium B.C., there was a very sophisticated stylization of animal forms to give designs that display a high artistic sense. This Mesopotamian pottery is remarkable for the combination of utility and elegance. Already they had invented the potter's wheel. Cultural evolution was well advanced and the ceramics of Susa represent their highest artistic performance in this field.

About 1000 years after its development in Mesopotamia, Neolithic culture had spread from there to Egypt, so seeding the great periods of Egyptian civilization. Later there was a wide dispersal to Europe and to Asia (first to the Indus valley and later to China) of this central feature of the Neolithic culture, namely farming with settled communities of villages and towns. Meanwhile great developments continued in Mesopotamia, which undoubtedly led the world during the magnificent periods of Sumerian civilization from 3,500 B.C. for more than a millenium. The Neolithic age gave place to the Bronze age at about 4,000 B.C. and, during the third millenium B.C., gold, silver and bronze workmanship was of a high order.

The greatest of all contributions of the Sumerians to culture was the development of a written language. The beginnings were about 3,300 B.C., but for some hundreds of years it was still in the form of ideograms that had been developed from pictograms. The Sumerians progressively simplified the forms so that eventually it was completely abstract, consisting of various arrangements of tapered signs inscribed in soft clay tablets by a stylus made like a wedge, hence the name "Cuneiform" for the first written language that was fully developed by about 2,800 B.C.

A written language must rank as one of the greatest discoveries in human history, for by means of it man could live beyond time. Thoughts, imaginings, ideas, understandings and explanations experienced and developed by men living in one age can be written down for distribution in that age and also for recovery in later ages. A man's creative insights need no longer die with him, but, when encoded in written language, can be re-experienced later by men who have the ability to decode. And so we enter into the historical epochs where the different civilizations have left records of their economic and political activities, their myths and legends, their drama, poetry, history, philosophy and religion.

Culture Exclusively Human

It must be recognized that each human individual has to be educated from babyhood to be able to participate even at the simplest level in the culture he has been born into, though of course he carries genetically the potentiality for this participation. This generalization applies to babies from all races. Their cultural development from that of the stone age culture of primitive men of today in which they may be born to that of the advanced technological cultures is dependent on their opportunities to learn. A very young child from a stone age culture can be assimilated readily to our culture, its achievement being of course dependent on what we may call "brain potentiality;" and, conversely, a very young child of our culture if immersed in a stone age culture would carry no genetic memory whatsoever of our culture, and merely be assimilated to the primitive culture of his society. Completely different propositions obtain for all of the instinctive behaviors of animals. This behavior is largely if not entirely inborn, but it is of course modified by environmental influences. Animals brought up in isolation exhibit a remarkable ability to develop the behavior patterns of the normal adult, for example nest-building or bird-song, but with birds and mammals the finesse of the performance is dependent on having examples on display, i.e., the details of the performance have an imitative basis.[11,12]

It can be concluded that animal behavior in constructions on the one hand and human purpose and design at all levels of doing and making on the other hand are quite distinct. The one belongs to the biological evolution, the other to the cultural evolution. Animals are innocent of culture and civilization, which are distinctively human. There is no trace of them in the whole of animal evolution, which is governed by trial and error acting blindly, but of course being guided by instinctive and learning behavior. I use the world "blind" because there is no evidence that animal behavior pattern is based on the understanding of a situation, in the way that we use the word "understanding" in respect of human behavior.

Culture and Man

Popper has expressed very well the specific relationship of World 3 (the world of objective knowledge or culture) to World 2 (the self of ego).

> "My central thesis . . . is that the self or the ego is anchored in the third world, and that it cannot exist without the third world. Before discussing this thesis more fully it may be necessary to remove the following difficulty. As I have here so often said, the third world is, roughly, the universe of the products of our minds. How can this be if, on the other hand, our minds or our selves cannot exist without the third world? The answer to this apparent difficulty is very simple. Our selves, the higher functions of language, and the third world have evolved and emerged together, in constant interaction; thus there is no special difficulty here. To be more specific, I deny that animals have states of full consciousness or that they have a conscious self. The self evolves together with the higher functions of language, the descriptive and the argumentative functions."[13]

In summary we can state that World 3 is a world of storage, for the whole of human creativity through the prehistory and the history of the cultures and civilizations. What we call in old-fashioned terminology a "cultured man" is a man able to retrieve from this storage and to enter into an understanding of it. But of course this retrieval is also right up to the contemporary scene, where critical evaluation is concerned with elimination of error or banality and in the setting of standards.

I believe that central to each human being is the primary reality of conscious experience in all the richness and diversity that characterizes World 2 existence. Furthermore this experience is self-reflective in the sense that we know that we can know. Our ultimate efforts are to understand this primary reality in relation to the secondary realities of the matter-energy world (World 1) and of the world of objective thought that embraces the whole of civilization and culture (World 3). We as experiencing beings must be central to the explanations, because all the experiences derived from Worlds 1 and 3 are recognizably dependent on the manner in which we obtain information by means of the transductions effected by sense organs and the coded transmission to our brains.

The story of man's thoughts on the meaning of life and on the ultimate human destiny in death provide a poignant testimony. Myths and religions and philosophies have been concerned with this tragic enigma of "ultimate concern" that faces each one of us. Is human destiny but an episode between two oblivions? Or can we have hope that there is meaning and transcendent significance in the wonderful, rich, and vivid conscious experience that is our birthright?

And that brings me to assert that any fundamental question in philosophy must be considered in the full context of related questions, and never in some arbitrary isolation. The question of death-awareness and self-annihilation must not be discussed except in relation to the question of birth and the subsequent self-actualization, which has been expressed by Plato in the Phaedo. As I have argued previously, I believe that my experiencing self is only in part explained by the evolutionary origin of my body and brain, that is of my World 1 component. It is a necessary but not a sufficient condition. About the origin of our world of conscious experience (World 2) we know only that it can be described as having an emergent relation to the evolutionary development of the human brain. The uniqueness of individuality that I experience myself to have cannot be attributed to the uniqueness of my genetic inheritance.[14] Our coming-to-be is as mysterious as our ceasing-to-be at death. Can we therefore not derive hope because our ignorance about our origin matches our ignorance about our destiny? Cannot life be lived as a challenging and wonderful adventure that has meaning to be discovered?

Let us look now at the future for cultural evolution. It is my thesis that this will provide man with virtually unlimited opportunities in the many rich fields of World 3. Even before the great and pioneering cultural achievements of Sumerian civilization, we can assume that the cerebral potentiality of man had evolved to the level of modern man. It seems that in this respect there has been no significant evolutionary advance in the last tens of millenia—perhaps from the latter part of the upper Paleolithic age. From then on biological evolution had given place to cultural evolution. And if we survey the recent history of man, century by century, we can see that there have been tremendous achievements in one or other aspect of culture. Not all aspects advance

267

continuously. Great creative discoveries and inspiring leadership by men of genius have led to a flourishing of now one great cultural discipline, now another. At one time it is in literature, at another in philosophy or in the plastic arts or in music or in science and technology. For example the classical age of Greece was remarkable for architecture, sculpture, literature and philosophy. In the Renaissance there were great developments in architecture, painting, sculpture and literature; later came music, philosophy, cosmology and science. There is generally agreement that for more than a century the greatest cultural achievements of man have been in science and technology.

I will now recapitulate my thesis. It has been argued that man differs *radically in kind* from other animals. As a transcendence in the evolutionary process there appeared an animal differing fundamentally from other animals because he had attained to propositional speech, abstract thought and self-consciousness, which are all signs that a being of transcendent novelty had appeared in the world—creatures existing not only in World 1 but realizing their existence in the world of self-awareness (World 2) and so having in the religious concept, souls. And simultaneously these human beings began utilizing their World 2 experiences to create another world, the third World of the objective spirit. This World 3 provides the means whereby man's creative efforts live on as a heritage for all future men, so building the magnificent cultures and civilizations recorded in human history. Do not the mystery and the wonder of this story of our origin and nature surpass the myths whereby man in the past has attempted to explain his origin and destiny?

We can have hope as we recognize and appreciate the wonder and mystery of our existence as experiencing selves. Mankind would be cured of his alienation if that message could be expressed with all the authority of scientists and philosophers as well as with the imaginative insights of artists. In *Facing Reality* I expressed my efforts to understand a human person, namely myself, as an experiencing being. I offered it in the hope that it may help man to discover a way out of his alienation and to face up to the terrible and wonderful reality of his existence—with courage and faith and hope. Because of the mystery of our being as unique self-conscious existences, we can have hope as we set our own soft, sensitive and fleeting personal experience against

the terror and immensity of illimitable space and time. Are we not
participants in the meaning, where there is else no meaning? Do
we not experience and delight in fellowship, joy, harmony, truth,
love and beauty, where there else is only the mindless universe?

Notes

1. J.C. Eccles, *Facing Reality* (Heidelberg, Berlin New York: Springer
   International, 1970).
2. K.R. Popper, *Objective Knowledge: An Evolutionary Approach* (Oxford: Clarendon Press, 1972).
3. E.P. Polten, *A Critique of the Psycho-physical Identity Theory* (The
   Hague: Mouton Press, 1973).
4. C.S. Sherrington, *The Integrative Action of the Nervous System* (London: Cambridge University Press, 1947).
5. E.P. Polten, *A Critique to the Psycho-Physical Identity Theory.*
6. C.S. Sherrington, *Man on His Nature* (London: Cambridge University
   Press, 1940).
7. T. Dobzhansky, *Mankind Evolving: The Evolution of the Human
   Species* (New Haven: Yale University Press, 1962).
8. J. Hawkes, "Prehistory in History of Mankind." *Cultural and Scientific
   Development*, Vol. 1, Part 1, UNESCO. (London: New English Library
   Limited, 1965).
9. T. Dobzhansky, *The Biology of Ultimate Concern* (New York: New
   American Library, 1967).
10. K.R. Popper, *Objective Knowledge: An Evolutionary Approach.*
11. N. Tinbergen, *The Study of Instinct* (Oxford: Clarendon Press, 1951).
12. W.H. Thorpe, *Learning and Instruct in Animals* (London: Methuen,
    1956).
13. K.R. Popper, Personal communication 1970.
14. J.C. Eccles, *Facing Reality*, Chapter V.

Part IV

Meaning of Life and Death in the Context of the Mind-Brain Problem

21.
Science and Man's Need for Meaning

W.H. Thorpe

In recent years a group of psychoanalysts in this country, and others elsewhere, have described how one of the major threats to health and sanity today is what they call the "existential vacuum" experienced by vast numbers of their patients: a feeling of inner emptiness, of aimless lives set down in a desert of meaninglessness. This is claimed as characteristic of modern scientifically oriented society—the result, in a word, of the widespread assumption that science is the only "philosophy" in which one can believe. The existential vacuum is regarded as due to the frustration of the most basic motivational force in man—the will to meaning. (In contrast to the Adlerian "will to power" and the Freudian "will to pleasure.") The argument is that people do not care for pleasure or for the avoidance of pain; but that they do crave profoundly for meaning. This need or demand for meaning is regarded as one of the most basic features of man.

Science, of course, as we all know, answers the need for "understanding" in the more limited sense, and is opening ever enlarging vistas of the stupendous complexity and beauty of the created universe. But in general, this does not, by itself, help to assuage the need for meaning. Belief in "meaning" in this sense, rests on religious faith or on an accepted philosophy or system of myths as to the nature of the world and the relation of man to it.

From the biological point of view the modern crisis was mainly generated by the theory of evolution by natural selection. I think that there is no doubt that, in Western countries, the retreat from organized religion is, in the long term, mainly based on the slow dissemination of the changed world picture, especially that originating from Darwin's work with the overwhelming evidence it *seemed* to supply of the importance of chance in the origin and development of man. For obviously mankind, before the nineteenth century, was by no means denied a measure of satisfaction of his needs: he had it of course in Western countries as a result of the Judaeo-Christian vision which gave man a clear place in the world system and a faith and hope in the future. But not only this: in Western Europe there was a very wide basic belief in (and acceptance of) a world system and man's place in it which could be held with or without the Judaeo-Christian picture and which in general reinforced some of the most important of its beliefs and attitudes. This was "The Great Chain of Being"—which served to express the unimaginable plenitude of God's creation, its unfaltering order, and its ultimate unity. This "chain" or "ladder," if one likes to regard it so, was thought of as stretching from the foot of God's throne to the meanest of inanimate objects. Every speck of creation represented a link in the chain. But its importance for my story now is that the top of every inferior class touched the bottom of a superior one—so that where the steps were in contact, as at the boundary between rocks and plants or between plants and animals or between animals and man there were transitional forms in which both higher and lower grades cooperated. And so at the top the noblest entity in the category of bodies, was the human body which touches the fringe of the next class above it—namely the human soul which occupies the lowest rank in the spiritual order.

As late as Elizabethan times awareness of this sophisticated system was widespread and basic. But by the eighteenth century the scheme was beginning to reveal flaws and was breaking down under philosophical and scientific criticism. And so the coming of evolution theory in the nineteenth century can in a way be regarded as ushering in the final destruction of that which had sustained man's thought for many centuries and had given him comfort in a mysterious world: indeed since Plato; from whose teaching the mighty plan originally grew.

I need not try to trace the process further; for threats to meaning are obvious everywhere—not least of these being the wide-spread monistic views of so many scientists and humanists of the present day; views which make man's spiritual side appear to be merely the superficial by-product of a material process. Again at the present day many scientists, and particularly scientific popularizers, have a lot to answer for in the way they have exhibited what has been called "the compulsive urge to disenchant," by being irresponsibly and irrepressibly smart and clever; often seeming to deliberately "bamboozle" the "common man" and his beliefs by shock and ridicule. The result has, I think, contributed to a sense of helplessness, a loss of nerve; indeed a sense of boredom and a failure to see (because life seems so complicated) that all the vast developments in science—dangerous as they are as threatening the very existence of life on this planet—have their beneficent side; and, if properly used and understood, can be, indeed must be, the means of progress to a new world order and re-awakening.

But how does today's scientific world picture affect man's view of himself and of his place in the universe? It seems to me that a very subtle and important series of changes has been taking place in recent years—changes which bear closely on our ideas of the emergence of new properties and values in the world. This is after all the key question—how and how far does quantity and complexification become quality? What is the real relation between wholes and parts? Emergent properties are the properties of a whole system not possessed by its parts. This is what one may call the *orthodox* scientific view. The program with which scientists commence, is that in principle, though not yet by any means in practice, the whole should be entirely explicable in terms of their parts; and for many branches of physical science it is indeed a sound research tactic. So it seems to me that this basic program of the physicist, though being very far from complete, is undoubtedly the one which he must pursue. But we all know that physical theorizing often leads to what seem to be absurdities—for instance the modern view is that, against all intuition (based on the special theory of relativity), there is no role for the "flow of time" or "now" in the physical world.

But before coming to biology I wish, at the risk of trespassing in the fields of the two other speakers today, to point out the extraordinary way modern cosmology seems to come nearer to asserting that the universe is, in some surprising ways, far more appropriate for life than was at one time thought. That although, as far as we *know*, life is only present in this solar system and on this planet, living beings, including ourselves, are perhaps more "at home" in the cosmos than we hitherto had reason to believe.

The first point that can be made with certainty is that if the universe were not much as it is, neither ourselves nor other forms of life could have come into existence. If the universe were not expanding, if there were no stars, if the proton-proton force were slightly different—without a certain ratio between the basic forces of interaction and a certain relationship between the fundamental constants—without all the space and time in the world, the "universe" would be dead. In particular the present theory of the periodic system explains the production of the heavier nuclei through the fusion of several hydrogen nuclei. These heavier elements, such as iron, are essential to life. All evidence at present points to the conclusion that it is only under the circumstances of intense gravitational contraction, which leads to supernova outbursts, that the heavier elements can have been formed; and it is only as another result of supernova explosions that these elements can have been spewed out into space and so made available to stars with solar systems such as ours. So it is this chain of events which during an estimated $10^{4.2}$ billion years, that has provided us with the heavy elements which we all of necessity carry around in our bodies. It is indeed the astounding coherence of the universe as a whole which had led to the present state of the cosmos being (according to current theory) due to events which took place a minute fraction of a second after the "big bang"—the very onset of time!

I have just said that the idea of the flow of time, of the present, and of "now," appear to be an emergent property of ourselves, and to have no counterpart in theoretical physics. Yet in the mental world such concepts have the unshakeable validity of direct experience. So here science seems to have brought us to the boundary between the material and mental worlds where there does seem to be an unbridgeable gap. Now the property above all properties which demarcates this gap is that of consciousness or self-awareness. So, in company with some neurophysiologists and philosophers, I see some form of dualism between "Matter" and "Mind" to be unavoidable in the future program for biology. Karl Popper for instance sees that no explanation of the physical world can be valid which regards the self-consciousness of man as being merely an epiphenomenon—an accidental outcome of the mechanical workings of a machine which we call the brain. This amounts to saying that there must in fact be two worlds—the world of self knowing and the physical world which is known by the operations of the scientific method as used by the physicists and biologists. The miracle is that the "big bang" created a situation such that thousands of millions of years later a part of the universe could study the rest of itself!

Now let us return to consideration of the evidence for what, if we are dualists in the sense above used, we are forced to describe as "Mind" or "The Mental" or "The Quality of Awareness" in the biological realm, apart from man himself.

In recent years the problem as to whether or not we are justified in the assumption that some animals have some kind of mental experiences—certainly not comparable in quality and scope to our own—but evolutionarily continuous with it—has come to the forefront of biology as the result of new and highly important experiments.

There are a number of lines of research which have provided new evidence, indeed key evidence, for this question of the "mentality" of animals; all of them concerned with the modern study of communication and an increased understanding of what the word can signify, when we are considering the coordination of behavior between individuals of the same species. It similarly arises from much modern work on the nature of animal orientation—in particular, studies of the hearing of bats, the orientation of the flights of migratory and homing birds, the underwater hearing of fish, whales, and, above all (in bats and fish), their ability to orient themselves by responding to echoes of their own "voices" (*i.e.,* by echolocation). But because of lack of time I must restrict myself to a very brief summary of recent work in two fields—namely the ability of primates such as the chimpanzee to acquire languages taught them by human beings; and secondly, the ability of the social insects, particularly the worker honey bee (*Apis mellifica*) to transmit information to other members of the colony with a subtlety and precision which hitherto had been regarded as quite unthinkable.

The first, and by now widely famous, study of the language learning of chimpanzees is that of R.A. and B.T. Gardner, who achieved remarkable success in teaching a young female animal in captivity the gesture language known as the American Sign Language (A.S.L.). This language is composed of manually produced avisual signals called "signs" which are strictly analogous to words used in speech. These are arbitrary but stable meaningless signal elements which are arranged in a series of patterns constituting minimum meaningful combinations of those elements. Not only did the Gardners' first chimp "Washoe" but also other chimps since studied, achieve surprisingly good learning of the varieties of signs; they also developed signs which can best be described as "straight inventions," in that they were quite different from signs which had, until then, been the models provided for them by their teachers. Moreover it is possible for such experimental animals to use pronouns appropriately. The animals can also combine previously learned signs into small groups in meaningful ways and apply them appropriately to new situations. For example the sign for "open," which was originally learned in regard to doors, was later used correctly in requesting the opening of boxes, drawers, brief-cases and picture books. All this provides clear evidence for elementary purposiveness.

The significance of these new results is strengthened enormously by the fact that there are at least three series of experiments (with different animals and using different techniques) in which the same results have been reached. One of the reasons why it has been necessary to consider so carefully the question of animal language is because it relates to the arguments put forward by Chomsky and others that the possession of language is indubitable evidence of mentality and of some basic and innate mental structure without which the acquisition of true language and its purposive use, whether by animals or men, is inconceivable.

There has of course been a great deal of pungent criticism of the results of these studies and their interpretation. But I think the experimenters have now gone a long way, if not the whole way, towards giving satisfactory answers. As a result of the totality of chimpanzee experiments nearly all the critical objections raised by scientists and philosophers against crediting animals with true linguistic developments have been answered by at least one animal and most of them by several. These objections amounted to the demand for the fulfilment of five criteria, namely that an animal must:

1. Demonstrate an extensive system of names for objects in the environment.

2. Sign about objects which are not physically present.

3. Use signs for concepts; not just objects, actions and agents.

4. Invent semantically appropriate combinations, and

5. Use correct order when it is semantically necessary.

Over and above the fact that all these questions have now been answered in the affirmative; still yet more relevant activities are coming to light. It has been shown that captive chimpanzees can communicate fairly complex information by some combinations of gestures or expressive movements that human investigators have not yet deciphered. In the light of these results it is very interesting to look at some of the more recent statements of philosophers and linguists; (who have argued that human language is closely linked with thinking, if not basically identical and inseparable from it). In 1968 we were assured that it would be astounding to discover that insects or fish, birds or monkeys are able to talk to one another—because man is the only animal which can talk and can use symbols, the only animal that can truly understand and misunderstand. Again:—"Language is an expression of man's very nature and his basic capacity . . . animals cannot have language because they lack this capacity. If they had it they would no longer be animals—they would be human beings."[1]

Now let us look for a moment at the communication of bees. The general story of the communication of the distance, the situation and the direction of a food source by the dances of the returning worker bee on the vertical comb of the hive, has been known in general outline from the work of Karl von Frisch in the middle 1950s. Philosophers and linguists have made the same kind of objection to the attempt to regard this as language as I have just referred to in relation to the use of ASL by apes.

The basic correctness of the original conclusions has now been amply confirmed and established. But, far more than this, recent observations have shown overwhelmingly how adaptable, flexible and "purposive" is the use of these signs. For instance it has been argued that the use of the dances is rigidly controlled by the circumstances (such as the absence or presence of food). This is not so. For the dances, though most frequently used to signal the location of a food source, are, under special conditions, also applied to other requirements of the mutually inter-dependent members of the colony of bees. After all they are not *rigidly* used for foraging flights. When food is plentiful returning foragers often do not dance at all. The odors conveyed from one bee to another always help to direct recruits to new sources and often they alone are sufficient. Independent searching by individual foragers seems to be adequate under many conditions. Thus the dance-communications system is called into play primarily when the colony of bees is in great need of food; but it is not tightly linked to any one requirement; on the contrary it may be used for such different things as food, water and resinous materials from plants (propolis). Moreover when a colony of bees is engaged in swarming, the scouts search for cavities suitable to serve as the future home for the entire colony and report their location by the same dances—which are now performed when crawling over the mass of bees which makes up the swarm cluster.[2,3] When Lindauer observed the scouts of a swarm of bees which had moved only a short distance away from the original colony he found that the same marked bee would sometimes change her dance pattern from that indicating the location of a moderately suitable cavity to one signalling a better potential site for a new hive. This occurred after the dancer had received information from another bee and had flown out to inspect the superior cavity. Thus the same worker bee can be both a transmitter and receiver of information within a short period of time; and in spite of her motivation to dance about one location, she can also be influenced by the similar but more intense communication of another dancer. As Griffin said in 1976, "There is no escape from the conclusion that, in the special situation when swarming bees are in serious need of a new location in which the colony can continue its existence, the bees exchange information about the location and suitability of a potential hive site. Individual worker bees are swayed by this information to the extent that after inspection of alternative locations they change their preference and dance for the superior place rather than for the one they first discovered. Only after many hours of such exchanges of information, involving dozens of bees, and only when the dances of virtually all the scouts indicate the same hive site, does the swarm as a whole fly off to it."[4] This consensus results from the communicative interactions between individual bees which alternately "speak" and "listen."

Here again the sweeping negativisms of Chomsky have been thrown into the arena. His main thesis as to the pre-eminence of human reason is sound and important and needs constant reiteration in these days when it is the fashion to denigrate man and all that is transcendental in his nature. But Chomsky does poor service to his cause, and merely weakens his case by scorning the proven abilities of animals. He says, "Human reason in fact is a universal instrument which can serve for all contingencies, whereas the organs of an animal or a machine have need of some special adaptation for any particular action . . . no brute (is) so perfect that it has made use of a sign to inform other animals of something which had no relation to their passions . . . for the word is the sole sign and the only certain mark of the presence of thought hidden and wrapped up in the body; now all men . . . make use of signs, whereas the brutes never do anything of the kind; which may be taken for the true distinction between man and brute."[5]

One of the philosophers (R.F. Terwilliger) who argues specifically against the evidence from honey-bees in his efforts to support his view of the animals as Cartesian machines, says, "No bee was ever seen dancing about yesterday's honey (he means of course *nectar*) not to mention tomorrow's . . . Moreover bees never make mistakes in their dance."[6]

One of the many facts that Terwilliger, and other authors of a similar persuasion ignore is that bees can be stimulated, by extreme food deficit, to dance during the middle of the night (a thing which they normally very rarely do) about a food source they have visited the day before, and will almost certainly visit again the next morning. In these circumstances a bee which has been dancing right up to sundown will, as soon as the morning comes, fly out to the same source, now, of course, *taking a very different direction relative to the sun, in its morning position.*

It is not so very surprising to find true linguistic ability in a primate with a brain-construction so similar to that of ourselves. But it is indeed in a sense "shocking" to find it in an insect, with its vastly simpler central nervous system.

A prominent student of "machine intelligence" has said "an organism which can have intentions is, I think, one which could be said to possess a mind, provided that it has the ability to form a plan and make a decision to adopt the plan."[7] And to "decide on and adopt a plan" implies purpose. From all this it appears that the presence of mental images and an ability to provide introspective reports on self-awareness and intentions or purposes emerge as criteria of mind. So again we must ask ourselves, do these studies of animal language show evidence of purpose or "intention?" It seems to me extremely difficult to support a negative answer. M.J. Adler argues that if it were discovered that animals differ from men only in degree and not radically in kind, this would destroy our moral basis for holding that all men have basic rights and individual dignity.[8] It would seem that Adler, now confronted with the present situation, would conclude that the study of communicative behavior in animals has more dangerous political consequences than nuclear physics had in the 1930s (Griffin).[9]

Such views raise the whole question of "emergence" which is, at rock bottom, what all this discussion is about. We have been considering the emergence of new properties in complex systems through physics up to the mind of man. In the physical sciences such emergence can often be fully accounted for in terms of the individual properties of the component particles in isolation. In a very large number of other cases this cannot be done—though it is the widely accepted research strategy to assume that, as the science develops further, it will prove possible to do so. As we proceed to biology and up towards the higher reaches of the subject, this goal appears increasingly remote and unattainable. So many are forced to the conclusion, that at least when we come to the development of the behavioral abilities of the "higher" animals and man himself, this reductive view can never suffice and we must perforce envisage truly unpredictable and unforeseeable events (emergents) for which no refinements of physical technique or theory can ever be able fully to account. If this conclusion is accepted and absorbed into the culture and consciousness of mankind—that there are real and what can only be defined as sacred values in the world which must *never* be denigrated or relinguished—then the dangerous moral and political consequences referred to just now can and must be avoided.

A.N. Whitehead said in 1938 "The distinction between man and animals is in one sense only a difference of degree. But the extent of the degree makes all the difference. The Rubicon has been crossed."[10] I believe this must be taken with the greatest seriousness.

To summarize, very briefly, the two aspects of the present world picture as it affects our estimate of our own situation:

1. I have little doubt that the cosmological revolution, provisional though it may be, has shown us a deep relationship between ourselves, the stars and space; and so has provided us with a universe more concordant with the life and aspiration of man than any which preceded it up to the 1930s. And although I have used the presently favoured "big-bang" model, I believe the same could be argued for a "steady-state" model; or indeed a combination of the two. This is not to say that there is now a sound basis for a new argument from design. But (to quote Dr. Carling) "It is a rather strong kind of coherence that can relate the present appearance of the universe back to events a minute fraction of a second after the 'big-bang'—approximately ten thousand million years ago."

2. When we come to realise the strength of the present evidence for the continuity of mental experience, we are led to postulate a real predisposition in the world for the evolution of mental awareness. And this brings us to contemplate a supreme miracle—"That the universe created a part of itself to study the rest of itself."

All this presents us with the great task of formulating the new prospect in a manner which the majority will welcome and understand. In this connection I cannot do better than paraphrase some remarks of Polanyi[12]: So far as we know we are the supreme bearers of thought in the universe. After five million centuries of evolution, we have been engaged for only fifty centuries in a literate process of thought. It has all been an affair of the last hundred generations or so. If this perspective is true, a supreme trust is placed in us by the whole creation; and it is sacrilege even to contemplate actions which may lead to the extinction of humanity or even its relegation to earlier or more primitive stages of culture. To avoid this is the particular calling of literate and scientific man in this universe.

In this task of re-formulation perhaps the key lies in the modern development of Process Philosophy and Process Theology—based upon the thought of Alfred North Whitehead.

During these three days we have been considering the human brain and have come to realize that, in spite of its overwhelming complexity, it has ultimate limitations as a machine. But I believe with Whitehead that in spite of these limitations the human mind and soul which operates in liaison with it, has latent possibilities and capacities for further emergence and transcendence —capacities to which we can set no limit.

And in conclusion I would like to paraphrase some words of Louis Pasteur: "Infinity stares us in the face, whether we look at the stars or search for our own identities. A true science of life must let infinity in and never lose sight of it." Hold fast to this and we shall find that the infinity of mind seems to encompass us everywhere.

Notes

1. M. Black, *The Labyrinth of Language* (New York: Praeger, 1968).

2. K. von Frisch, *The Dance Language and Orientation of Bees* (Cambridge, Mass: Harvard University Press, 1967).

3. M. Lindauer, *Communication Among Social Bees* (revised edition, Cambridge, Mass: Harvard University Press, 1971).

4. D.R. Griffin, *The Question of Animal Awareness* (New York: Rockefeller University Press, 1976).

5. N. Chomsky, *Language and Mind* (New York: Harcourt, Brace, Jovanovich, 1972).

6. R.F. Terwilliger, *Meaning and Mind: A Study of the Psychology of Language* (London and New York: Oxford University Press, 1968).

7. H.C. Longuet-Higgins, in A.H.P. Kenny, J.R. Lucas, and C.H. Waddington, *The Nature of Mind* (Edinburgh: Edinburgh University Press, 1970).

8. M.J. Adler, *The Difference of Man and the Difference It Makes* (New York: Holt, Rinehart & Winston, 1967).

9. D.R. Griffin, *The Question of Animal Awareness.*

10. A.N. Whitehead, *Modes of Thought* (Cambridge and London: Cambridge University Press, 1938).

11. J.C. Lilly, *The Centre of the Cyclone* (London: Paladin, p. 215 1973).

12. M. Polanyi, *The Study of Man* (Chicago: University of Chicago Press, 1959).

In addition to the work by Donald Griffin, the following may be found useful as providing general summaries:

A) W.H. Thorpe, *Animal Nature and Human Nature* (London: Methuen and New York: Doubleday-Anchor, 1974).

B) J.B. Cobb and David Ray Griffin, eds., *Mind in Nature: Essays on the Interface of Science and Philosophy* (Washington, D.C.: University Press of America, 1977). (This constitutes a general summary of the present position of Process Philosophy. Readers may find the contributions of J.B. Cobb, Theodosius Dobzhansky, Charles Hartshorne, R.H. Overman, C.H. Waddington and Sewell Wright of particular relevance.)

C) W.H. Thorpe, *Purpose in a World of Change* (London: Oxford University Press, 1977). (This is written from a biological standpoint.)

Acknowledgments

I have been indebted to many colleagues and friends in the preparation of this paper. Among them, it is an especial pleasure to acknowledge the following:

The late DR. E.M.W. Tillyard, the first to introduce me to the subject of the Great Chain of Being. His book *The Elizabethan World Picture* (London: Chatto and Windus, 1945) and the admirable earlier work of the American scholar Professor A.O. Lovejoy, The Great Chain of Being (Cambridge, Mass: Harvard University Press, 1936), proved to be of much value.

For the section on Cosmology, I became acquainted with facts and theories from a number of astronomy colleagues at Cambridge University—particularly Dr. W. Saslaw, Professor M.J. Rees and Professor Anthony Hewish. But, for the first part of the section, I am especially indebted to Mr. C.D. Curling, Sub-Dean of the Faculty of Natural Science of King's College, University of London. However, none of these may be blamed for any errors; which are mine alone.

While I was engaged in writing a new book, *The Question of Animal Awareness* (New York: Rockefeller University Press, 1976), by a friend of many years, Professor Donald R. Griffin, this material landed on my desk. This was remarkably fortunate in that it enabled me to substantially improve the section on mind and mentality. It also provided me with some new references.

22.

The Scientist at His Last Quarter of an Hour

Duke L.V.P.R. de Broglie

When we have reached the end of our lives (and which of us, whatever his age may be, is sure of not being about to reach it?), it is only natural that we should try to understand the meaning of life and to pass judgment on the activities we may have carried out during our existence. In particular, anyone who has devoted the greater part of his time in scientific research must of course be led during his "last quarter of an hour" to consider the material and spiritual value of Science, the place it occupies in the progress of civilization and in the general evolution of the human race, the prospects which we may see as to the significance and the destiny of the Universe and of Thought. On the assumption that we have come to our last quarter of an hour, let us therefore ponder over these grave problems.

A few billion years ago, Life appeared on the surface of the Earth, no doubt in a very humble form in which living matter was hardly distinguished from inert matter. Then over the centuries and millenaries, driven by a mysterious force whose true nature we are still far from understanding, it spread through the waters, into the air and on firm land, producing more and more complicated organisms, which were better and better adapted to very diverse conditions of life. According to the data of Paleontology, it is most probable that all the species have arisen from one another, although we do not know by what continuous or discontinuous processes (progressive evolution of sudden mutations) have successively come about the living forms which have existed or still exist on the earth. During this long and astounding history of the development of Life on our planet, of this grandiose epic which Mr. Jean Rostand has given the striking name of "the adventure of protoplasm," living organisms have adapted themselves with incredible flexibility to the conditions of existence offered to them and have reached that degree of prodigious complexity and admirable precision to be found in the evolved species and, in particular, in the higher vertebrates. Apart from the astonishing physico-chemical mechanisms that ensure the continuation of life in individuals and its perpetuation through successive generations, how can one fail to admire the perfection of those "sense organs" which allow a living being to know its environment and, thanks to its mobility, to find there what can be useful to it and to avoid as far as possible the dangers which may lie in wait for it. The marvelously precise structure, the extraordinary sensibility of organs such as the eye and the ear of the higher animals stagger the imagination and it seems incredible that such organs could have been produced by mere chance, even over enormous periods of time. The realizations of Life seem to result from a kind of organizing force which does not manifest itself in inert matter and whose true nature is totally unknown to us.

Linked to the mobility of living beings and to their faculty of perception, there appeared one of the most astonishing phenomena in the world such as we know it; I am referring to the phenomenon of "consciousness," that is, to the fact that living beings, at least those whose organization is sufficiently high, are aware that they constitute a unit endowed with autonomy in the physical world and consciously "perceive" the messages sent to them from the outer world through their sensory organs and which, so to speak, are reflected on their autonomy. A deeply mysterious faculty! We clearly understand how, for instance, light may be collected by our eye, act on our retina, induce in our optic nerve an electrical influx which excites certain nerve cells in our brain, but the transformation of these purely physical phenomena into the conscious perception of a luminous sensation remains astounding and almost inconceivable.

The appearance of thought marked a new and prodigious step forward in Life, linked to the existence of consciousness which is its necessary condition. Thought is superior to it. Its higher forms which tend, by abstraction and generalization, to break away from the always limited and particular data of perception, go far beyond simple consciousness. Whilst consciousness no doubt already exists in an elementary state in relatively inferior species, though is certainly still only very rudimentary even in the most intelligent higher vertebrates. It really appears in all its fullness in man only and, as has often been said, it is that which constitutes Man's eminent dignity and gives him the exceptional place he holds in nature.

The appearance of Man on earth, the development in him, thanks to a prodigious complexity of the cerebral mechanisms, of thought and reason, marked a decisive turning-point in the history of Life on our planet and a new phase of that history began as human intelligence improved. Having acquired the capacity for reasoning, man endeavored to understand what we observed, to classify the phenomena, to discover their regularity. He has unceasingly acquired knowledge through this rational observation of things and his knowledge has been preserved in the individual by memory, soon to be assisted by books, and handed down from generations to generations by oral or written teaching—such knowledge increases continually. In its endeavor to discover laws and causes, the human mind wants to understand the "how" and the "why" of things, and this noble aspiration, though an audacious one, has led man to tackle scientific and metaphysical problems which are both a credit to him and a torment.

If one thinks of it, it is most surprising and incomprehensible as well, that this progressive appearance of consciousness and thought should have occurred in the midst of a physical world which, it would seem, might well have remained totally and eternally unconscious and inert. Is it not a strange fate for the small pieces of animated matter that we are to have succeeded, at the cost of long efforts often pursued for generations, to reconstitute laboriously a few elements of that Nature from which however we derive? Our body is made up of atoms teeming with electrons, protons and other elementary particles, and in which quantic transitions follow one another unceasingly; our nervous system, the essential tool of our activities, is the seat of innumerable electrical phenomena required for its functioning, the whole balance of our body and of the processes that ensure the continuation of our existence depends upon the action of hormones, vitamins and a large number of complicated organic substances. And yet, it needed the whole slow development of modern science to make known to us all these things *which are in us!* Scientific work therefore consists in a kind of strange "reconquest" whereby, by reflecting itself in men's consciousness and reason, the World learns to know itself. An astonishing outcome of the adventure of protoplasm!

Thus is revealed the outstanding value of human thought in general, of scientific thought in particular. Through it, the Universe becomes slightly conscious of itself, and to a certain extent, we are the consciousness of the Universe and each advancement in our Science marks an advancement in that consciousness.

That is what reveals the grandeur of Science in its disinterested aspect. But there is another way of considering things when seen from the standpoint of action. We have said that as there appeared on the earth more complicated organisms in which consciousness showed itself more and more clearly, Life entered upon a new course. Sprung from inert matter and undergoing incessantly its obsessing pressure, living matter breaking up into units conscious of their autonomy began in turn to exert a voluntary action on the exterior environment and thus to modify somewhat the evolution thereof. Furthermore, man endowed with consciousness, intelligence and liberty may influence the material world surrounding him. To acquire a deeper knowledge of the physical world and to act upon it, man uses means totally different from those used by the other living beings. Until the appearance of man, Life, which had already launched forth on the conquest of the World by the organizing impulse that characterizes it, had increased its means of perception and its possibilities of action through anatomical and physiological channels thanks to a complexity and gradual refinement of the living structures and their organs.

With the intervention of human intelligence, Life will extend its power by other means—in man, the sense organs no longer evolve perceptibly, but instruments which science enables him to design and bring into being will considerably extend the field of his perceptions. The telephone and radio enable him to hear at great distances, optical instruments enable his eyes to scan the depths of the heavens and the innermost part of matter. A still more extraordinary process because more subtle principles are involved, the electron microscope further extends indirectly his field of vision in the realm of the infinitesimally small. Whilst his power of perception is constantly increasing and gaining in refinement, man also acquires through science means of action which formerly could never have been imagined. The railway, the steamer, the submarine, the car, the airplane enable him to travel at increasing speeds on land, on the sea, under water and in the air. The steam-engine, the production and transport of electric power make considerable energies available to him whenever and wherever he wishes. Chemistry, by supplying him with an ever increasing number of bodies with diverse properties offers wider and wider possibilities to his industry. Sustained by the rapid progress of physiology and the natural sciences, Medicine and Surgery hold back sickness and death, whilst Biology is beginning to cast a somewhat disturbing beam of light on the mysteries of Life itself and particularly on the mechanism of heredity. And in the recent and remarkable developments of biology, we again see, in accord with previous remarks, how Life by applying itself to its own study, is beginning to understand itself.

Thus, thanks to Science and its technical applications, man is going to domineer over the Earth and transform its history. He knows its whole surface, goes across it rapidly and can act more and more on it as well as on the flora and fauna that cover it. Through atomic energy and other discoveries to be made, man will be more than ever the Master of the Earth—no one knows how far his work will stop in this field. And who knows whether one day, perhaps in the not too distant future, some mutation either accidental, or brought about by man himself, may give rise to a superman with a far greater intelligence than ours who, with means of which we have no idea, will pursue the work we have begun and carry still further the triumphs of Life.

Fired with the enthusiasms for the prospects disclosed to him by such thoughts, the scientist may grow excited at the idea that he participates more than anyone in this progressive evolution of the World. He will be tempted to cry out with Jean Perrin: "Thanks to the more and more differentiated living beings in which its structure is building up, the Universe is gradually rising to an ever extending Thought, so much so that it may become a Will governing its own history."

And yet, there is a formidable argument which may make us fear that our hopes are vain and our enthusiasm is ingenuous.

Life, Thought, Will, we know these only on the surface of the Earth, this small planet, and then on limited regions of its surface. No doubt we can imagine that in other solar systems there exist other planets where Life may appear, where perhaps beings somewhat similar to us and likewise endowed with thought pursue a task akin to ours. It may also be presumed (not in the near future no doubt) that man may succeed in leaving the Earth, in extending his presence or at least his influence to more or less vast parts of the solar system. But how insignificant all this is in comparison with the immensity of the heavens, with the illimitable dimensions of that Universe where the galaxies float like isolated islands at distances of hundreds of millions of light-years! The progressive evolution of Life on Earth, the achievements of our intelligence and of our will, all these things which formerly made us feel proud and confident now appear to us as having been reduced to nothing by the immensity of space. Moreover, there is the immensity of time, the final death which threatens the Earth, the solar system, the whole present or future theatre of our activities. We are oppressed by such thoughts and are tempted to sink into despair.

We are perhaps the victims of an illusion and give too much importance to space and time, which are just the *frames* of our perceptions. Maybe we are wrong to admit implicitly that the value of a thing is to be measured according to the volume it occupies in space or to its duration in time. Perhaps the whole Universe which we know by our perceptions from the atom to the spiral nebula is only a very small fraction of a much greater Reality which some superman may succeed one day in knowing partially. Within the framework of this vaster Reality, our effort, which from the standpoint of Sirius seems to us so localized and so temporary, might resume all its value. The worker who, facing the reverse side of his work, weaves a high-warp tapestry, may not realize the real work he is performing, but he would perceive this day when he could turn the tapestry back and contemplate it. Thus, when human thought has reached a higher stage of its development, it may perceive some day, beyond the reaches of Space and Time, the true meaning of the work which, extending and crowning Life's effort, it will have endeavored untiringly to accomplish. Such is the supreme hope, which, at the close of his existence, may comfort the scientist who has reached the end of his task.

23.

Bridging Science and Values: A Unifying View of Mind and Brain

Roger Sperry

Introduction

General acceptance of the inadequacy of science in the realm of ethics and moral judgment is reflected in the old adage that "Science deals with facts, not with values," and its corollary that "Value judgments lie outside the realm of science." In other versions it is stated that science may tell us *how* but not *why*, or that science may show us how to achieve defined goals, but not which are the right goals to aim for. A further pronouncement holds that science can tell us what *is* but not what *ought* to be: science *de*scribes but cannot *pre*scribe.

Although this time-honored dichotomy between science and value judgment has not gone unchallenged,[1, 2, 3] the great majority in science, philosophy and related fields continue today to accept the tradition that science as a discipline must by its very nature operate in the realm of objective fact and that science, either as a method or as a body of knowledge, can neither formulate value standards nor resolve issues in the domain of subjective value. When it comes to value conflicts and ethical validation, we are told that we must seek our answers elsewhere—in the humanities, in ethics and philosophy, and particularly in religion, long held to be the prime custodian of human value systems. In what follows, my aim, in large part, is to try to show that this traditional separation of science and values and the related limitations it has implied for science as a discipline are no longer valid in the context of current mind-brain theory.

The issues at stake, even by the most hard-nosed, pragmatic standards, are neither trivial nor ivory tower. Human values, in the framework to be spelled out below, become a practical concern of concrete consequence. In addition to their commonly recognized significance from a personal, religious, or philosophic standpoint, human values can also be viewed objectively in scientific terms as universal determinants in all human decision making. All decisions boil down to a choice among alternatives of what is most valued—for whatever reason; and are determined by the particular value system that prevails at the time. Viewed objectively, human value priorities stand out as the most strategically powerful causal influence now shaping events on the surface of the globe. More than any other causal system with which science now concerns itself, it is variables in the human value factor that will determine the future.

I have rated human values as a social problem above the more concrete crisis conditions like poverty, population, energy or pollution, on the following grounds.[3] First, all these crisis conditions are man-made and very largely products of human values. Further, they are not correctable on any long-term basis without first changing the underlying human values involved. And finally, the more strategic way to remedy these conditions is to go after the social value priorities directly in advance, rather than waiting for these value changes to be forced by changing environmental conditions. Otherwise we are doomed from here on to live always on the margins of intolerability, because it is not until things get rather intolerable that the voting majority gets around to changing its established values.

The importance of value issues is apparent also in other perspectives. From the standpoint of brain function, it is clear that a person's or a society's values directly and constantly shape its actions and decisions. Any given brain will respond differently to the same input, and will tend to process the same information in quite diverse ways depending on its particular system of value priorities. In short, what an individual or a society values determines very largely what it does. As human numbers increase, and science and technology advance, the regulative control role of the human value factor (that directly determines how all this growing human impact will be applied and directed) will become correspondingly more powerful.

In a different vein we are informed that the prevailing social neurosis of our times is a growing sense of valuelessness, apathy, a sense of hopelessness and loss of purpose and ultimate meaning. One is reminded of the generalized disintegration of long established values and belief systems and the grasping in all directions for new answers, new life styles, and the reviving in radical form of some of the old answers. From still other directions come warnings that we need a whole new system of social value guidelines if civilized man is to survive, "new ethics for survival" as Hardin puts it,[4] that would act to preserve man's world instead of destroying it.

Accepting the enormous control power of human values and the critical key role their shaping will play in determining the future, it follows that if science is inherently inadequate to deal with value problems, we are indeed confronted with a profound shortcoming in science and all it stands for. On these terms perhaps it is for the best that government should be tightening the screws on the funding of science, especially pure science; and that public confidence in science generally should be in question, while the forces of antiscience gain new ground fostered by the eloquent and often cogent writings of critics like Roszak and Mishan.[5, 6] Certainly the future of science will be very different depending on whether science is, or is not, recognized in the public mind to have competence in the realm of values. Of greater importance, the future of civilized society and of the ecosystem generally will also be very different, depending on the extent to which future social values are shaped from the world view of science or from various alternatives.

Grounds for Reappraisal

While the epistemological separation of science and values has seemed logically justified in the past, especially with respect to physical science, and still applies in practice to many aspects of scientific methodology, new grounds can be seen today to directly question the main philosophic validity of the science-vs.-values dichotomy. Recent developments, especially in the behavioral sciences, reopen central questions and greatly strengthen arguments for a revised, almost diametrically opposed philosophy in which modern science is advanced as man's prime hope in the quest for new values and a sense of meaning. Problems of values, ethics and morality (questions, i.e., of what is *good, right* and *true* and of what *ought* to be) become, on these revised terms, something to which science can, in the most profound sense, contribute fundamentally and in which science should be actively and responsibly involved.

Although proposals along similar lines since Francis Bacon have failed to gain any wide acceptance and have been largely written off under the label "scientism" by detractors, conceptual developments during the last decade in the area of mind-brain relations introduce an interpretation of conscious mind and a related philosophical framework that substantially alter the picture. The scope of science in respect to mental activity and its qualifications for dealing with subjective experience are directly affected. A modified concept of the relation of subjective experience to brain mechanisms and to external reality has emerged, that involves a direct contradiction of the central founding thesis of Behaviorism in this country and of the materialistic philosophy in Russia and elsewhere.[7-10] Important departures from long-established determinist and materialist doctrine follow with extensive implications for the philosophy of science and derivation of values.

Current mind-brain theory no longer dispenses with conscious mind as just an "inner aspect" of brain activity, or as some passive "epiphenomenal," metaphysical, or other impotent by-product, as has long been the custom; nor does it reject consciousness as merely an artifact of semantics or as being identical to the neural events. Consciousness, in these revised terms, becomes an integral, dynamic property of the brain process itself and a central constituent of brain action. Subjective experience is viewed in operational terms[11] as a causal determinant in brain function and acquires emergent control influence in regulating the course of physico-chemical events in brain activity. No metaphysical interaction in the classical sense is implied; the causal relation primarily involves the power of the whole over its parts. In a sense, mind moves matter in the brain just as an organism moves its component organs and cells, or a molecule governs the molecular course of its own electrons. In the case of conscious phenomena, it is the dynamic enveloping power of conscious high order cerebral processes over their constituent neural and chemical elements.[12] As an emergent interpretation of mind, it differs from the concepts of Gestalt psychology[13] in that the conscious effects are not ascribed to isomorphic field forces, nor are they considered to be mere correlates of neural activity. The conscious mind is put to work and given a reason for being and for having been evolved in a material world.

Although inseparably tied to the physical brain process, conscious awareness is conceived to be something distinct and special in itself, "different from and more than" the collected sum of its physico-chemical components. Values and other mental phenomena, though built of neural events, are no longer conceived to be reducible to, nor identifiable with, those events, nor to be mere parallel correlates.

This modified approach to the status of mind emerged largely out of efforts to account for the unity and/or duality and related aspects of conscious experience in split brain studies. I described the scheme initially[14] as a swing toward mentalism that puts conscious mind in the driver's seat in command over matter, gives ideas and ideals control over physico-chemical interactions, and recognizes conscious mental forces as the crowning achievement of evolution. It provides a conceptual explanatory formula for the interaction of mind with matter that does not violate the principles of scientific explanation and is expressed in terms acceptable to modern neuroscience. Conscious mind is reinstated in the brain of objective science and scientific theory is squared with common sense on the mind-controlling-behavior issue.

A New Outlook

The involved change in the status of conscious mind in objective science carries with it a renunciation of much of the mechanistic, behavioristic, deterministic, and reductionistic thinking that formerly has characterized behavioral science and scientism. Long-standing epistemological paradoxes involving the separation of mind and matter, subjective and objective, fact and value, free will and determinism, and *is* and *ought* that have long puzzled and polarized ethical and scientific thinking, seem now to begin to resolve in principle. The current interpretation brings together selected aspects of prior materialist, mentalist, gestalt, monist and dualist doctrine. Some of its implications are explored here, not with any presumption that the present view offers definitive solutions, but only that it seems to represent an advancement containing certain features that differ from those on which value-belief systems have previously been built.

297

On the present terms it becomes increasingly impossible, among other things, to accept the idea of two separate realms of knowledge, existence, or truth: one for objective science and another for subjective experience and values. Old metaphysical dualisms and the seemingly irreconcilable paradoxes that have prevailed in psychology between the realities of inner experience on the one hand and those of experimental brain research on the other,[15] disappear in a single continuous hierarchy. Within the brain, we pass conceptually in a hierarchical continuum from the brain's subnuclear particles on up through atoms, molecules, and brain cells to nerve circuit systems without consciousness, and finally to cerebral processes with consciousness. Objective facts and subjective values become parts of the same realm of discourse. The hiatus between science and values is eraseed in part by expanding the scope of science to encompass inner experience, and also by altering the status of subjective values so that they are no longer set off in an epiphenomenal or other parallelistic subjective domain beyond the reach of science.[16] "Science" is used broadly here to include the knowledge, insight, perspectives, beliefs, and understanding that come from science as well as the relative validity, credibility, and reliability of the scientific method itself as an approach to truth so far as the human brain can know it. Also, one needs to remember in this connection that modern science includes the behavioral, political, social and related sciences and does not on the above terms imply the traditional hardcore materialism and strict objectivity of a decade ago.[17]

So long as science was lacking a plausible account of mind in relation to matter, and excluded on principle the whole realm of inner subjective experience, the worldview of science remained incomplete and inadequate to provide answers in the realm of subjective moral value or higher meaning. Alternative world views built around more wishful metaphysical dimensions were not only more appealing to the public majority, but also remained competitive in credibility. With the value-rich world of inner experience no longer excluded on principle from the realm of science, scientism (i.e., the search for values and higher meaning through science) takes on added humanistic dimensions and a whole new look. On these revised terms the emotional, interpersonal, and aesthetic dimensions in ethical systems no longer exclude a scientific approach nor are they either excluded from an ethic based on science. Many of the antiscience and counterculture objections leveled against materialistic science no longer apply.

From the outset it has been recognized that this compromise operational interactionist approach to consciousness would provide in theory a long sought unifying view of mind, brain and man in nature and would go far to restore to the scientific image of man some of the freedom, dignity, and other humanistic attributes of which it has long been deprived.[18] An antireductionist worldview and interpretation of reality are also implied in which the qualitative pattern properties of all entities are conceived to be just as real and causally potent as are the properties of their elements or their quantitative measurements and abstractions. This preservation of the qualitative value and pluralistic richness of reality helps to counter antiscience views[19] that correlate science with reductionism.

The reductionist approach that would always explain the whole in terms of "nothing but" the parts leads to an infinite nihilistic regress in which eventually everything is held to be explainable in terms of essentially nothing. By our present interpretation, it is better science to conceive wholes and their properties as real phenomena with their own meaning and causal efficacy. This means essentially that the pattern relationships of the component parts to each other in time and space are recognized to be of critical importance in causation and in determining the nature and meaning of all things and that these configurational relationships are not reducible to properties of the parts alone. The message will not be found in the chemistry of the ink. Thus, the search in science for a unifying explanatory formula for the universe is discouraged in favor of the recognition and sanction of pluralism.

Further Implications

A substantially altered picture of scientific determinism is also implied.[20, 21] Subjective values of all kinds, even aesthetic, spiritual and irrational come to be recognized as having causal control potency in the brain's decision-making process—along with all other components of the world of inner experience. Even such factors as one's subjective feelings about predicted outcomes anticipated to result from a given choice as long as 25 or 100 years in the future, may be entered proactively as causal determinants in the cerebral operations that lead to a given choice. In terms of the degrees and kinds of freedom of choice introduced thereby into the causal sequence of decision making, the human brain is clearly set apart above all other known systems, at an apex post in the deterministic universe of science.

Issues raised in the foregoing are central and fundamental to ethics and value questions at all levels. Value priorities especially in the ideological, religious, and cultural areas, are heavily dependent, directly or by implication, on concepts and beliefs regarding the properties of the conscious mind, and on the kinds of life goals and worldviews which these permit. Directly and indirectly, the latter depend on whether consciousness is believed to be mortal or immortal, or reincarnate or cosmic; and whether consciousness is conceived to be localized and brain-bound or essentially universal as in pan-psychism or Whiteheadian theory —or perhaps capable of "supracoalescence" in a megamind. Where formerly there were seemingly unlimited degrees of freedom for speculation in these areas, advances in neuroscience during the last few decades substantially narrow now the latitudes for possible realistic answers. In modern neurology it is no longer a question of whether conscious experience is tied to the living brain, but rather to what particular parts of the brain, or to which neural systems and under what physiological conditions.[22]

As the brain process comes to be understood objectively, all mental phenomena, including the generation of values, can be treated as causal agents in human decision making. The origins, directive potency, and the consequences of values all become subject, in principle, to objective scientific investigation and analysis. This applies at all levels, from that of the brain's pleasure-pain centers and other reinforcement systems on up through the forces that mold priorities at the societal, national, and international plane. Modern behavioral science already treats value variables and their formation as important causal variants in behavior, and it also deals analytically with goals, needs, motivation, and related factors at individual, group, and societal levels. Value variables are in principle reproducible through replication of similar brain states. What amounts to a separate science of values in the context of decision theory becomes conceivable, extending into all branches of behavioral science and forming a skeletal core for social science. Any advances in our understanding of the origins and logical structure of value systems can be expected to result in wiser selection and ordering of social values, and better value judgments and decisions generally.

Remaining Obstacles

Once it is possible, in principle, to resolve epistemological differences between mind and brain, subjective value and objective fact, determinism and free will, and to treat values objectively in the context of decision making, it then follows that other remaining obstacles and objections to an approach to values and meaning through science tend to disappear. The old argument of professional philosophy that it is logically impossible to determine what *ought to be* from what *is*, or to derive ethical values from scientific facts may hold on paper in the abstract. It carries little practical significance, however, when values are viewed pragmatically as above in a brain-behavior framework. Human values are inherently properties of brain activity and it invites logical confusion to try to treat them as if they had independent existence artificially separated from the functioning brain. In the operations of the brain, incoming facts regularly interact with and shape values. In terms of cerebral processing, it is difficult to see a better way to determine "what ought to be" than on the basis of factual information, especially facts and deductions therefrom that have been scientifically verified. History and common observation confirm that nothing tells better than science what ought to prevail in order to achieve any defined aim, whether the aim be a landing site on Mars, improved health or whatever.

The human brain comes already equipped in advance with established value determinants and with inbuilt logical constraints that have their origins partly in biological heritage, partly in prior experience, and may even come through formal acceptance of ethical axioms. In practice, therefore, it is not a question of deriving values from the facts per se. Incoming factual information interacts as a cofunction with intrinsic cerebral value determinants in hen-egg fashion in the building of one's sense of value. The value system of any adult or society is determined in large part by objective facts. The mutual interactions through time between the inbuilt systems of values inherent in human nature and the developing worldview determinants form a complex manifold. Value judgments will never be made simple by a scientific approach and in some respects promise to become more complicated. One can hope only for improved value judgments through error correction and advanced insight. The worldview of science includes, of course, a growing understanding of the origins and structure of the inherent value functions and of their chronological shaping during development.

The question at issue may thus be framed more usefully in terms of the impact of a set of facts upon ongoing brain processes wherein values and related logical determinants already are operative. If one asks accordingly whether a set of facts can shape value priorities, the answer, of course, is "yes." We are constantly adjusting our values to conform logically with new factual information. The advance of science historically has always had a deep inevitable influence on social value systems. For present purposes, the innate primal system of values inbuilt in human nature (the personal and social aspects of which tend to form a large common denominator for any human value system) is treated largely as constant in order to focus on the more extrinsic variables that involve science and its alternatives. Our concern here is specifically with those value system variables introduced by acceptance of the method and worldview of science. Many advances of past teachings in the area of personal and interpersonal relations would not be changed. The related problem of starting axioms or premises and prime determinants in ethical systems is considered separately below.

Science, as man's number one source of factual information, may be enlisted in the realm of value judgment on the simple and straightforward rationale that an informed judgment is generally preferable to one that is uninformed or misinformed. Merely to close the value gap that currently exists around the world between the informed and the uninformed might in itself go a long way to help counter current disaster trends. Similarly, if judgments about right and wrong are best arrived at on the basis of what is true, avoiding what is false, science would seem on this count as well to deserve a lead role in determining ethical values instead of being disqualified.

Some of the arbitrariness and endless complexity of human values that have always seemed forbidding to any approach through science disappear in part if one agrees to exclude the metaphysical and mythological, and to hold to a frame of reference supported by science. Societal values of the category that get written into law can be shown to be largely goal-dependent directly or by implication and arrangeable into logical hierarchical systems with major and subsidiary goals superseded by ultimate goals and conditioned throughout by inherent traits and needs of the species.[23]

A quite different view would renounce any rational approach to ethics through science, not because social values should be left to the humanities, the church, the courts, or to Karl Marx, but rather on grounds that it is wiser that values be left to themselves to change spontaneously, by collective intuition as it were, in response to changing environmental conditions. Some economic realists assert that this is the only way that values change and eschew any moral philosophizing and idealizing as ineffectual. This latter overlooks the strong reciprocal interaction between mental concepts and environmental conditions and the tremendous impact that ideology and value systems have always had on the course of human history. It overlooks also the fact that social values formed merely on this situational feedback basis as a reflection of prevailing conditions tend in the democratic process to be locked to levels of tolerability.

Science and the Prime Determinants of Value

It is not only the value systems of formal religion that have been found wanting today, but also those based in humanist, communist, existentialist, and even in common humanitarian persuasions. Contemporary recourse to alternatives like the "lifeboat ethic" or that of "triage" hardly offer inspired solutions. The global ecospheric nature of current world problems calls for value perspectives built on something higher than just the human species or its societal dynamics, something that will include the welfare of the entire biosphere and ecosphere on a long term basis.[24] It becomes a logical necessity also in efforts to perceive any higher meaning or purpose, that humanity see itself in terms of a meaningful relation to something more important than itself.

The more critical value issues that must be faced in the near future will involve decisions that ultimately require appraisals of the relative worth of human life in various contexts. As terrestrial crowding conditions get tighter, for example, the value of human life must be balanced increasingly against that of other species. Having already destroyed the natural meaning and dignity of life for a number of subordinate species and permanently extinguished others, man will be forced to judge how much farther the violation of species' rights should be carried and by what ethic. Many more examples can be listed where scientific advancements, coupled with mounting population and related pressures, raise a growing host of moral dilemmas that resolve finally around the question of the ultimate worth and meaning of life itself. Possible answers become relative with alternatives that call for assessment within some larger ethic yet to be found. What is needed ideally, of course, to make decisions in these areas is a consensus on some supreme comprehension and interpretation of the universe and the place and role within it of man and the life experience.

The same position is reached by way of abstract value theory, in which values are shown to depend largely on goals, and that any concept or belief regarding the goal and value of life as a whole, once accepted, then logically supersedes and conditions values at all subsidiary levels. Value priorities become ordered and ethical issues judged in accordance with the conceived ultimate goal. This latter will imply in turn an associated "worldview" or universal scheme that is consistent.

By one route or another, then, we come down to these prime determinants of value priorities—these "life-goal," "worldview" concepts and beliefs, explicit or implied, that lie at the heart of the problem of values and pose the central challenge for a scientific or any other approach. This is where the great unknowns lie and also where the great differences of opinion are found. This is where answers are most needed and where any answers, once accepted, right or wrong, have the greatest impact. And it is here also that the competence of science in the arena of values and any new ethic must eventually prove itself. The scientist, trained to rigorous reasoning and skepticism, to checking against empirical evidence, and above all, to avoiding false conclusions, may easily be persuaded at this point that value problems are not for science. It must, however, be remembered that final, absolute, or perfect answers are not demanded, only improved ones; and that society has in the past and probably will continue in the future to find and abide by some kind of answers from somewhere.

Actually, modern science, with its concepts of cosmology, evolution and the nature of conscious mind, reaching into all levels and aspects of the natural order from subnuclear particles on up through galaxies millions of light years away, has a considerable amount to say about most of those fundamental cornerstone concepts upon which man's great mainline value systems have built through history. The worldview of modern science renders all previous schemes simplistic by comparison and provides man's most reliable understanding of, and rapport with those forces that move the universe and control creation. What has been accepted most commonly in the past as the highest reference for ethical standards and moral authority, man's creator, becomes in the eyes of science the vast interwoven fabric of all evolving nature. Each new scientific discovery and insight increases by that much more man's comprehension of the total design of evolving nature which, as indicated, implicates value and meaning in our current concept of mind and makes a final referent and framework for any ethical or moral system.

Some of the kinds of social value changes that might inhere in an ethic founded in science can be foreseen in broad outline,[25, 26] but these remain for the most part still to be developed. Social decisions on ethical issues, however, do not require and frequently do not involve, nor wait on precise logical answers. Decision making proceeds commonly on the basis of vague impressions, inclinations, doctrinal perspectives, emotional learnings and convictions, personal biases, and the like. Even a slight shift in the ethical norms of society, as along the science-antiscience axis, could set in motion, through a vast complex of decisional differences, changes affecting population policy, global conservation, and ecosystem planning generally, the overall future impact of which would make that of other top goals in science, like a cure for cancer, appear insignificant by comparison. Progress along the above lines could be greatly speeded on many fronts if we can merely clear the way by making it intellectually respectable and scientifically sound to think that "Science deals with values as well as with facts."

Notes

1. Clyde Kluckhohn. 1959. *Proceedings of the American Philosophy Society* 102, p. 469.

2. Ralph W. Burhoe. 1973. *Zygon* 4, p. 65; *Zygon* 8, 412.

3. R.W. Sperry. 1972. *Perspectives on Biological Medicine* 16, 115; reprinted in *Zygon* 9, p. 7 (1974).

4. Garrett Hardin, *Exploring New Ethics for Survival* (New York: Viking Press, 1972).

5. Theodore Roszak, *Where the Wasteland Ends: Politics and Transcendence in Postindustrial Society* (New York: Doubleday, 1973).

6. Ezra J. Mishan, *The Costs of Economic Growth* (New York: Praeger, 1969). See Chapter 12, sections d and e.

7. R.W. Sperry. 1966. *Bulletin on Atomic Science* 22, p. 2; John Platt, *New Views of the Nature of Man*, Chap. 4 (Chicago: University of Chicago Press, 1965).

8. R.W. Sperry. 1969. *Psychology Review* 76, p. 532.

9. R.W. Sperry. 1970. *Psychology Review* 77, p. 585.

10. R.W. Sperry. in *Consciousness and Brain*, Gordon Globus, G. Maxwell, I. Savodnik, eds. (New York: Plenum, p. 198).

11. R.W. Sperry. 1952. *American Scientist* 40, p. 291.

12. For an expanded discussion on holistic causality, see Edward Pols. 1971. *International Philosophy Quarterly* 11, p. 293.

13. Wolfgang Kohler and Richard Held. 1949. *Science* 110, p. 414.

14. R.W. Sperry. 1966. *Bulletin on Atomic Science* 22, p. 2.

15. T.W. Wann, ed., *Behaviorism and Phenomenology: Contrasting Bases for Modern Psychology* (Chicago: University of Chicago Press, 1965).

16. R.W. Sperry. 1969. *Psychology Review* 76, p. 532.

17. See also Michael Polanyi, *The Tacit Dimension* (New York: Doubleday, 1966).

18. R.W. Sperry, *Bulletin on Atomic Science* 22, p. 2.

19. Theodore Roszak, *Where the Wasteland Ends*.

20. R.W. Sperry, *Problems Outstanding in the Evolution of Brain Function* (New York: American Museum of Natural History, James Arthur lecture, 1964).

21. R.W. Sperry, *Bulletin on Atomic Science* 22, p. 2.

22. John C. Eccles, *The Understanding of the Brain* (New York: McGraw-Hill, 1973), *Brain and Conscious Experience* (New York: Springer-Verlag, 1966).

23. R.W. Sperry, *Perspectives on Biological Medicine* 16, p. 115.

24. Garrett Hardin, *Exploring New Ethics for Survival*.

25. Ralph W. Burhoe, *Zygon* 7, p. 412.

26. R.W. Sperry, *Perspectives on Biological Medicine* 16, p. 115.

24.
Individual Existence

Bradley T. Scheer

H. D. Lewis begins, in *Persons in Recent Thought*, by listing metaphysical bases for consideration of persons, under the classical headings of idealism and materialism. I consider that the prevailing metaphysics of natural scientists, and of all those multitudes whose thought is formed on theirs, may be designated monistic naturalism. This is the position that nature, defined as the sensible universe accessible to human senses, aided or supplemented by suitable instruments of known mechanism of operation, is the only reality. This is a form of materialism in that, according to the prevailing reductionist ontology, all nature can be understood in terms of a single entity, matter-energy, and therefore nature, and all reality, are comprehended in this single entity.

Henry Margenau, in a treatment which has had less notice than it deserves,[1] presents a different metaphysics, and Weisskopf, in a recent article,[2] has joined the small heretical party of those who recognize some limitations of natural science in understanding nature. According to Margenau, physical reality consists in those sets of verifacts (deductively verified mental constructs) categorized as systems, observables, and states. I consider this to be a form of idealism, though Margenau attempts to refute any such intention. In his system, reality does not reside in the "P-plane" of perceived objects and phenomena, but rather in the "C-plane" of, as I should put it, mappings of perceptions into constructs, using accepted epistemic rules. We may, however, apply Margenau's system to our consideration of Lewis' question as to the meaning of individual existence. From a naturalistic point-of-view—which is by no means my only personal viewpoint—the question is whether the system designated "person," and the states of that system, can be fully defined by a limited set of observables.

A person may be thought of as a member of the larger category of living systems. I shall consider three properties of living systems under the headings of individuality, continuity, and ectropy. Individuality is apparent in the common observables of size or mass, color, and form. For legal purposes, a single feature of form, the fingerprint, is considered sufficient to identify a person, and for many purposes a signature, which is a product, is sufficient. Evidently, however, to say that we know a person, in the sense of the French verb *connaitre*, requires much more information and long acquaintance or observation. All these modes of knowing clearly reveal individuality or observation. All these modes of knowing clearly reveal individuality as a characteristic of persons. The basis of individuality of all living systems is a genome or set of genes, a unique body of information constituted, in all species with a sexual process in the life history, at the moment of conception when one gene set, from one parental strain, is united with another from the other parental strain to constitute the genome of the individual.[3] I should not wish to be interpreted, however, as proposing a genetic determinism of persons, for individuality is also a matter of the history of the individual.

Weisskopf notes that living systems are different from most physical systems in that the properties of a living system reveal the history of the system.[4] The genome of every member of a species contains something of the entire history of the species and its predecessors from The Beginning. This is expressed in the biochemical and physical properties of individuals which constitute the taxonomic characteristics used by systematists in classification. On these common specific properties, incorporating a large element of variance introduced by random processes in the transmission of a genome from one generation to the next, is imposed the record of the history of the individual from the moment of conception. The expression of genes in the biochemical and physical characteristics of the individual is subject to a variety of environmental influences, and heredity is much less determinate than some writers would have us believe.

Beyond these developmental influences, the brain, once it

begins to function, preserves the record of a large part of the history of the individual, including not only external stimuli and their perception, but also a record of the responses to those stimuli and their interpretation. The identity of a person, and the sense of continuity as Lewis notes, is rooted in memory. Psychological experimentation has shown that the erasure of the past by post-hypnotic suggestion results in the immediate appearance of schizophrenic symptoms, loss of identity and modification of personal expression in behavior. Our identity is in the past, and not only in our personal past but in that of our ethnic, regional, and national forebears. I am an American, not only because I was born in this state and nation, but because my ancestors for at least nine generations were born in some part of this nation.

We come then to the matter of the states of the system we have denoted by person. In the interests of brevity, I shall only consider the states of consciousness and its opposite, unconsciousness. These states are evident in terms of the observables of activity and responsiveness. Sir Charles Sherrington has given us an unforgettable picture of the spread of nervous activity through the "great ravelled knot" of nerve fibers we call the brain, during the process of awakening.[5] Since he wrote, we have learned more than he knew about the localization of the events he described, and with the elaborate instrument known as an encephalograph electrical correlates of nervous activity in the brain can be detected in the wavy lines and spikes of an encephalogram. Although the nerve impulse itself, the source of these electrical events, is now fully understood in terms of events at the level of atoms and molecules, we still do not understand the connection between the functions of the brain and the electrical events detectable with the encephalograph. This is a scientific mystery which, in Weisskopf's terms, evades our understanding because it is too complex, rather than because we have no principles of explanation. In effect, we have more principles than we can usefully employ. The "higher functions" of the brain in a state of consciousness are not understood in naturalistic terms, even though we have a working model of the memory and logical functions in electronic computers. There thus remain important aspects of the system person which are not defined by common physical observables, and are not explained by known physical principles. In my opinion, the mystery of the person is the sort for which the requisite explanatory principles have not yet been discovered. My intuition, for I can claim no more than that, is that the key to our understanding of persons will be found in the concept of information, at the interface between thermodynamics and information theory, and I shall outline the sketch of my thinking here. Information is a matter of pattern or order. The information which I may convey in my speech is conveyed by means of elaborate patterns of sounds in time. The same or other information may be conveyed in an elaborate pattern of conventional marks on paper, or in any suitable code, even the system of dots and dashes in the traditional telegraphic code.

The information which I attempt to convey has its source and seat in my brain, where it has been assembled by the organization and integration of elements from perception and from memory. When I say "my brain" I am manifesting that property of proprietary self-awareness mentioned by Lewis as an important characteristic of persons. I hope that I am also manifesting two other characteristics, namely spontaneity and self-transcendence. Spontaneity is the creative property of persons, whereby we create new patterns of order by the manipulation of objects, symbols, or constructs. The property of self-transcendence, a term I owe to the late Reinhold Niebuhr, is the ability to "stand outside oneself and look at oneself."[6]

The history of a person is a history of the expression, reception, creation, and transmission of information. The information that is transmitted from one generation to the next in the genome is expressed materially during the process of development, which continues throughout life from conception to death. Development is epigenetic, in that each stage or step is dependent on those that precede it, and provides the necessary conditions for those that follow.

The genome of an individual may be described as a program for the life processes and development of the individual, written in the genetic code, which has a well-defined material basis. The expression of that program depends to a considerable degree on external influences. During the lifetime of the individual there is a continuing process of reception, selection, integration, and accumulation of information beyond that contained in the genome,[7] and the creation of information by rational construction and imagination beyond that contained in the input from the environment. Some of this accumulated information is transmitted during the lifetime of the individual, and the ultimate question concerning persons is that of the survival of the distinctive pattern of information that characterizes the individual after the death and disintegration of the material vehicle of that information. I have defined the person in terms of individuality, historicity, and information, and concluded that the body of information carried in and by the body of a human person defines that person as a continuing entity, and the question is primarily one of continuity. The psychological experiments I mentioned earlier showed that, when the future was erased by post-hypnotic suggestion, the result was lethargy and a complete lack of interest in the life of the present. And when both past and future were erased in a single suggestion, the subject fell into a coma. Our identity as persons is the past, and our hope is in the future. Many of the symptoms of society at the moment can be traced to the absence from the information content of many persons of any definite constructs of the past or of the future, and the fear of death so markedly evident in Western society today results from the absence of future, and is, in effect, the fear of ceasing to exist as a person.

Information is immaterial, though it is ordinarily carried by or embodied in a material medium or vehicle. The challenge to nonidealistic philosophies is the undoubted reality of information, independent of its medium or vehicle. The production of information—order, pattern, negentropy, or ectropy—has been recognized as the distinctive property of living systems, and pre-eminently of persons, by Auerbach, Schrodinger, Schoffeniels, and the present writer. Weisskopf has suggested that the principle according to which a flow of energy from high to lower potential, with increase in entropy, engenders a smaller decrease in internal entropy (increase in ectropy) could be called the fourth law or principle of thermodynamics.[8, 9, 10, 11] This is a form of the principle stated by Prigogine as the principle of minimum entropy production.[12]

Even the monistic naturalist, who regards only the material expression of information and not its content, sees in the fundamental and universal laws or principles of natural science, invariant in time, something of absolute value. In the contemplation of these principles and their operation we come in touch with eternity. The theist may, as I do, regard these principles as the expression of the Will of the Creator. From either viewpoint, it is possible to envision a philosophy of values, comprising ethics and

311

esthetics, founded on the ectropy principle. I can see no difficulty, on that foundation, with the conclusion that the information content or ectropy which defines a person has the property of eternity, and is of the highest absolute value.

Notes

1. H. Margenau, *The Nature of Physical Reality* (New York: McGraw-Hill, 1950).

2. V.F. Weisskopf, "The Frontiers and Limits of Science," *American Scientist*, pp. 65–4, 405–11.

3. B.T. Scheer, *Patterns of Life* (New York: Harper's College Press, 1977).

4. V.F. Weisskopf, "The Frontiers and Limits of Science."

5. C. Sherrington, *Man on his Nature* (Cambridge, Mass: Cambridge University Press, 1940).

6. R. Niebuhr, *The Nature and Destiny of Man*, Vol. 1, Human Nature (New York: Charles Scribner's and Sons, 1941).

7. B.T. Scheer, *Patterns of Life.*

8. F. Auerbach, *Ektropismus oder die Physikalisches Theorie des Lebens* (Leipzig: Englemann, 1910).

9. E. Schrodinger, *What is Life?* (New York: Macmillan, 1945).

10. E. Schoffeniels, *L'Anti-Hasard* (Paris: Gauthier-Villars, 1973).

11. V.F. Weisskopf, *The Frontiers and Limits of Science.*

12. I. Prigogine, *Introduction to the Thermodynamics of Irreversible Processes* (Springfield: Thomas, 1955).

25.
Death and the Meaning of Life

Kai Nielsen

For intellectuals, at least, the effects of the posture of modernity is very pervasive. It characteristically leaves us with a fear of being caught out in trivialities and with a fear of saying the obvious.[1] This leads us to indirect discourse, to a penchant for being clever and, because of that very fear of saying the obvious, into triviality. Certainly on a topic such as our present one such anxieties readily surface and no doubt have a reasonable object. However, without any posturing at all, I shall simply brush them aside and plunge into my subject.

Most of what I say here I have said before and has, as well, been said before by many others.[2] Moreover, it is my belief that most of the claims made here should be a series of commonplaces, but, given the direction of our popular culture, they are not. I repeat them because they seem to me to be true, to be truths which are repeatedly avoided and which need to be taken to heart.

J.M. Cameron, a distinguished Roman Catholic philosopher whose work I admire, has remarked that more and more people today think "that to die is to be annihilated."[3] Particularly for very many of us who are intellectuals and are touched by modernity and the swarth of our secular culture, belief in the survival of bodily death is an impossibility. It seems to many of us at best a groundless bit of fantasy and at worst a conception which is through and through incoherent.[4] It is an interesting point, a point which I shall not pursue here, whether the philosophical

313

arguments purporting to establish these thoroughly secular beliefs are sound or whether they simply reflect the *Weltbild*—itself without grounds—of the dominant secular culture with its deeply scientistic orientation.[5] Whatever we should say about this, it remains the case that among the intelligentsia, and to a not inconsiderable degree elsewhere as well, belief in the survival of death is either a very considerable stumbling block or something dismissed out of hand as something which is simply "beyond belief" for anyone who can look at the world non-evasively and think tolerably clearly.

Even Cameron, who presumably does believe in some form of the survival of the death of at least our present bodies, recognizes that for most men "the hypothesis of survival" is "impossibly difficult."[6] Annihilation seems plainly and evidently to be our end. Yet he thinks that the "full terror of death" and the need to give some significance to our lives will drive us, if we are honest with ourselves and probing, to such an at least seemingly implausible belief.[7]

I want to resist this. I shall argue that, even if death is, as I believe it to be, utter annihilation, we can still find significance in our lives and that, if we will think carefully and indeed humanly —from the emotions or existentially if you will—we need not, and indeed should not, feel death to be such a stark terror. Cameron, like Kierkegaard, seems to take it as almost true by definition that to be fully human is to react to death. But why should we accept this conventional wisdom?

I shall, for a moment, as seems to me appropriate in this context, speak personally. Even though Tolstoy, Dostoevsky and Pascal have deeply touched my life, I do not feel terror when I dwell on death. Yet I know full well it must come and I firmly believe —believe without a shadow of doubt—that it will mean my utter annihilation. Yet I am without such a dread of death, though, of course, when I think of it, I feel regret that I must die, but, unlike Ivan Ilyitch, I do not feel that "before its face" all life is meaningless: nothing is worth experiencing or doing. As I am now in possession of the normal powers of life, with things I want to do and experience, with pleasure in life and with people I very much care for and who care for me, I certainly do not want to die. I should very much like, in such a state, to go on living forever. Yet plainly I cannot. In the face of this, it seems to me both a sane response and a human response to that inevitability to rather wistfully regret that fact about our common human lot and to want to make the most of the life one has. But I see no reason to make a mystery of death. And I see no reason why reflecting on my death should fill me with terror or dread or despair. One takes rational precautions against premature death and faces the rest stoically, as Freud did and as Samuel Johnson came to do, and as I am confident countless others have as well. Death should only be dreadful if one's life has been a waste.

By a conventionalist's sulk such an attitude, as I have just evinced, is thought to be a shallow one devoid of the depth and the *angst* that Cameron evinces or that he finds in Ernest Becker's *The Denial of Death* or that we find in the existentialists. (I do not speak here of Nietzsche.) John Austin, when he was dying of cancer and knew that he was dying of cancer, but when others did not, was reported to have responded to a talk by Gabriel Marcel on death by remarking "Professor Marcel, we all know we have to die, but why do we have to sing songs about it?" The conventional wisdom would make this a shallow response, but, coupled with an understanding of the integrity and importance of Austin's work and with a knowledge of Austin's fierce determination to work right up to the end, it seems to me to be just the opposite. We know we must die; we would rather not, but why must we suffer *angst*, engage in theatrics and create myths for ourselves. Why not simply face it and get on with the living of our lives?

There is a tradition, finding its most persistent expression in Christianity, which contends that without life everlasting, without some survival of the death of one's present body and without the reality of God to ensure that such a life will have a certain character, life will be pointless and morality without significance. I shall now argue that these beliefs, common as they are, are not true.

It is indeed true that mortal perplexity runs deep and moral ambivalence and anguish should be extensive. A recognition of this should be common ground between morally sensitive believers and skeptics. But there is no need to have the religious commitments of Christianity or its sister religions or any religious commitment at all to make sense of morality. Torturing human beings is vile; exploiting and degrading human beings is through-and-through evil; cruelty to human beings and animals is, morally speaking, unacceptable; and treating one's promises lightly or being careless about the truth is wrong. If we know anything to be wrong we know these things to be wrong and they would be wrong and just as wrong in a Godless world and in a world in which personal annihilation is inevitable as in a world with God and in which there is eternal life.

There is indeed a philosophical problem about how we know these things to be wrong, but this is as much a problem for the believer as for the skeptic. I would say that for anyone—for believer and skeptic alike—if he or she has an understanding of the concept of morality, has an understanding of what it is to take the moral point of view, he or she will, *eo ipso*, understand that it is wrong to harm others, that promises are to be kept and the truth to be told. This does not mean that he or she will be committed to the belief that a lie *never* can rightly be told, that a promise *never* can be broken or that a human being in *no circumstance* can rightly be harmed. But, if there is no understanding that such acts always require very special justification and that the presumption of morality is always against them, then there is no understanding of the concept of morality. But this understanding is not intrinsically or logically bound up with knowing God or knowing about God or the taking of a religious point of view or knowing or even believing that one will survive the death of one's "earthly body."

It might be responded that such an understanding does imply a knowledge of the reality of God because we *only* know these things to be wrong because we know they are against God's will and something is only good because God wills it and is only wrong because God prohibits it. Leaving aside skeptical questions about how we can know, or whether we can know, what God does and does not will, the old question arises whether something is good simply because God wills it or does God will it because it is good? What is plain—leaving aside God for a moment—is that something is not good simply because it is willed or commanded; indeed it is not even morally speaking, a good thing to do simply because it is willed or commanded by an omnipotently powerful being, unless we want to reduce morality to power worship, as has one rather well known but (on this issue) confused philosopher.[8] But might—naked power—doesn't make right. And there is no implication that it will become right even when conjoined with faultless intelligence. There can be—and indeed are —thoroughly ruthless, exploitative, manipulative people who are very intelligent indeed. Neither omnipotence nor omniscience imply goodness.

However, it is still not implausible to say that it is *God's* willing it which makes all the difference, for God, after all, is the supreme, perfect good. But I in turn ask, how do we know that or do we know that? If we say we know it through studying the Scriptures and through the example of Jesus, then it should in turn be responded that it is only in virtue of our own quite independent moral understanding of the goodness of his behavior and the behavior of the characters in the Bible that we come to recognize this. Moral understanding is not grounded in a belief in God; just the reverse is the case: an understanding of the religious *significance* of Jesus and the Scriptures presupposes a moral understanding.

If, alternatively, we claim that we do not come to understand that God is the supreme and perfect good in that way but claim that it is a necessary truth—a proposition, like "Puppies are young dogs," which is true by definition—then we still should ask: how do we understand that putatively necessary proposition? But again we should recognize that it is only by having an understanding of what goodness is that we come to have some glimmering of the more complex and extremely perplexing notions of supreme goodness or perfect goodness. The crucial thing to see is that there are things which we can recognize on reflection to be wrong, God or no God, and that we can be far more confident that we are right in claiming that they are wrong, than we can be in claiming any knowledge of God or God's order.

Finally, someone might say that since God is the cause of everything, there could be no goodness or anything else if there were no God. But this confuses *causes* and *reasons*, confuses questions about causally bringing something into existence or sustaining its existence and justifying its existence. If there is the God of the Jews and the Christians everything causally depends on Him, but still, even if there were no God who made the world, it would still be wrong to torture little children, and even if there were no people to be kind, it would be timelessly true that human kindness would be a good thing and that the goodness of human kindness does not become good or cease to become good by God's fiat or anyone else's. And it is in no way dependent on whether we live out our fourscore years and ten or whether life is everlasting.

In terms of its fundamental rationale, morality is utterly independent of belief in God or a belief in immortality. To make sense of our lives as moral beings there is no need to make what may be an intellectually stultifying blind leap of religious faith or to in any way believe in an afterlife. Such a moral understanding, as well as a capacity for moral response and action, is available to us even if we are human beings who are utterly without religious faith.

Furthermore, it does not follow that our lives are pointless, empty or meaningless if there is no God and if death is unequivocally our lot. There is no good reason to believe that because of these things we are condemned to an Oblomov-like, senseless existence. There is no reason why we must despair if God is dead and if life must come to an end. If there is no God, it is indeed true that we are not blessed with the questionable blessing of being made for a purpose; furthermore, if there is neither God nor *Logos*, there is no purpose to life, no plan for the universe or providential ordering of things in accordance with which we must live our lives. Yet, from the fact, if it is a fact, that there is no purpose to life or no purposes for which we are made, it does not at all follow that there are no purposes *in* life that are worth achieving, doing or having, so that life in reality must be just one damn thing after another that finally senselessly terminates in death. "Purpose of life" is ambiguous: in talking of it we can, on the one hand, be talking of "purpose to life," or, on the other, of "purposes in life" in the sense of plans we form, ends we seek, etc., that result from our deliberate and intentional acts and our desires, including our reflective desires. The former require something like a god or a *Logos*, but the latter most certainly do not. Yet it is only the latter that are plainly necessary to make life meaningful in the sense that there are in our lives and our environment things worthwhile doing, having or experiencing, things that bring joy, understanding, exhilaration or contentment to ourselves or to others. That we will not have these things forever does not make them worthless any more than the inevitability of death and the probability of decay robs them, or our lives generally, of their sense. In a Godless world, in which death is inevitable, our lives are not robbed of meaning.

Some might concede all this and still respond that I am leaving out something crucial from the religious traditions. They could agree I have shown that life for an atheist can very well have meaning. But what I have not shown is that with the loss of the kind of hope and the kind of perspective that have gone with Judaism, Christianity and Islam something has not been irreparably taken from us, the loss of which is increasingly felt as the managed society of the Twentieth Century closes in on us.

What I am alluding to can perhaps best be brought forward if I turn to a famous trio of questions of Kant's: "What can I know?," "What ought I to do?" and "What may I hope?."[9] Max Horkheimer, in commenting on them, remarks that an examination of the "third question leads to the idea of the highest good and absolute justice."[10] He then adds that the "moral conscience . . . rebels against the thought that the present state of reality is final. . . . "[11] In the struggles of our everyday life, in the world as we know it, our hopes for a realization, or even approximation, of a truly human society, a society of human brotherhood and sisterhood, a just society or even a rational society are constantly dashed, constantly defeated. This led Kant, Lessing and even Voltaire to postulate immortality in order to make some match between our aspirations and what is realizable. Such postulations are indeed easy to satirize and indeed it is folly to try to argue from such hopes to any likelihood at all that such a reality will obtain.[12] But one can understand it as a hope—a hope which a person who truly cares about his fellows and has lost all faith in anything like a Marxist humanist future, might well keep close to his heart. If we believe, as Horkheimer and Adorno do, that we live in a world where we grow lonelier, more isolated, more caught up in meaningless work routines, more passive, more and more incapable of seeing things as a whole and of having any believable sense of where we come from, who we are or where we are going, we may perhaps rightly become "knights of faith" and make such an otherwise absurd postulation.

Yet, if we can rightly live in hope here, can we not, even more rightly, live in accordance with the less intellectually stultifying hope that we humans can attain a certain rationality and come to see things whole and in time make real, through our struggles, a truly human society without exploitation and degradation in which all human beings will flourish? Even *if* this hope is utopian—another dream of the "dreamers of the absolute"—it is still far less utopian, and far less fantastical, than the hope for "another world" where we will go "by and by." Moreover, such secular hopes are in the various Marxisms (reified and otherwise) as alive in traditions as are the otherworldly conceptions of Christianity.

Notes

1. The sense of this is very acute in Stanley Cavell's *Must We Mean What We Say* (New York: Charles Scribner's and Sons, 1969). This sense is further astutely conveyed in Francis Sparshott's discussion of it in *The Times Literary Supplement*, July 22, 1977, p. 899.

2. *My Ethics Without God* (London: Pemberton Books, 1973), *Scepticism* (London: Macmillan, 1973), "Linguistic Philosophy and The Meaning of Life," *Cross-Currents*, Vol. XIV (Summer, 1964), "Linguistic Philosophy and Beliefs," *Philosophy Today*, No. 2, Jerry H. Gill ed., (London: Collier Macmillan Ltd., 1969), "An Examination of the Thomistic Theory of Natural Moral Law," *Natural Law Forum*, Vol. 4 (1959), and "God and the Good: Does Morality Need Religion," *Theology Today*, Vol. XXI (April, 1964).

3. J.M. Cameron, "Surviving Death," *The New York Review of Books*, Vol. XXI, No. 17 (October, 1974), pp. 6–11.

4. Anthony Flew, "Is There a Case for Disembodied Survival?", *The Journal of the American Society For Psychical Research*, Vol. 66, (April, 1972), pp. 129–44, Part III of Anthony Flew, *The Presumption of Atheism* (New York: Barnes and Noble, 1976), Terrence Penelhum, *Survival and Disembodied Existence* (London: Routledge & Kegan Paul, 1970), and my "Logic, Incoherence and Religion", *International Logic Review*, 1979.

5. Ludwig Witthenstein, *On Certainty*, translated by Denis Paul and G.E.M. Anscombe (Oxford: Basil Blackwell, 1969) and G.H. von Wright, "Wittgenstein on Certainty," *Problems in the Theory of Knowledge*, ed. by G.H. von Wright (The Hague: Martinus Nijhoff, 1972) pp. 47–60.

6. J.M. Cameron, "Surviving Death," p. 11.

7. *Ibid.*

8. Peter Geach, *God and the Soul* (London: Routledge & Kegan Paul, 1969), pp. 117–129.

9. Immanuel Kant, *Critique of Pure Reason*, tr. by J.M.D. Meiklejohn (New York: Dutton, 1934), p. 457.

10. Max Horkheimer, *Critique of Instrumental Reason* (New York: The Seabury Press, 1974), p. 2.

11. *Ibid.*

12. J.L. Mackie 1976. "Sidgwick's Pessimism," *Philosophical Quarterly*, pp. 326–7.

26.
Death and the Meaning of Life In the Christian Tradition

W. Norris Clarke, S.J.

The purpose of this morning's symposium is to discuss what light death, or more precisely the meaning of death, sheds on the meaning of life. And my particular task is to present this as interpreted by the Christian tradition in contrast with Professor Nielsen, who will discuss it, I presume, from a naturalist viewpoint. I must say it caused me some surprise at first that such a topic should be on the program at a non-theological conference, since up to the very recent years in most American intellectual and social circles death was a subject that was ordinarily veiled in a conspiracy of silence and brushed under the rug as much as possible; it was considered bad taste to bring it up, at least in any personal existential way, i.e., in any way other than as a practical technical problem concerning practical adjustments among those on this side of death. A striking example of this technical viewpoint was given me by one of my students recently, who is doing a doctoral thesis on the philosophical dimensions of death. He was interviewing a distinguished doctor at the famous Sloan-Kettering Institute for the treatment of cancer in New York, and was trying to get at the doctor's own personal attitude toward death as a human experience, since he was dealing with it in his patients every day. When he was asked, "Doctor, what does death mean to you personally?" the answer was: "To me, death is the ultimate challenge to my expertise." Hardly a personalist response. But in recent years there has been a sudden and dramatic rise in interest in the subject, as we all know. Courses in colleges and universities proliferate on it, books pour out, symposia are held, etc. This is quite a healthy sign, it seems to me, since it would appear all to obvious that the end of human life should throw a great deal of light on the significance of what has gone before. Hence I welcome our frank discussion of the subject in the context of this conference on ultimate values and their relation to the work of science.

I shall treat the question primarily from the point of view of the Roman Catholic side of the Christian tradition, since it is this that I know best,[1] though I suspect that most of it will apply, *mutatis mutandis*, to the other branches of Christianity. I shall examine first the meaning of death itself in the Christian view of human destiny, then the light that this sheds on the meaning of life itself this side of the grave.

The Meaning of Death

Let us go at once to the heart of the matter. The essence of the Christian teaching on death is that it proclaims the victory over death through the life-giving power of the risen Christ. As St. Paul cries out in those exultant phrases that have echoed and reechoed all down through Christian history, "Death is swallowed up in victory. O death, where is thy victory? O death, where is thy sting? Thanks be to God who has given us the victory through our Lord Jesus Christ" (I Cor. 15:54–57). In this conception death in its present painful form is viewed as having exercised domination over man even since the sin or fall of early man, personified in Adam and Eve. It is thus looked on as a punishment for sin. This reign of death over mankind is overthrown by the voluntary death of Jesus on the Cross and his resurrection by the power of the Father, who now appoints him as the Giver of Life—eternal life—to all who believe in him (and indeed to all who seek God with a sincere conscience and thus implicitly believe all that God wishes them to believe).

The exact meaning of the doctrine that death is the punishment of sin is veiled in considerable obscurity. Contemporary theological speculation is more or less agreed that it does not mean necessarily that man would not have died at all without the sin of Adam. Karl Rahner speculates that even without sin man would have had to pass through death as an end to his biological life, but a death chosen by his free decision as the completion of his life and not a painful death forced upon him from without and veiled in fear and obscurity as at present.[2] We do not wish to delay any further here on this more technical question but will concentrate on the more positive Christian vision of victory over death at least in its present human modality, whatever the latter's origin.

Death has always haunted the consciousness of man, as a source of fear, of sadness at the threat of ultimate defeat and extinction, or at least the uncertainty of what lies beyond this impenetrable veil. The Greek elegiac poetry, with its muted but deeply moving chords of resigned sadness over the death of a loved one or the anticipation of one's own death, bear eloquent witness to man's sense of profound disappointment and frustration at the apparent ultimate victory of death over all his projects, his loves, his life itself. Death, as Rahner puts it, is "the point where man in the most radical way becomes a question for himself, a question which God himself must answer."[3]

Most, if not all, religions promise man some victory over death, some form of immortality, even though not always by the preservation of his own distinct individuality (as in some Hindu and Buddhist traditions). But the distinctive character of the Christian vision of the victory over death is that not only does it preserve the individuality of each person in the future life, but this overcoming of the domination of death is brought about by the special intervention of God himself becoming incarnate in the man Jesus, through his voluntary acceptance of death as taking on the burden of the sins of all mankind, and then breaking the power of death as the last word in man's destiny by rising from the dead in a transformed state beyond the reach of death to enjoy the fullness of eternal life with God his Father. And it is by voluntary participation in the death and resurrection of Christ that each man can pass over to eternal life with Christ. As St. Paul often says, just as we have died with Christ in baptism, so too we have risen with him, and our life is now hidden with Christ in God,[4] and, as St. John adds, we now have within us the seeds of eternal life, though they will not blossom fully till the resurrection.[5]

One could put this same central message more precisely by saying that the victory of Christ over death is not so much a destruction of death itself, since all men must still pass through death, as a transvaluation of its meaning. Death now becomes no longer the ultimate darkness, the end without issue, but rather the gateway to a new and indestructible fullness of life. Death is no longer the end of the journey but a passage to a new and definitive chapter of life.

Before we pass on to consider the light shed upon the meaning of life by this vision of death as the passage to eternal life by participation in the death and resurrection of Christ, we would be failing in our duty if we did not point out one implication of the traditional Christian view of death. This is the rejection of any literal doctrine of *reincarnation* of the human soul in other bodies after the present life. The grounds of this tradition are as follows: (1) the clear text of St. Paul: "It is appointed for man to die once, and then the judgment" (Hebrews 9:27), though the import of this canonical text may be somewhat weakened by the fact that the *Epistle to the Hebrews* is now widely acknowledged not to have been written by Paul himself; (2) a clear implication of the doctrine of redemption through Christ: those who die "in Christ," as St. Paul says, are definitively saved and sure of their resurrection to eternal life in and through him (one might also mention the indelible mark of baptism: once baptized, always baptized): (3) a long tradition of the Church reaffirming this, although not explicitly mentioning reincarnation. This long but still sparse documentary tradition is summed up admirably by the unofficial summary of the main doctrines of the Christian faith in a Schema presented by the theologians of the Second Vatican Council but which for lack of time never came to an official vote:

> Those who die in this grace (of Christ) will, with certainty, obtain eternal life, the crown of justice, and just as certainly, those who die deprived of this grace will never arrive at eternal life. For death is the end of our pilgrimage, and shortly after death we stand before the judgment seat of God "so that each one may receive what he has won through the body according to his works, whether good or evil" (II Cor. 5:10). And after this mortal life there is no place left for repentance or justification.[6]

As Karl Rahner puts it, commenting on this text and the foregoing tradition in his recent *Encyclopedia of Theology*: "In this way any doctrine of transmigration of souls is rejected as incompatible with the conception of the uniqueness and decisiveness of human history and the nature of freedom as definitive decision."[7]

Despite the solidarity of this tradition, which some, however, think may not be quite as airtight as it seems, I must note that in very recent years a small but growing number of Christians, especially those interested in Eastern religions, are raising the question again as to the absolute incompatibility of Christian doctrine with that of reincarnation—including some in this room, if I am not mistaken. Although I do not share this view, it might well be a subject for discussion.

Implications for the Meaning of Life

1. *Optimistic View of Human Life.* One implication of seeing death as a passage of eternal life and ultimate human fulfillment is that one also sees our present human life as a prelude and preparation for this same eternal life. This sets the short and precarious span of our earthly human existence in a much vaster framework that should take away the sting of most of our fears, anxiety, a frustration in the face of a precarious existence whose course and outcome we can only partially control and which is doomed to be cut short eventually, unpredictably, and ineluctably by death as the end of all our projects. Seeing this present life as a prelude and preparation for eternal life where total and truly authentic human fulfillment can be ours if we sincerely will it (coming at once as a gift of God and yet as matched to our own good will and moral effort) illumines our present life with the light of a magnificent destiny extending far beyond it, of which the uncontrollable accidents and even mistakes of this life cannot rob us unless we stubbornly cling to them. All this gives both a profound meaning and purpose and an indestructible hope to the project of the earthly part of our existence. This lifts from us the burden of either desperate urgency to achieve as much happiness and fulfillment as possible in this life or the sad, bitter resignation at seeing it slip from our hands or receded beyond our reach—attitudes all too natural to fall into—if we believe that this short life is all that there is for this self-conscious "I" with its inexhaustible reach of longings and desires.

The positive vision of man thus becomes that of an image of God, in process of development toward transformation and final union with Infinite Intelligence, Goodness, and Love. This vision and the hope that it nourishes makes of man's earthly life a project of immense dignity and eternal importance for which death is no longer the cruel and inscrutable end to all hopes, the passage to final extinction, but the passage to a new and definitive chapter of fulfillment. As a result, the ultimate importance in themselves of our possessions and achievements, whether successes or failures, in this earthly chapter of our history becomes profoundly relativized, so that we do not have to seek for or cling to them desperately, as though it is all or nothing in this life alone, as though failure here is ultimate and unredeemable. An authentic Christian should thus be characterized by a certain liberating freedom and detachment from the fruits of his earthly efforts, which should also give him a special readiness and willingness to sacrifice without anxiety not only his possessions but even his physical life for the sake of some proportionate value, even if it be for the welfare of another. It is not clear to me how the readiness to sacrifice one's own life for another, no matter how much one may admire the courage and generosity of the person acting thus, can make truly good sense, satisfying sense, if one believes that death is the absolute and total end of oneself. But this too is a point open for the most fruitful discussion. It seems to me that it is a crucial test for the viability of any ethics and overall vision of the dignity of man that one should be able to make good sense of the act of giving up one's life for another.

Before we leave this point, it should be noted that man's earthly life, viewed in this Christian perspective of the meaning of death, appears as at once a project of man's own self-development and fulfillment and at the same time the carrying out in loving obedience of a project first conceived and given to us with our being by our Creator, the Father of life, hence a project not subject merely to our own arbitrary will. This existential synthesis of authentic self-interest and loving obedience to a Higher Will, where loving obedience and service become in fact identical with our own authentic self-fulfillment, is one of the hallmarks of the Christian vision of the meaning of human life. Life for a Christian is both his own and God's project.

2. *The Urgency of Living Well This Present Life*. We have said above that the perspective of an eternal life after death implies a notable relativization of our achievements in this life, whether successes or failures, since our definitive fulfillment far transcends them, and all their immediate fruits must be let go of as we pass through the purifying emptiness of death. Yet on the other hand there is a peculiar urgency to our moral life on this earth resulting from the fact that we have only this one life to live, this

one preparation for eternal life, since there is no reincarnation or second chance. Although our outer historical achievements and possessions are indeed relativized, the inner quality of our moral life, of our pursuit of and response to primary values, which depends on our own free decision, takes on an enhanced import and urgency because of the eternal significance of what we do with our freedom in time. Even though one's external successes and failures in this life can and should be taken lightly, the moral portrait which we slowly forge out of our truly authentic acts of free moral decision during our lives, and which receives final and definitive ratification at the moment of death, is to be taken with the utmost seriousness. Yet even here, because of the Christian doctrine of forgiveness available to every man for even the most evil act, through the salvific death and resurrection of Christ, the moral portrait of every man remains unfinished, capable of even the most drastic remodeling, up to the moment of death. As you perhaps may know, though it is not a question of official Catholic doctrine one way or the other, and opinions are about equally divided over it, many Catholic theologians today hold for a theory of *final option* at the moment of death. This means that at the time of death, either at the moment before or at the moment of actually leaving the body, each person has the opportunity to pull together the meaning of his whole life, which may never have been clear to him before, and decide definitively in full clarity and self-possession just what he wishes the radical meaning and commitment of his life to be, which at this point would be a commitment either to God as the center of value and meaning, or to oneself as the center, or perhaps to meaninglessness and despair. There is much to be said both for and against this appealing doctrine, and I am not too sure just where I stand on it, though I do lean toward it. In any case, it would be highly imprudent even for someone who believes in it to bet on the chance that his final option would, with no prior preparation, be somehow radically different from the freely and deliberately forged moral portrait characteristic of his whole prior life.

It seems to me that here, if one compares this view of human life and death with the traditional Hindu and Buddhist belief in reincarnation, insofar as this doctrine is to be taken literally—as most ordinary Hindus and Buddhists seem to do—we come face to face with at least one clear-cut point of difference between these two great traditional views of human life and death. And there is no doubt that the practical ethical and religious consequences of this difference are considerable. The belief that we have only one life to live, and that our eternal destiny depends on how we live it, insofar as this comes under the control of our freedom, invests each human life-span and one's personal moral decisions within it with a unique dignity, decisiveness, and urgency. For the Christian, this life is an all or nothing deal, not an indefinitely repeated series of new starts and new chances, both for good and evil. But this again is a fine subject for discussion. How different in practice is the moral pressure exerted by the desire to escape the wheel of *karma* from the urgency for the Christian to live his one life well? Surely there must be a difference in the psychic and spiritual tonality of one's inner life, as one lives within one or the other of these two spiritual universes.[8]

3. *Mindfulness of Death in the Midst of Life.* Since the meaning of death, as we have seen, plays such an important role in determining the meaning of life for a Christian, one of the characteristic spiritual attitudes that should mark the entire life of an authentic Christian—though this is more honored in the breach than in the observance by most, I fear—is the *mindfulness of death* as a guide for life, rather than a deliberate forgetfulness of it, as has become the custom in our contemporary secular culture. For the Christian, death is one of what have been traditionally called "the four last things"—namely death, judgment, heaven, and hell—which should be kept permanently in his mind as part of the abiding background or horizon of his spiritual consciousness, as a positive beacon to guide his way on this earth. Thinking of these "last things," rather than being an escape from the present, has a way of illuminating and setting in proper perspective all that is prior to them. In the tradition of Christian spirituality it has always been a potent device for preventing us from being hypnotized by the often apparent urgency and absorbing fascination of the immediate moving present, for cutting through the insidious spell of self-deception, and for arranging our practical priorities in harmony with our deepest beliefs—in a word, for testing the Christian authenticity of our moral decision-making. Thus St. Ignatius uses it as one of his key rules in his famous *Spiritual Exercises* for making an important decision in one's life. He recommends that one put himself in his imagination on his death-bed and ask himself: "How at that moment would I feel disposed towards the present

decision now facing me? Which alternative would I feel better then, as I am about to face God in judgment, about having made now?"

4. *The Spirit of Detachment.* Another key spiritual attitude that flows immediately from the above is a certain permanent spirit of inner freedom from attachment, that is, possessive clinging attachment, to any of the created goods (possessions, projects, pleasures, modes of enjoyment even of persons) that will pass away with death. This does not mean that we have nothing to do with them, which would be impossible anyway, or that we do not respect and love them according to their value, enjoy them as temporary gifts of God, and use them to help us along the way to Him. But it does mean that we do not *cling* to them tenaciously, anxiously, as though we could not do without them, as though God alone were not enough for us. In a word, we are spiritually *free* with respect to them, can take them or leave them according to the will of God as manifested in our lives at the time. Another traditional name for this is "poverty of spirit": "Blessed are the poor in spirit, for theirs is the Kingdom of Heaven" as the First Beatitude in Jesus' Sermon on the Mount puts it. The purpose of such "detachment" is not purely negative, emptying for the sake of emptying. It is a form of self-emptying in order to open ourselves more fully to the fullness of God Himself, who wishes to give Himself to us as fully as we are able and ready to receive.

Seen in the light of the Christian meaning of death, this spirit of detachment from all creatures during life appears as a progressive, freely willed preparation throughout one's life for negotiating well what should be the supreme *act* of a human life for a Christian, that is, death itself. For death by nature is that radical moment which forces upon us a total self-denudation of all the possessions, projects, and modes of activity and relationship we have enjoyed upon earth, a total emptying and withdrawal of all that seemed to support us here, to be left naked and alone in the presence of the living God. This cannot help but awaken a certain natural fear in us. But this unavoidable moment can be met either as something undergone purely passively, as something we are dragged reluctantly into, desperately and vainly trying to hold on to as much of our possessions as possible; or it can be accepted freely, willingly, even joyously, as a deliberately willed act of total detachment, self-emptying, in order that we may open ourselves as fully as possible for the final gift of Himself that God alone can give, in whom alone we believe and hope our total fulfillment will lie. There is no other way, really, it seems, for man as a creature of the earth to prepare himself adequately for the final gift of God than by passing through this freely accepted moment of total self-denudation as condition to his transformation to a new mode of life unrestricted by the bonds of space and time-bound matter. The same held true for Christ himself as man, whose freely accepted death in loving obedience to his Father was the very instrument for making available to all men the final victory over death by transforming it into a passage to eternal life.

Here the marvelous yet fearful paradox of death comes fully to light as mystery-filled coincidence of opposites. As Karl Rahner puts it so strikingly: "Consequently in death the act of human life . . . finally comes to its sharpest contradiction, the simultaneity of highest will and extreme weakness, a lot which is actively achieved and passively suffered, plenitude and emptiness."[9] That we prepare well and with eyes open to meet this supreme challenge and opportunity at our best, rather than stumble into it terrified and unprepared, is surely a significant part of the meaning of human life for a Christian—as also, I might add, for a sincere Hindu or Buddhist.

5. *The Intrinsic Value of Man's Earthly Activities: Two Christian Views.* What has gone before I think would find fairly wide acceptance in all Christian traditions. Let me conclude now with a more controverted question among Christians regarding the Christian meaning of man's secular activities during his earthly life. What is the intrinsic value of man's work in the world such as culture, civilization, science, technology, art, etc., in a word, the work of building the human city on this earth? Secular humanists of various kinds, including Marxists, have often criticized Christianity for being as preoccupied with the next life as to have little real interest in or wholehearted commitment to the betterment of this world, compared to the secularist for whom this life is the only one and hence deserving of his total attention and commitment. It is true that Christian thought has shown a certain ambivalence on this point down the ages, tending to oscillate between two different if not opposed attitudes.[10] One has been called the *eschatological* view (i.e., focused primarily on the *eschata*, the last things) for whom this world and all its activities are merely the theater or testing ground for man's inner moral and spiritual growth, which alone has intrinsic permanent value.

In themselves apart from their purely instrumental character they have no value in the eyes of God and no intrinsic relation to man's true goal, eternal life.

The other attitude, called the *incarnational* view, so called for its focus on the incarnation as God's act of assuming, consecrating, and conferring intrinsic value forever to the world of matter, regards man's work of culture in the world as having not merely instrumental but intrinsic value of its own in the eyes of God, and hence some direct proportion and significance even for man's eternal life. Secular history is not merely an external foil or framework for sacred history but bears an intrinsic relation to it as built into the latter's own growth and destined to be not merely swept away as useless straw at the end of history but to be somehow assumed in a transformed way into the eternal life itself of man. St. Augustine may be taken as a type of the first attitude, Teilhard de Chardin of the second.

The second naturally appeals more to contemporary Christian man, with his strong commitment to social action, and gives him a more secure stance in meeting the challenge of the secular humanists. I must admit it appeals more to me too. And it is, I think, one genuine Christian view of the world and the meaning of human life, though the dyed-in-the-wool eschatologist looks on it as a compromise with worldliness. But it is not the only authentic Christian view, one reason being that the basic Christian sources give no sufficient grounds for a clear-cut choice between them. It may be that for the full dimensions of the Christian mystery to remain intact and not be arbitrarily truncated by our limited human wisdom, both attitudes must remain in vital and creative tension within Christian thought, so that each will help to keep the other honest and humble in not believing too easily that it has mastered the mystery of the total meaning of human life, as seen in the partly revealing, partly concealing light of death.

Notes

1. Here are a few key references from which one can follow up with bibliography: Karl Rahner, *The Theology of Death* (New York: Seabury Press, 1961), together with an excellent condensation of its main points in the *Encyclopedia of Theology* edited by him in 1 volume (New York: Seabury Press, 1975), article on "Death." See also Ladislaus Boros, *The Mystery of Death* (New York: Seabury Press, 1965); M.M. Gatch, *Death:*

Meaning and Mortality in Christian Thought and Contemporary Culture (New York: Seabury Press, 1969); E. Kubler Ross, *Death and Dying* (New York: Macmillan, 1969); M. Simpson, *Theology of Death and Eternal Life* (University of Notre Dame, 1971). See also the magisterial work of the Protestant theologian John Hick, *Death and Eternal Life* (New York: Harper and Row, 1976).

2. Article "Death" in *Encyclopedia of Theology*, p. 329.

3. Article cit., p. 329.

4. Colossians 2:22–3; p. 4.

5. I John 2–3.

6. In *The Church Teaches*: Documents of the Church in English Translation, ed. by J.F. Clarkson, et al. (St. Louis: Herder, 1955), no. 891, pp. 352–53; it should be noted that this text comes from the *Schema* prepared by the theologians of the Council as a summary of the principle mysteries of faith, but the Council ended hastily before the *Schema* could be brought to the floor of the Council for formal approval; hence it is not an official document but clearly reflects Catholic teaching. The more official documents through history can be found in the same book under the heading "The Last Things," esp. nos. 878, 881, 883–84, 886, 887, 889; these maintain that we rise in this flesh in which we now are and not some other, that soon after death, or the purification needed in Purgatory—during which there is no more place for merit, increase of charity, or loss of salvation—the souls of those who die in Christ receive the beatific vision forever, while the souls of those who die in mortal sin go to eternal punishment.

7. Article on "Death," p. 330.

8. Cf. F.H. Holck, ed., *Death and Eastern Thought* (New York: Abingdon, 1974).

9. Article cit., p. 333.

10. A spirited controversy on this aspect of the theology of history broke out in the 50s and 60s; a few samples are: H. Urs von Balthasar, *A Theology of History* (New York: Sheed & Ward, 1965); J.V.L. Casserley, *Toward a Theology of History* (New York: Holt, Rinehart & Winston, 1965); H. Butterfield, *Christianity and History* (New York: Charles Scribner's and Sons, 1950); O. Lewry, *Theology of History* (Notre Dame: Fides, 1969).

27.
Death and the Meaning of Life—A Hindu Response

Ravi Ravindra

Since the "Hindu Response" covers a wide spectrum, I shall base my remarks mainly on the *Bhagavad Gita*; this, however, being the most popular scripture in India may fairly be taken to be representative of Hindu views. There is, first of all, a relativity of life and death, and a definite continuity across the barrier represented by physical death, a barrier which appears permanent and massively opaque. What really is, cannot cease to be; just as death is certain for those who are alive, rebirth is certain for those who are dead. Man's existence thus includes both sides of the apparently uni-directional divide called death. Therefore, the problem of death is not essentially different from the problem of life.

What changes is the form of manifestation: from gross to subtle and back to gross, and so on endlessly. This process will go on forever according to the laws of nature, which revels in the subtle no less than in the apparent, and all beings, human as well as others, are compulsively born again and again, and die repeatedly. This process of repeated births and deaths, that is, a continual change of form, is an outcome of cosmic causal necessity and operates for all existences, at all scales, for all time. This is what is called *sam sara*.

To be free of the entire inherent compulsion of sam sara is the only real freedom. This freedom is no more in "death" than in "life," these being the two sides of the same ceaselessly changing coin. From this point of view, death lends no more immediacy to the question about the meaning of life than life does itself. What then is the meaning of life? The general Hindu response is that the meaning of life consists in the opportunity it affords for this radical liberation—deliverance from the endlessly repetitious, unconscious nature, outside as well as inside man, driven by mechanical necessity.

This unconscious nature includes not only our bodies but also our minds. But man is more than that. He is spirit as well. According to most Hindus, man is essentially nothing but spirit, which by some illusion identifies itself with a part or the whole of his psycho-somatic complex (*sarira*). The real man (*puru sa*, spirit) is incarnated, that is he takes on a *sarira*, for the explicit purpose of seeing through the illusion that keeps him in bondage; and he gives up the *sarira* when it is no longer able to be useful to him in his essential purpose. It is *sarira* which is born and which dies, and we mistakenly think that it is the real man who is born and who dies. At "death" what is said is that the person has given up the *sarira* (in contrast to saying that he has given up the ghost).

This process of birth and death will go on, for millions of lives if necessary, until the spiritual principle in man realizes its true nature and is freed. Then there will be no more need of being born or dying. Until then "death" is as necessary for the purposes of the spirit as "life."

28.
Natural Theological Speculations on Death and The Meaning of Life

Sir John Eccles

On all materialist theories of the mind there can be no consciousness of any kind after brain death. Immortality is a non-problem. But with dualist-interactionism it can be recognized from the standard diagram (Fig. 2 of Chapter 7) that death of the brain need not result in the destruction of the central component of World 2. All that can be inferred is that World 2 ceases to have any relationship with the brain and hence will lack all sensory information and all motor expression. There is no question of a continued shadowy or ghost-like existence in some relationship with the material world, as is claimed in some spiritualist beliefs. What then can we say?

Belief in some life after death came very early to mankind, as is indicated by the ceremonial burial customs of Neanderthal man. Our earliest records of beliefs about life after death however, were most unpleasant. This can be seen in the Epic of Gilgamesh or in the Homeric poems, or in the Hebrew belief about Sheol. Hick (1976) points out that the misery and unhappiness believed to attend the life hereafter very effectively disposes of the explanation that such beliefs arose from wish-fulfillment![1]

The idea of a more attractive after-life is a special feature of the Socratic dialogues, being derived from the Orphic mysteries. After the poignant simplicity of Socrates' messages before death, it is quite an experience to contemplate the many kinds of immortality that have been the subject of speculation. The idea of immortality has been sullied over and even made repugnant by the many attempts from the earliest religions to give an account that was based on the ideologies of the time. Thus today intellectuals are put off by these archaic attempts to describe and depict life after bodily death. I am put off by them too.

A more interesting and meaningful disputation concerns the recognition of self after death. We normally have the body and brain to assure us of our identity, but, with departure of the psyche from the body and brain in death, none of these landmarks is available to it. All of the detailed memory must be lost. If we refer again to Fig. 2 of Chapter 7, memory is also shown located in World 2. I would suggest that this is a more general memory related to our self-identity, our emotional life, our personal life and to our ideals as enshrined in the values. All of this should be sufficient for self-identity. Reference should be made to the discussion on the creation of the psyche by infusion into the developing embryo.[2] *This divinely created psyche should be central to all considerations of immortality and of self-recognition.*[3]

Our life here on this earth and cosmos is beyond our understanding in respect of the Great Questions. We have to be open to some deep dramatic significance in this earthly life of ours that may be revealed after the transformation of death. We can ask: What does this life mean? We find ourselves here in this wonderfully rich and vivid conscious experience and it goes on through life; but is that the end? This self-conscious mind of ours has this mysterious relationship with the brain and as a consequence achieves experiences of human love and friendship, of the wonderful natural beauties, and of the intellectual excitement and joy given by appreciation and understanding of our cultural heritages. Is this present life all to finish in death or can we have hope that there will be further meaning to be discovered? In the context of Natural Theology I can only say that there is complete oblivion about the future; but we came from oblivion. Is it that this life of ours is simply an episode of consciousness between two oblivions, or is there some further transcendent experience of which we can know nothing until it comes?

Man has lost his way ideologically in this age. It is what has been called the predicament of mankind. I think that science has gone too far in breaking down man's belief in his spiritual greatness, as exemplified in the magnificent achievements in World 3, and has given him the belief that he is merely an insignificant animal that has arisen by chance and necessity in an insignificant planet lost in the great cosmic immensity. I think the principal trouble with mankind today is that the intellectual leaders are too arrogant in their self-sufficiency. We must realize the great unknowns in the material makeup and operation in our brains, in the relationship of brain to mind and in our creative imagination. When we think of these great unknowns as well as the unknown of how we come to be in the first place, we should be much more humble. The unimaginable future that could be ours would be the fulfillment of this our present life, and we should be prepared to accept its possibility as the greatest gift. In the acceptance of this wonderful gift of life and of death, we have to be prepared not for the inevitability of some other existence, but we can hope for the possibility of it.

This is the message we would get from what Penfield and Thorpe have written;[4, 5] and I myself have also the strong belief that we have to be open to the future. This whole cosmos is not just running on and running down for no meaning. In the context of Natural Theology I come to the belief that we are creatures with some supernatural meaning that is as yet ill defined. We cannot think more than that we are all part of some great design, which was the theme of my first Gifford series.[6] Each of us can have the belief of acting in some unimaginable supernatural drama. We should give all we can in order to play our part. Then we wait with serenity and joy for the future revelations of whatever is in store after death.

Notes

1. J. Hick, *Death and Eternal Life* (London: Collins, 1976).

2. J.C. Eccles, *The Human Psyche* (Heidelberg, Berlin, New York: Springer International, 1979).

3. H.D. Lewis, *Persons and Life After Death* (London: Macmillan, 1978).

4. W. Penfield, *The Mystery of the Mind* (New Jersey: Princeton University Press, 1975).

5. W.H. Thorpe, *Biology and the Nature of Man* (London: Oxford University Press, 1962).

6. J.C. Eccles, *The Human Mystery* (Heidelberg, Berlin, New York: Springer International, 1979).

Contributors

W. Norris Clarke is Professor of Philosophy, Fordham University, New York, New York.

Duke L.V.P.R. de Broglie, (deceased) Secretary of the Academy of Science, Academie Francaise, Paris, France.

Sir John Eccles is Distinguished Emeritus Professor, State University of New York, Buffalo, New York, USA/Switzerland and Past Chairman of the International Conference on the Unity of the Sciences V and VI.

William Horsley Gantt, (deceased) Emeritus Director, Pavlovian Laboratory, Johns Hopkins University, Baltimore, Maryland.

Ragnar A. Granit is Professor of Neurophysiology, The Medical Nobel Institute, Stockholm, Sweden.

Holger Hyden is Professor and Director of The Institute of Neurobiology, University of Goteborg, Goteborg, Sweden.

Harry J. Jerison is Professor of Psychiatry, University of California, Los Angeles, California.

Marius Jeuken is Professor of Theoretical Biology, State University, Leiden, Netherlands.

Brian D. Josephson is Professor of Physics, University of Cambridge, Cambridge, England.

H.B. Jones, (deceased) Professor of Medical Physics and Physiology, University of California, Berkeley, California.

Benjamin Libet is Professor of Physiology, University of California Medical School, San Francisco, California.

H.D. Lewis is Professor of History and Philosophy of Religion, King's College, London, England.

K.B. Madsen, Professor of General Psychology, Royal Danish School of Educational Studies, Copenhagen, Denmark.

Grover Maxwell is Professor of Philosophy, University of Minnesota, Minneapolis, Minnesota.

Diane McGuinnes is Lecturer in Psychology, Stanford University, Stanford, California.

Kai Nielsen is Professor of Philosophy, University of Calgary, Alberta, Canada.

Karl H. Pribram is Professor of Neuroscience, Stanford University, Stanford, California.

J.W.S. Pringle is Linacre Professor of Zoology, Oxford University, Oxford, England.

Ravi Ravindra is Associate Professor of Physics and Religion, Dalhousie University, Halifax, Nova Scotia.

Mary Carman Rose is Professor of Philosophy, Goucher College, Towson, Maryland.

Bradley T. Scheer is Professor of Biology, Westmont College, Santa Barbara, California.

Roger Sperry is Hixon Professor of Psychobiology, California Institute of Technology, Pasadena, California.

Gunther S. Stent is Professor of Molecular Biology, University of California, Berkeley, California.

W.H. Thorpe is Professor of Zoology, Jesus College, Cambridge, England.

J.W.N. Watkins is Professor of Philosophy, London School of Economics, London, England.

Roger W. Westcott is Professor of Anthropology, Drew University, Madison, New Jersey.

Robert J. White is Professor and Co-Chairman of Neurosurgery, Case Western Reserve University, Cleveland, Ohio.

Sources

The primary sources for this volume are the Proceedings of the Second, Third, Fourth, Fifth, Sixth and Seventh International Conferences on the Unity of the Sciences. The two exceptions are "Human Evolution: His and Hers" by Roger W. Wescott, a paper originally read at ICUS VII in Boston, 1978, and first published in *Mind and Brain: The Many-Faceted Problems*, pp. 41–44, by Paragon House Publishers, Washington, D.C., copyright 1982; and "Natural Theological Speculations on Death and the Meaning of Life" by Sir John Eccles, also first published in *Mind and Brain: The Many-Faceted Problems*, pp. 365–367.

Papers included in *Modern Science and Moral Values*, Proceedings of the Second ICUS (Tokyo, November 18–21, 1973), International Cultural Foundation Press, copyright 1973, are: "The Science of Behavior and the Internal Universe" by W. Horsley Gantt (pp. 499–514); "Cerebral Activity and the Freedom of the Will" by Sir John Eccles (pp. 35–53); and "Culture: The Creation of Man and the Creator of Man" by Sir John Eccles (pp. 23–34).

Those works included in *Science and Absolute Values*, Volumes I and II, Proceedings of the Third ICUS (London, November 21–24, 1974), International Cultural Foundation Press, copyright 1974, are: "Structuralism and Biology" by Gunther S. Stent (Volume II, pp. 845–858); "Commentary" by Marius Jeuken (Volume II, pp. 858–862); "Adaptability of the Nervous System and Its Relation to Chance, Purposiveness, and Causality" by Ragnar A. Granit (Volume II, pp. 1373–1392); and "The Scientist at His Last Quarter of an Hour" by Duke L.V.P.R. de Broglie (Volume I, pp. XVII–XXIII).

A paper originally published in *The Centrality of Science and Absolute Values, Volumes I and II*, Proceedings of the Fourth ICUS (New York, November 27–30, 1975), International Cultural Foundation Press, copyright 1975, is: "Bridging Science and Values" by Roger Sperry (Volume I, pp. 247–259).

Works from *The Search for Absolute Values: Harmony Among the Sciences, Volumes I and II*, Proceedings of the Fifth ICUS (Washington, D.C., November 26–28, 1976), International Cultural Foundation Press, copyright 1977, are: "The Brain, Learning and Values" by Holger Hyden

(Volume II, pp. 671–683); "Commentary" by Robert J. White (Volume II, pp. 685–688); "The Mechanism of Knowledge: Limits to Prediction" by J.W.S. Pringle (Volume II, pp. 961–976); "Commentary" by B.D. Josephson (Volume II, pp. 977–980); and "Science and Man's Need for Meaning" by W.H. Thorpe (Volume II, pp. 1011–1022).

Papers first published in *The Search for Absolute Values In a Changing World, Volume I and II*, Proceedings of the Sixth ICUS (San Francisco, November 25–27, 1977), International Cultural Foundation Press, copyright 1978, are: "Some Thoughts on the Matter of the Mind-Body Problem" by Daniel N. Robinson (Volume II, pp. 933–941); "A Basic Difficulty in the Mind-Brain Identity Hypothesis" by J.W.N. Watkins (Volume II, pp. 943–953); "Unity of Consciousness and Mind-Brain Identity" by Grover Maxwell (Volume II, pp. 955–959); "A Critical Appraisal of Mind-Brain Theories" by Sir John Eccles (Volume II, pp. 961–967); "Commentary" by Hardin B. Jones (Volume II, p. 969); "The Mind-Brain Issue as a Scientific Problem" by Karl H. Pribram (Volume II, pp. 979–985); "Persons in Recent Thought" by H.D. Lewis (Volume I, pp. 249–258); "Commentary" by Mary Carman Rose (Volume I, pp. 259–262); "Subjective and Neuronal Time Factors in Conscious Sensory Experience, Studied in Man, and Their Implications for the Mind-Brain Relationship" by Benjamin Libet (Volume II, pp. 971–973); "Commentary" by K.B. Madsen (Volume II, pp. 975–977); "Death and the Meaning of Life" by Kai Nielson (Volume I, pp. 483–490); "Individual Existence" by Bradley T. Scheer (Volume I, pp. 263–267); "Death and the Meaning of Life in the Christian Tradition" by W. Norris Clarke (Volume I, pp. 493–504); and "Death and the Meaning of Life—A Hindu Response" by Ravi Ravindra (Volume I, pp. 491–492).

Papers from *The Re-Evaluation of Existing Values and the Search for Absolute Values, Volumes I and II*, Proceedings of the Seventh ICUS (Boston, November 24–26), International Cultural Foundation Press, copyright 1979, are: "The Human Brain and the Human Person" by Sir John Eccles (Volume II, pp. 1125–1140); "Experimental Transference of Consciousness: The Human Equivalent" by Robert J. White (Volume II, pp. 705–710); "Evolution of Consciousness" by Karl H. Pribram (Volume II, pp. 701–703); "The Evolution of Consciousness" by Harry J. Jerison (Volume II, pp. 711–723); and "The Evolution of Sexual Consciousness: Was Darwin Conscious of His Mother?" by Diane McGuinness (Volume II, pp. 725–735).

Index

Index